COOKING

with *Music*

Celebrating the tastes and traditions
of the Boston Symphony Orchestra

The Boston Symphony Orchestra – Boston – 1999

Library of Congress Catalogue Number: 99-73276

Cooking with Music:
Celebrating the Tastes and Traditions of the
Boston Symphony Orchestra

ISBN 0-9671148-0-2

Cooking With Music is a fund-raising project of the
Boston Symphony Association of Volunteers (BSAV), under the auspices of the
Boston Symphony Orchestra, Inc. Favorite recipes were solicited from orchestra
members (current and retired), staff, guest artists, Tanglewood Festival Chorus members,
staff of the Tanglewood Music Center, Trustees, Overseers and the Boston and
Tanglewood volunteers. Recipes were tested and selected with complete anonymity.
The BSO and BSAV are not responsible for the originality of the recipes used in the book.

Cover photograph © Jim Scherer, '99
Cover concept and design by Sametz Blackstone Associates, Boston
Cover recipe from The Four Seasons, Boston (page 176)

Printed in the USA by

WIMMER
The Wimmer Companies
Memphis
1-800-548-2537

BSAV

BOSTON SYMPHONY ASSOCIATION OF VOLUNTEERS

Salute to Symphony Weekend

Photo by: Ginny Martens

3

Photo by: Margaret Williams-DeCelles

BSAV members at work

ALL PROCEEDS
FROM THE SALE OF
GLASS HOUSE ITEMS
DIRECTLY BENEFIT
THE BOSTON SYMPHONY
ORCHESTRA.

THE
BOSTON
SYMPHONY
ORCHESTRA

SEIJI OZAWA
MUSIC DIRECTOR

Photo by: Mary M. Blair

Glass House gift shop at Tanglewood

THE HISTORY AND MISSION OF THE BSAV

Carrying out the mission of a world-class orchestra requires an enormous cast of supporting players, and volunteers have played a pivotal role in the BSO's efforts for thirty years.

The Boston Symphony Association of Volunteers evolved from diverse volunteer groups. The Council of the BSO, which existed for over a decade as an all-women's committee, was joined in 1974 by the Junior Council, a volunteer organization of young professional men and women. In the Berkshires, a dedicated and active group, the Tanglewood Association, had provided support for the BSO at its summer home and for the Tanglewood Music Center for many years. In 1984, all these volunteers were invited to become members of the BSAV.

The BSAV is dedicated to supporting the mission of the BSO as directed by the Board of Trustees. Members contribute 40,000 hours annually to increase community awareness of the BSO, support fund-raising initiatives, and assist with hall services in Boston and public services in Tanglewood. The BSAV is grateful for the ongoing support and guidance provided by BSO Trustees and Overseers, and from BSO Managing Director Mark Volpe.

BSAV members' varied talents are reflected in projects that range from education to flower arranging and event planning. Volunteer tour guides and ushers welcome the public to Symphony Hall and Tanglewood and share the orchestra's history with visitors. Youth concert volunteers illuminate orchestral music for school children with hall tours and "petting zoos" for musical instruments. The BSO has two gift shops available to the public on a seasonal basis: the Symphony Shop in Boston and the Glass House in Tanglewood. They are both fully dependent on volunteer staffing, which further enhances the revenue produced for the BSO. The dedication and enthusiasm of the volunteers are very much evident to anyone who attends such gala events as Opening Night at Symphony or Opening Night at Tanglewood.

Cooking with Music has been a two-year fund-raising project. One hundred and fifty volunteers donated their time and talents to the project and collaborated with BSO staff and orchestra members. Proceeds from the cookbook will enable the BSAV to continue to make significant contributions to help sustain the excellence of the BSO for future audiences.

Berlioz the Bear at the BSAV Orchestrated Event

Courtesy of BSAV

BSO Music Director Seiji Ozawa

A MESSAGE FROM THE MUSIC DIRECTOR

I love to eat. Part of our performing life is fellowship, and nowhere it is more keenly felt than at the dinner table after a concert. Whether it is *linguine vongole* in Milan, a bowl of *soba* noodles in Tokyo, or a cup of clam chowder right here in Back Bay, food is an integral part of the rhythm of my life. Whether it's relaxing alone or enjoying a cast party with 200 singers, eating is an essential aspect of music!

I want to thank all the members of the BSAV who have worked so hard on this book. I look forward to combing through the recipes and trying some with my family.

The last time we published a BSO cookbook, I was finishing my tenth season as Music Director. This time, it's twenty-five years since I first was awarded that position, and I am prouder than ever to be associated with this remarkable institution. Bravo to everyone who contributed, and who continue to work together to make this such a singular organization.

Seiji Ozawa

Seiji Ozawa

May 1999

A young Seiji Ozawa conducts

SYMPHONY HALL

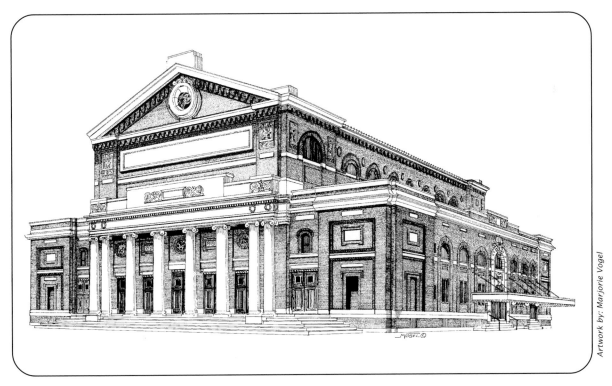

Symphony Hall, Boston

Major Henry Lee Higginson
Founder of the Boston Symphony Orchestra

SYMPHONY HALL

When Symphony Hall opened its doors in preparation for the formal dedication on Monday, October 15, 1900, the residents of Boston had never seen anything like it. The air was filled with excitement as they entered the main hall through the leather-studded doors and ascended marble staircases to the balconies. They marveled at the gilded proscenium, the great organ pipes towering over the stage, and the 65-foot coffered ceiling and chandeliers.

Today, as it approaches its centennial, Symphony Hall continues to inspire performers and amaze and charm music lovers. Recently designated a national historic landmark, Symphony Hall has legendary acoustics, considered the finest in the United States. In addition to its acoustical perfection, the hall is historically significant because of the Boston Symphony's influential role and that of other performing artists and groups in shaping American musical culture.

Photo by: © Steve J. Sherman

The orchestra did not always have the luxury of owning its own home. Since its founding in 1881 it had performed in the old Boston Music Hall between Winter and Bromfield Streets; but in 1892 that building was threatened by a proposal to relieve downtown traffic congestion by running a rapid transit line directly through its site. Fortunately, Major Henry Lee Higginson, the BSO's founder and benefactor, knew of an alternative location in the Fenway area and had already commissioned Charles Follen McKim, of the New York architectural firm of McKim, Mead and White, to draft plans for a new concert hall on the Huntington Avenue site. A public subscription launched in June 1892 raised over $400,000 toward the cost of what was originally referred to as the "New Boston Music Hall."

Although the rapid transit scheme was soon afterward rejected by the voters, Major Higginson and his associates still wished to provide the city with a better concert space; but they were uneasy about McKim's unconventional design for the building, based on a plan of a Greek amphitheater. Widely hailed for its esthetic merits, that scheme gave rise to serious doubts about its acoustical suitability.

By 1898, McKim was encouraged to shelve the Greek theatre scheme and work out a new plan based on the traditional rectangular model exemplified by such buildings as the old Music Hall and the celebrated *Gewandhaus* concert hall in Leipzig. Assisting on the acoustical side, at Higginson's invitation, was Harvard physics professor Wallace C. Sabine, whose recent work in Cambridge had laid the foundations of the modern science of acoustics. Every detail of the new hall's interior—its 2,625 seats, the narrow balconies with their lattice work, the coffered ceiling, even the niches for statuary above the second balcony—were carefully scrutinized for their potential acoustical effect.

Actual construction began June 12, 1899, barely fifteen months before the scheduled opening of the hall and of the BSO's twentieth season. In the days before the formal dedication on October 15, 1900, the local and national press indulged in glowing accounts of the building's spaciousness and tasteful decor, its modern heating and ventilation systems, hopeful acoustics, fireproofing, and the great organ with its movable console.

In a program chosen in part to show off the new organ, the published order of events began with Wilhelm Gericke conducting the orchestra and the Cecilia Society in the Bach chorale *Grant us to do with zeal*. This was followed by a report by Major Higginson and a reading of the poem *The Bird of Passage: an Ode to Instrumental Music* by Owen Wister. The program closed with a performance of the Beethoven *Missa Solemnis*.

Photo by: © Ira Wyman

Listening from the first balcony was flamboyant society matron and arts patron Isabella Stewart Gardner. Like all of Boston's elite, attendance at the symphony opening was a must for Gardner. She wore her famous diamond tiara and sat beside a young music student who turned the pages of her musical score. Her exact seat location for the inaugural concert is not known; however, for the Saturday evening series she had secured two season tickets on the right side of the first balcony, numbered First Balcony A15 and A16.

Unoccupied on opening night were all but one of the sixteen statuary niches, the one exception being that of the Apollo Belvedere at the rear of the hall. Most of the remaining statues were procured and hoisted into place the following winter, thanks largely to the efforts of Mrs. Mary Elliot, a cousin of Major Higginson and the wife of Dr. John Wheelock Elliot. Mrs. Elliot headed a committee of 200 women who selected and raised money for the statues. Many Bostonians were horrified at the committee's choice of plaster copies of ancient Greek and Roman statues representing music and the arts. They especially frowned on the nude Greek poet Anacreon, and the committee admirably resisted their suggestions that a cloak be thrown over his shoulders.

The statues were cast in the Boston studio of Pietro Caproni, and the project took more than two years to complete. The statues' gradual installation made headlines in the local newspapers.

The interior of the hall remains unchanged from McKim's and Sabine's designs of a century ago. But the offices and hallways surrounding it reflect a modern corporation. The Hatch Room (once the lobby and called the "vestibule") and the Cabot-Cahners Room above are filled with tables and chairs where light refreshments are available. Located down a flight of stairs from the Hatch Room, the Cohen Wing houses the Symphony Shop, the Miller Room, Higginson Hall and several BSO departments. This addition was completely renovated and dedicated in 1990.

Each spring, Symphony Hall invites the community to its free "Salute to Symphony" Open House, organized by the Boston Symphony Association of Volunteers. More than 8,000 visitors of all ages enjoy the extravaganza and the chance to learn about music and musicianship. It is a wonderful opportunity, especially for first-time visitors, to experience the magic and magnificence of this hall that has been characterized as "a hospitable house for music".

After 100 years, Higginson's vision for the corner of Huntington and Massachusetts Avenues remains alive and ready to embark on its second century.

Photo by: © Ira Wyman

SYMPHONY HALL

HUNTINGTON AND MASSACHUSETTS AVENUES

Inaugural Concert

MONDAY EVENING, OCTOBER FIFTEENTH
NINETEEN HUNDRED, AT EIGHT O'CLOCK

L. van Beethoven

Missa Solennis

in D, for Chorus, Solo Quartet, Orchestra, and Organ

PERFORMED BY

THE BOSTON SYMPHONY ORCHESTRA

ASSISTED BY

THE CECILIA SOCIETY AND OTHER SINGERS

AND THE FOLLOWING SOLOISTS:

Mme. CLEMENTINE De VERE
Miss GERTRUDE MAY STEIN
Mr. EVAN WILLIAMS
Mr. JOSEPH S. BAERNSTEIN

Conductor, WILHELM GERICKE
Solo Violin, Mr. FRANZ KNEISEL
Organ, Mr. J. WALLACE GOODRICH

Courtesy of BSO Archives

Symphony Hall Inaugural Concert
October 15, 1900

TABLE OF CONTENTS

The Four Conductors: (left to right) John Williams,
Harry Ellis Dickson, Seiji Ozawa and Keith Lockhart

Youth Education

Days in the Arts (DARTS) at Tanglewood

Keith Lockhart
and his young audience

Project STEP students

YOUTH EDUCATION

For one week every spring and autumn, Symphony Hall resounds with the conversation and laughter of excited young people exploring the musical arts at BSO Youth Concerts. The hall rings with the same enthusiasm during the Saturday Family Concerts. That young energy is music to the BSO's ears. Getting schoolchildren excited about classical music is what the orchestra's Youth Education Programs are all about.

Such programs date back to the first concert for young people in 1888. Today the BSO supports a rainbow of musical programs for young people, including Potpourri, Community Partnerships, Professional Development Workshops, and Concerto Competitions.

The most ambitious program is the Youth and Family Concert series, which reaches 45,000 people every year. Harry Ellis Dickson's creativity and energy launched the series in 1959. Dickson is one of Boston's most beloved conductors, and he has touched many young lives with his musicianship, humor, and rare gift for reaching out to his audience. His baton has now been passed on to Keith Lockhart, who has stepped into the role with equal musicianship and his own knack for charming young audiences.

Photo by: © Miro Vintonir

Offering a week long arts celebration is Days in the Arts at Tanglewood, a unique summer program for middle-school students. Over eight weeks, 400 participants from fifth through seventh grade and from all parts of Massachusetts share a week of recreation and immersion in the arts. For many, the fun-filled days of classical music, dance, theater, and visual art—and the exposure to the arts—are an experience they never forget. The students might spend an afternoon at Jacob's Pillow meeting with dancers, find themselves backstage at the Berkshire Theatre Festival, or attend a master class with young musicians of the Tanglewood Music Center.

DARTS participants gain new friends, master new skills, and discover ways in which the arts can enrich their lives. One fifth grader, climbing onto the bus to return home, asked the driver, "Did you see our show last night? Weren't we amazing?" DARTS gives every camper the opportunity to be amazed and amazing.

If DARTS is about engaging young people in music with fun, then Project STEP is about preparing them for musical careers once they've developed their talents. Project STEP opens the doors to a career in classical music for talented schoolchildren. The program, formally called String Training and Educational Program for Students of Color, was founded in 1982 to address the under-representation of musicians of color in the classical music profession. Its mission is to identify, educate, and guide students to fulfill their music potential as soloists, teachers, chamber music performers, and orchestra members. String instruments were chosen for emphasis because they represent the largest number of available positions in orchestras and ensembles.

The program started with eight students and now includes twenty-eight students each year. Participants enjoy weekly private and class instruction, master classes taught by established artists, chamber music coaching, and student recitals. To date, the program has involved several hundred talented young people and prepared them to enter prestigious conservatories and universities, and then go on to a rewarding career in classical music. Project STEP has graduated students to Juilliard, New England Conservatory, MIT, Oberlin College, and other fine institutions.

Photo by: © Miro Vitoniv

Project STEP in action

APPETIZERS ~ SOUPS & STEWS

Seafood Scampi Pizza

1 ½ teaspoons olive oil
1 package (about 1 pound) prepared bread dough
3 cloves garlic, finely chopped
1 tablespoon chopped parsley
½ teaspoon black pepper
16 ounces ricotta cheese
⅓ pound bay scallops, cut into pieces
14 medium shrimp, peeled, deveined and split
¾ cup freshly grated Parmesan cheese
3 tablespoons melted butter

Preheat the oven to 425°.

Brush the olive oil in a jelly-roll pan to cover. Press dough into the prepared pan.

Mix the garlic, parsley and black pepper into the ricotta cheese. Spread the mixture evenly over dough. Place the scallops and shrimp alternately on the cheese. Sprinkle the Parmesan cheese over the pizza. Then drizzle the melted butter over all.

Bake in the oven for about 10 to 15 minutes, or until the cheese is melted and the crust is browned. Cool the pizza slightly before cutting into squares.

Yield: 8 to 10 servings

Note: It is preferable to serve the pizza pieces on a plate with a fork, since the ricotta mixture and resulting softer slices make it difficult to serve as a finger food.

Prosciutto-Escargot Appetizer

12 ounces (3 sticks) unsalted butter, softened
3 cloves garlic, minced
2 shallots, minced
¾ cup minced fresh parsley, divided
½ cup freshly grated Parmesan cheese
1 tablespoon dry vermouth
2 teaspoons lemon juice
Salt and black pepper
36 thin slices prosciutto
36 canned snails, rinsed and drained
French bread, for serving

Preheat oven to 400°.

In a mixing bowl, beat the softened butter until light and fluffy. Beat in the garlic, shallots, ½ cup of the parsley, and the Parmesan cheese. Blend in the vermouth and lemon juice. Season with salt and pepper to taste.

Spread each slice of prosciutto with a generous tablespoon of the garlic-butter. Place a snail in the center of each slice and roll it up tightly around each snail. Arrange the snails close together with the seam side down in a baking dish.

Bake the escargot for 10 minutes; then broil close to the heat source until the butter is sizzling - about 1 minute. Sprinkle with the remaining parsley. Serve with toothpicks, and with bread to soak up the garlic-butter.

Yield: 6 servings, as a first course

Shrimp Curry on Toast Points

1 pound small shrimp, shelled and deveined
1 ½ cups mayonnaise
2 tablespoons curry powder
1 teaspoon milk
6 slices bread

Cover the shrimp with cold water in a pan; place over high heat. When the water comes to a boil, the shrimp will be cooked. Immediately remove the shrimp and plunge into cold water to stop further cooking.

In a large bowl, mix together the mayonnaise, curry and milk. Add the shrimp, cover, and refrigerate overnight.

When ready to serve, toast the bread; then remove the crusts and cut each slice into 4 squares.

Place one shrimp and some of the sauce on each toast square. Place under broiler for approximately 1 minute, or until browned. Serve hot.

Yield: 24 appetizers

This is a wonderful and easy appetizer to make!
It also makes a lovely lunch, served on a whole slice of toast.

Toasted Almond Party Spread

8 ounces cream cheese, softened
1 ½ cups freshly shredded Swiss cheese (about 6 ounces)
⅓ cup mayonnaise
3 tablespoons chopped green onion
⅛ teaspoon grated nutmeg
⅓ cup sliced almonds, toasted
Additional almonds, for garnish (optional)

Preheat oven to 350°.

In a bowl mix the cream cheese, Swiss cheese, mayonnaise, green onion, nutmeg and sliced almonds. Spread the mixture in a 9-inch pie plate or a small casserole.

Bake for 15 minutes.

Garnish with additional almonds, if desired. Serve with crackers.

Yield: about 2 ½ cups

BOSTON SYMPHONY ORCHESTRA
SEIJI OZAWA
Music Director

Professional Development Workshops

The BSO's professional development program includes workshops for classroom teachers and music specialists as well as special sessions geared to school systems' arts curriculum. The workshops help teachers with pre-concert preparation and activities for integrating music into the educational experience. Participating teachers receive credit toward recertification of their teaching licenses.

BOSTON SYMPHONY ORCHESTRA
SEIJI OZAWA
Music Director

Charles Smith
Percussion

Josephine and Charlie Smith sent us this recipe. Charlie Smith will long be remembered as the orchestra member who played the Remington typewriter for the Pops' performances of Leroy Anderson's "The Typewriter," while wearing a baseball cap and smoking a fat cigar. Audiences loved him, and there was always a roar of applause after his performance.

The typewriter was not Charlie's only instrument. He played in the BSO percussion section for many years before retiring in 1990.

Olive Cheese Balls

1 cup shredded sharp cheese
⅓ cup softened butter
¾ cup flour
⅛ teaspoon salt
½ teaspoon paprika
1 (5¾-ounce) jar small pimento-stuffed green olives (about 35 count)

Preheat oven to 400°.

Blend together the cheese and butter in a mixing bowl. Sift together the flour, salt and paprika into the cheese mixture. Mix together to form a dough.

Shape about 1 teaspoon dough around each small pimento olive. Place the balls on an ungreased cookie sheet. Bake for 12 to 14 minutes.

Yield: 30 to 35 cheese balls

Note: The olive-cheese balls can be frozen.

Easy Quesadilla Pie

Oil for cooking and browning
1 small onion, chopped (scallions may be used)
½ green bell pepper, chopped
1 jalapeño pepper, chopped (optional)
1 cup sliced mushrooms
½ to ⅔ cup tomato salsa
2 large flour tortillas
1 cup cooked chicken (or ham), diced
1 cup shredded Monterey Jack cheese

In a sauté pan, heat some oil and cook the onion, green pepper, jalapeño pepper (if desired) and mushrooms until tender and done. Add the salsa to the vegetable mixture, and set aside.

Heat a large skillet on the stove top. Brush one side of a tortilla with some oil and lay it oiled side down in the skillet over medium heat. Add the vegetable mixture, chicken and cheese on top of the tortilla. Top with the other tortilla and brush the top with some oil. When the tortilla's underside is browned, flip it carefully. (Flip the tortilla over by placing a plate face down on the tortilla "pie" in the skillet; then, holding the plate in place, turn the skillet over. Remove the skillet and slide the tortilla "pie" back into the skillet to cook the other side.) Cook the second side for 1 minute, and check for doneness.

Slide the pie out of the skillet onto a serving board. Cut into wedges.

Yield: 3 servings

Note: It is advisable to wear gloves when handling jalapeño peppers.

Petits Quiches

Cream Cheese Pastry:
3 ounces softened regular or low-fat cream cheese
½ cup softened butter or margarine
1 ½ cups flour

Filling:
1 (2¼-ounces) can deviled ham spread
1 medium onion, finely chopped
⅓ cup grated cheddar cheese
2 eggs
½ cup fat-free coffee cream
¼ teaspoon grated nutmeg
¼ teaspoon ground pepper
Dash of Tabasco

Make the pastry: Cut the soft cheese and butter into the flour. Form a ball. Wrap the ball and chill for 1 hour or more. (It will keep in the refrigerator for up to 4 days.)

Divide the pastry into 24 balls. Place one ball into each of 24 mini-muffin cups. (These may be covered and refrigerated at this point, to be finished later.) When ready to bake, press and spread the dough mixture to make a small shell in its muffin cup.

Preheat oven to 450°.

Make the filling: Beat the deviled ham, onion, cheddar cheese, eggs, coffee cream, nutmeg, pepper and Tabasco together in a bowl. Spoon a small amount into each shell, leaving about ¼ inch for expansion.

Bake in the oven for 10 minutes. Lower the oven temperature to 350° and bake for an additional 10 minutes.

Serve hot, warm or cold. (After baking, they may be frozen and reheated at a later date.)

Yield: 24 petits quiches

Crab-Artichoke Dip

¼ cup cream cheese, at room temperature
½ cup mayonnaise
Salt and pepper
¾ cup drained crabmeat (about 4 ounces)
¼ cup plus 2 tablespoons grated Parmesan cheese, divided
3 tablespoons chopped and drained marinated artichoke hearts
2 tablespoons sliced green onion
2 tablespoons diced red bell pepper
2 tablespoons diced celery
1 tablespoon finely chopped fresh Italian flat-leaf parsley
1½ teaspoons sherry wine vinegar
½ teaspoon Tabasco

Preheat oven to 400°.

Beat the cream cheese with a mixer until smooth. Add mayonnaise; beat until just blended. Season with salt and pepper to taste.

Using a rubber spatula, fold in the crabmeat, the ¼ cup of Parmesan cheese, the artichokes, green onion, red pepper, celery, parsley, vinegar and Tabasco. Transfer the mixture to a 2-cup ovenproof dish. Top with the remaining 2 tablespoons of Parmesan cheese.

Bake for 15 minutes.

Yield: about 2 cups of dip

BOSTON
SYMPHONY
ORCHESTRA
SEIJI OZAWA
Music Director

Since 1995 Keith Lockhart has introduced children to the wonders of conducting.

After taking a turn with the baton to lead "The Washington Post March" with a brass ensemble, the young conductors join Keith for an ice cream party.

All proceeds from the class benefit the education and outreach programs of the BSO.

Courtesy of BSAV

Curriculum Resource Kits

Extending the reach of the BSO's education programs into school classrooms, the orchestra's resource kits are designed to enhance core curriculum.

The interactive materials readily fit into existing teaching plans and address both state and national standards. The kits are available on diverse topics that include exploring the world of percussion, Stravinsky's Firebird, opera, and string instruments.

The resource materials range from curriculum guides to books, videos, CDs, and even costumes. All are interdisciplinary multimedia units with flexible lesson plans that can be used for up to four weeks. The BSO education department develops new resource kits each year.

Mushroom Dip

*Butter, for cooking
2 large onions, sliced
8 ounces mushrooms (preferably Portobello),
lightly chopped
8 ounces cream cheese, cut into chunks
(to facilitate melting)*

In a pan, melt some butter; then add the onions. Cook the onions until they are browned. Add the mushrooms to the browned onions, and sauté until they are soft. Add the cream cheese chunks to the mushroom mixture and cook, stirring until the cheese is melted. Serve with pita chips, crackers, or cut-up veggies.

Yield: 3 cups

Note: This recipe can be doubled or halved.

Variation: Adding $1/8$ teaspoon cayenne will give the dip a little "zip"!

This dip is even better the next day!

Marinated Chicken Wings

3 to 4 pounds chicken wings (about 24)
1 ½ cups orange-pineapple juice
5 ounces soy sauce
2 cloves garlic, crushed

Marinate the chicken with the juice, soy sauce and garlic in a covered container at least 6 hours or overnight. Turn or stir at least once.

Preheat the oven to 375°.

Bake the wings on a cooking pan with a rack for 1 ½ hours.

Yield: 6 to 8 servings (3 to 4 pieces for each person)

BOSTON
SYMPHONY
ORCHESTRA
SEIJI OZAWA
*Music
Director*

Godparent Program

Since 1993 the BSO and the Boston Music Education Collaborative have been bringing musicians and schoolchildren together. BSO members visit fourth-, fifth-, and sixth-grade classrooms as teaching artists and provide the kind of first-hand experience that only professional musicians can offer.

Through performances and hands-on activities, the BSO hopes students will gain a life-long connection to and interest in classical music and the BSO as well as a deeper understanding of musical artistry.

For example, violinist Amnon Levy has been an active participant in the Godparent Program at the Philbrick School since its inception and feels that the experience with the inner city school has enriched his life deeply.

Frank Epstein
Percussion

Amsterdam native Frank Epstein has been percussionist with the BSO since 1968.

After moving to California in 1952, he graduated from the University of California and later earned a master's degree from the New England Conservatory. His interest in new music led to the founding of Collage New Music in 1972, and he has overseen the commissioning and performance of 200 new works written for the ensemble.

Frank and his wife Mary are particularly fond of this delicious appetizer.

Spinach Balls with Lemon-Mayonnaise Dip

2 pounds fresh spinach
3 cloves garlic, minced
¾ cup melted butter
4 eggs, beaten
2 cups herb-seasoned stuffing
1 large onion, finely chopped
½ cup freshly grated Parmesan cheese
¼ teaspoon black pepper

Dip:
½ cup mayonnaise
1 tablespoon fresh lemon juice
1 tablespoon Dijon mustard
¼ cup sour cream
Dash of hot pepper sauce

Preheat oven to 350°.

Stem and tear the spinach into 2-inch to 3-inch pieces. Sauté the spinach and garlic in the butter for 3 minutes (maximum).

In a bowl beat the eggs with a whisk. Mix in the stuffing, onion, cheese and black pepper; stir until evenly distributed. Add the sautéed spinach and garlic; mix well. Set aside.

Make the dip: Mix the mayonnaise, lemon juice, mustard, sour cream and hot pepper sauce in a bowl. Set aside.

Make the balls by shaping the mixture into 40 to 50 balls about 1-inch in diameter. Place the balls on a nonstick cookie pan. Bake until golden brown, about 10 minutes. Serve immediately with the mayonnaise dip.

Yield: about 40 to 50 spinach balls

Note: Spinach balls may be frozen on the cookie pans instead of baking them immediately. After they are thoroughly frozen, remove them from the pans and place them in a ziplock plastic freezer bag. When you are ready to use them, remove an appropriate number of spinach balls; defrost and bake them.

Russian Appetizer

½ cup sour cream
1 tablespoon snipped fresh dill
1 loaf dried pumpernickel bread, sliced and cut into quarters
8 ounces pickled herring

In a bowl mix together the sour cream and snipped dill.

On a piece of pumpernickel place a piece of herring. Top with a dollop of the sour cream mixture

Note: Dried dill may be substituted for the fresh dill, using 1 teaspoon as a measurement. However, the dried dill must be combined with the sour cream one day earlier and refrigerated until used.

Do not use low-fat sour cream as a substitute in the recipe.

BOSTON
SYMPHONY
ORCHESTRA
SEIJI OZAWA
Music Director

Potpourri

The Potpourri program opens the doors of Symphony Hall to musically advanced high school students. Each year, as many as 300 students attend BSO chamber recitals, open rehearsals, and full concerts. They engage in lively discussions with artists, managers, and others involved in the production of concerts.

BOSTON
SYMPHONY
ORCHESTRA
SEIJI OZAWA
Music
Director

Asparagus-Prosciutto Rollups

*32 medium-size asparagus spears
(approximately 2 pounds)
16 thin slices provolone cheese
(about ½ pound), at room temperature
⅓ cup purchased or homemade pesto sauce (p.102)
16 thin slices prosciutto (about 3 ounces)
Fresh basil sprigs, for garnish (optional)*

Trim the tough ends from the asparagus spears.

In a 10 to 12-inch frying pan, over high heat, bring 1 inch of water to a boil. Add the asparagus and simmer, covered, until tender-crisp to the bite, about 2 to 3 minutes. Drain the asparagus, immerse it in ice water until cold, and drain again.

Separate the cheese slices; cut each in half. Spread each piece with ½ teaspoon pesto.

Separate prosciutto slices. Cut each slice in half lengthwise.

To make each roll, wrap a cheese slice around an asparagus stalk. Then spiral a prosciutto slice around the cheese to hold it in place.

Serve, or chill airtight up to 6 hours. Garnish with basil sprigs when serving.

Yield: 32 rollups

This is an easy and elegant recipe with a fine presentation.

Crostini with Roast Beef

24 slices baguette or small crusty bread, cut into
¼ to ½-inch slices
2 tablespoons olive oil
½ cup mayonnaise
¼ cup freshly grated Parmesan cheese
2 tablespoons snipped fresh chives
2 to 4 tablespoons drained capers
1 to 2 teaspoons horseradish (optional)
¼ teaspoon garlic powder
½ pound thinly sliced cooked roast beef
(Italian-style preferably),
cut into 24 thin slices
2 to 3 plum tomatoes, cut into 24 thin slices
Additional snipped chives, for garnish (optional)

Preheat oven to 350°.

Place the bread slices on ungreased cookie sheets, and brush them with the olive oil. Bake for 8 to 10 minutes, or until crisp. Remove from the oven.

Meanwhile, combine the mayonnaise, cheese, chives, capers, horseradish (if used), and garlic powder; mix well. Spread the mayonnaise mixture on the bread slices; top with a slice of roast beef, then a tomato slice. Garnish with additional chives, if desired.

Yield: 24 crostini

Variation: Use full-size bread for a delicious open-face sandwich.

Gorgonzola-Pistachio Loaf

1 pound cream cheese, at room temperature
½ pound Gorgonzola cheese, at room temperature
8 ounces (2 sticks) unsalted butter, at room temperature
1 cup chopped fresh parsley
1 cup shelled chopped pistachios
French bread or crackers, for serving

Line a pretty mold with plastic wrap, draping excess over sides.

Combine the cream cheese, Gorgonzola cheese, and butter in a bowl. Blend well. Spread one third of the cheese mixture in the prepared mold. Sprinkle with the parsley. Cover with one half of the remaining cheese mixture. Sprinkle with pistachios. Top with the remaining cheese mixture. Fold the ends of the plastic wrap and press down lightly. Let the mold sit for 30 minutes; then, refrigerate for 1 hour, or until ready to use.

To serve, invert the mold onto a serving plate and remove the wrap. Serve at room temperature with French bread or crackers.

Note: It is vital that the two cheeses and butter be at room temperature when combining, and that the mold sits prior to refrigeration. This will allow the flavors to "marry" properly when the mixture is refrigerated.

Profiteroles with Smoked Salmon

½ cup water
3 tablespoons unsalted butter
¼ teaspoon salt
¾ cup sifted flour
2 to 3 eggs

Filling:
1 pound smoked salmon, cut julienne
1 small Bermuda onion, minced
1 bunch fresh dill, finely snipped
1 cup sour cream

Preheat oven to 425°.

Boil the water in a heavy saucepan; add the butter. Melt the butter and add the salt. Add the flour all at once; mix until a ball forms. Remove from the heat; cool slightly.

While the dough is still warm, beat in the eggs one at a time until a smooth, sticky dough forms. Drop by teaspoon onto an ungreased cookie sheet. Bake for 5 minutes. Then reduce oven to 375° and bake for an additional 15 minutes, or until firm and golden. Cool on a cake rack.

Make the filling: Mix well together the salmon, onion, dill and sour cream. Cut and fill the cooled profiteroles with the mixture.

Yield: 12 profiteroles

The profiteroles also make a very nice lunch.

BOSTON
SYMPHONY
ORCHESTRA
SEIJI OZAWA
Music Director

Barbara Bonney
Soprano

This is one of Barbara Bonney's most frequently used recipes. In her own words:

"This recipe stems from my eight years living in Sweden, where one is always looking for new ways to present smoked salmon. I once had some profiterole shells and smoked salmon left from a dinner party, and I threw this together for a quick lunch. As they say in Swedish: 'Mumsfillibabba!'"

Barbara Bonney is a superlative opera, concert and recital artist, and is a favorite with both Boston and Tanglewood audiences for her radiant tone and the engaging warmth of her personality. At the end of a Tanglewood rehearsal, a member of the audience in the Shed was heard to exclaim: "She is just like the girl next door, but she sure doesn't sound like her!"

I			
Adagio molto	C ♪	=	88
Allegro con brio	¢ ♩	=	112
Andante cantabile con moto	3/8 ♪	=	120
Allegro molto e vivace	3/4 ♩	=	108
Adagio	2/4 ♪	=	63
Allegro molto e vivace	2/4 ♩	=	88

II			
Adagio molto	3/4 ♪	=	84
Allegro con brio	C ♩	=	100
Larghetto	3/8 ♪	=	92
Allegro	3/4 ♩	=	100
Allegro molto	¢ ♩	=	152

III			
Allegro con brio	3/4 ♩	=	60
Adagio assai	2/4 ♪	=	80
Allegro vivace	3/4 ♩	=	116
Allegro molto	2/4 ♩	=	76
Poco andante	2/4 ♪	=	108
Presto	2/4 ♪	=	116

IV			
Adagio	¢ ♩	=	66
Allegro vivace	¢ o	=	80
Adagio	3/4 ♪	=	84
Allegro vivace	3/4 ♩	=	100
Allegro ma non troppo	2/4 ♩	=	80

Eggplant Caviar

1 large, or 2 small, eggplants
3 tablespoons olive oil, divided
1 onion, minced
1 tomato, peeled, seeded and chopped
¼ cup chopped pitted Greek black olives
2 teaspoons lemon juice
1 teaspoon salt
¼ teaspoon pepper
Tomato wedges and additional pitted Greek black olives,
for garnish

Place the whole eggplant in a large pot of boiling water. Cover and boil 20 minutes, or until the eggplant is tender when pierced with a fork. Remove the eggplant from the kettle. When it is cool enough to handle, peel and finely chop the eggplant.

Heat 1 tablespoon of the olive oil in a large skillet, add the onion and cook until tender, but not browned. Add the eggplant, tomato and the remaining 2 tablespoons of oil.

Cook until juices running from the tomato and eggplant have evaporated. Stir in the chopped Greek olives. Add the lemon juice, salt and pepper. Remove the eggplant mixture from the skillet into a bowl; cover and chill thoroughly.

Serve in a chilled bowl surrounded with additional Greek black olives and tomato wedges. Use as a spread for crusty bread.

Yield: 12 servings

Salmon Appetizer

3 (8-ounce) packages cream cheese
16 ounces sour cream
3 eggs
1 ½ teaspoons salt
1 tablespoon horseradish
⅓ cup fine dry breadcrumbs
1 tablespoon lemon zest
1 tablespoon finely chopped parsley
1 tablespoon snipped chives
1 ½ cups crumbled smoked salmon

Preheat the oven to 350°.

Coat a springform pan well with a nonstick spray. Distribute crumbs in the pan.

In a bowl, beat the cheese, cream, horseradish and salt. Gradually mix in any or all of the lemon zest, parsley and chives.

Bake for 60 minutes. Turn off the oven, cover the pan and allow the mixture to stand for 30 minutes in the oven.

Cool the salmon mixture, then wrap in plastic wrap or refrigerate until ready to serve.

Yield: about 5 cups of appetizer

Serving Suggestion: Serve on large decorative plate with various crackers, rye bread or dried pita bread.

V			
Allegro con brio	2/4 ♩	=	108
Andante con moto	3/8 ♪	=	92
Allegro	3/4 ♩	=	96
Allegro	C ♩	=	84

VI			
Allegro ma non troppo	2/4 ♩	=	66
Andante molto moto	12/8 ♩	=	50
Allegro	3/4 ♩	=	108
Allegro	2/4 ♩	=	132
Allegro	C ♩	=	80
Allegretto	6/8 ♩	=	60

VII			
Poco sostenuto	C ♩	=	69
Vivace	6/8 ♩	=	104
Allegretto	2/4 ♩	=	76
Presto	3/4 ♩	=	132
Assai meno presto	3/4 ♩	=	84
Allegro con brio	2/4 ♩	=	72

VIII			
Allegro vivace e con brio	3/4 ♩	=	69
Allegretto scherzando	2/4 ♪	=	88
Tempo di menuetto	3/4 ♩	=	126
Allegro vivace	¢ 𝅝	=	84

The Concerto Competition for talented high school instrumentalists was launched in 1959, the same year Harry Ellis Dickson founded the Youth Concerts.

The competition is close to the BSO's heart. Not only does it provide young musicians a chance to perform in competition, but it has also produced two winners who have become BSO members: Larry Wolfe has played in the bass section for many years, and Nurit Bar-Josef joined the violin section in 1998.

Dolma
(Stuffed Grape Leaves)

1 jar preserved grape leaves (about 40 to 50)
2 onions, chopped
2 teaspoons salt
1½ cups rice
½ cup olive oil, divided
1 pound ground beef
1 teaspoon finely chopped fresh mint
1 teaspoon finely snipped fresh dill
½ cup finely chopped fresh parsley
Dash of garlic powder
Juice of 1 lemon, divided
2 beef bouillon cubes, dissolved in 2 cups hot water

Drain the grape leaves, separate them, and rinse well under running water, taking care not to tear them. Set aside.

Cook the onions in a little salted water over low heat for 5 to 10 minutes. Add the rice, one half of the olive oil and mix. Add the raw meat, mint, dill, parsley, garlic powder and one half of the lemon juice. Mix well.

In the bottom of a pot, place a few flat grape leaves. Add the remaining olive oil, lemon juice and the prepared bouillon. On a working surface lay a grape leaf, vein side up, with the stem toward you. Place a tablespoon of the meat mixture at the base of the leaf and roll it up, tucking in the excess leaf at the sides to make a tiny bundle. Repeat with the remaining leaves and filling, packing the bundles in the pot tightly together and in layers. Add additional water or bouillon, if necessary, to nearly cover the dolma.

Cover the pot, bring to a boil, then reduce to simmer. Cook the dolma until the rice stuffing is completely cooked, about 25 to 30 minutes. If served as an appetizer with a dipping sauce, it is best to cut into thirds and to provide toothpicks.

Yield: about 150 pieces for a dipping appetizer; 40 as a whole appetizer.

Variation: Additional mint may be substituted for some of the parsley.

Tomato Chipotle Salsa

25 tomatillos (about 2 pounds) (see note)
3 cloves garlic, unpeeled
1 medium white onion, finely chopped
3 tablespoons olive oil
4 canned chipotle chiles (see note), in adobo sauce
1 packed cup cilantro leaves (about 1 bunch cilantro)
1 teaspoon salt
Juice of 1 lime

Preheat oven to 375°.

Husk and wash the tomatillos under hot water. In a cast iron skillet, cook the tomatillos for 20 to 25 minutes over medium heat until soft and blackened all over, but not dried out. (Shake the pan every couple of minutes while cooking.)

Roast the garlic on a pan in the oven until soft, but not burned - about 15 minutes. Place the tomatillos, garlic, onion, olive oil, chiles, cilantro and salt in a blender. Blend until combined. The consistency should be even, with no lumps. (Add water, if necessary, to obtain desired consistency.)

Add the lime juice, and blend for a few seconds. Add more cilantro, if desired.

Serve either warm, at room temperature, or chilled.

Yield: 4 cups

Note: It is advisable to wear gloves when working with chili peppers.

Tomatillos (tohm-ah-TEE-ohs) are small green tomatoes with a thin, papery husk. Chipotle chiles (chih-POHT-lay) are smoked jalapeños. Both are available in large markets and in some food specialty shops, especially in the southwestern United States.

Serving Suggestion: Serve with tortilla chips.

Daniel Katzen
Horn

Daniel Katzen is the author of the official eggnog of the BSO horn section.

A native of Rochester, New York, he joined the BSO in 1979. He also serves on the faculty of the Boston University School for the Arts and the New England Conservatory. Danny's love of music also prompts him to keep a busy playing schedule. He has performed with the Boston Symphony Chamber Players, has joined BSO colleague Frank Epstein for Collage New Music, and has recorded with the Empire Brass.

"At our informal holiday party, I make a big batch of this low-fat delicious drink and give some to each member of our section for a warm holiday season," says Danny. "When we and our families go out to play Christmas carols on our horns, we take some along to share (but omit the alcohol, so it's family-friendly). Either way, it's sure to bring holiday cheer to your festivities."

Eggnog

*1 quart plus 2 cups milk, divided
2 sticks cinnamon
6 cloves
8 to 12 egg yolks (see note)
1½ cups confectioners' sugar
12 to 16 egg whites (see note)
2 to 3½ cups dark liquor (optional)
2 cups cream
1 teaspoon vanilla extract
Grated nutmeg*

In a large pot heat 1 quart of the milk, the cinnamon and the cloves. Let the mixture sit for 15 minutes. Strain the mixture into a bowl. Set aside.

In a medium bowl, beat the egg yolks and confectioners' sugar. Slowly drizzle the strained milk into the egg mixture. Return the mixture to the pot and cook over high heat for only 2 minutes. Cool.

In another bowl lightly beat the egg whites. Strain; then beat into the cooled mixture. Stir in the liquor, cream, the remaining 2 cups of milk, vanilla and a sprinkle of nutmeg. Chill.

Serve cold.

Yield: 8 to 12 servings

Note: For a low-cholesterol version, you may substitute egg whites for some of the yolks at a 2 whites-per-1 yolk ratio. Use a total of 24 yolks and whites combined to equal a total of 1 dozen eggs.

Either way you make this eggnog, your guests are sure to love it!

Soup à Sara

1 medium onion, grated
1 tablespoon butter
1 (10-ounce) package frozen green peas
1 (10¾-ounce) can beef consommé, mixed with 1 can water
1 tablespoon sugar
1 scant teaspoon dried leaf thyme
Pinch of garlic powder
1 cup heavy cream
½ cup milk
Croutons
½ cup champagne (optional)

In a saucepan, cook the onion in butter until soft and transparent, about 5 minutes. Stir often, being careful not to burn it. Add the peas and consommé, bring to a simmer, and cook over low heat for 10 minutes.

Add the sugar, thyme, and garlic powder. Stir and cook for another few minutes.

Put the mixture in a blender, add the cream and milk, and blend to desired consistency. Serve chilled or hot with croutons.

Yield: 4 servings

Note: For those with a bottle of champagne in the fridge, add an optional ½ cup of the wine.

Frederica von Stade
Mezzo-soprano

Frederica von Stade is a favorite with Boston and Tanglewood audiences, and has thrilled European music lovers when on tour with the BSO. She is an artist who traverses the world of opera and the concert stage with ease and exceptional musicianship.

Her career was launched with a great leap when she auditioned for the Metropolitan Opera and was immediately offered a contract by Rudolph Bing. Since her 1970 debut, she has sung nearly all of her great roles with the company.

Ms. von Stade is a repeat contributor; she also shared one of her favorite recipes with us for our first cookbook.

Wheatleigh

Wheatleigh is a small country hotel on 22 wooded acres in Lenox, Massachusetts, offering charm and a world class cuisine to visitors to the Berkshires and to Tanglewood.

Chef Peter Platt generously shares this Butternut Squash Soup recipe with us.

Butternut Squash Soup with Fig Quenelles

Quenelles:
6 dried figs, stems removed
1 tablespoon dark rum
1 cup heavy cream

2 butternut squash (about 3 pounds)
1 quart chicken stock
3 onions, thinly sliced
4 tablespoons butter
1 cup heavy cream
1 teaspoon powdered ginger
¼ teaspoon cayenne
½ teaspoon salt
Grated nutmeg
Prosciutto, sliced thin and cut into julienne, for garnish
Chopped parsley or snipped chives, for garnish

Make the quenelles: Cook the figs in water to cover for 30 minutes, or until soft. Purée and cool. Whip the cream with rum and fold in proportionately ⅓ fig mixture to ⅔ cream. Mix well. (At this point the mixture will hold well in the refrigerator.) When ready, form into quenelles (balls) with demitasse spoons.

Make the soup: Preheat the oven to 375°. Slice the squash in half and place upside down on a sheet pan with a little water. Cook in the oven for 1 hour, or until a knife passes through easily. Remove the squash from the oven and set aside.

Meanwhile, cook the onions and butter in a covered pot large enough to hold the finished soup. Cook over low heat as long as possible without browning them. (If they do brown a little, this is not a problem.) Scoop out the cooked squash and add it to the onions along with the chicken stock. Purée the mixture in a food processor or blender in batches; return to pot. Add the cream, ginger, cayenne, salt, and nutmeg to taste. If the soup is too thick, thin it with more chicken stock or milk; then double-check the seasoning. Garnish the soup with fig quenelles, prosciutto and chopped parsley or chives.

Yield: 4 to 6 servings

Note: Alternatively, the squash may be peeled, cut into chunks and cooked in chicken broth until tender. It will then be ready to be added to the onions and chicken stock.

Butternut Squash, Orange and Pear Soup

6 tablespoons (¾ stick) butter
1 large onion, roughly cut
1 large butternut squash, peeled and roughly cut into pieces
4 cups chicken stock
Pared rind of 1 orange, and its juice
2 Bosc pears, peeled, cored and cut into pieces
Salt and pepper
Pinch of nutmeg
Pinch of allspice

Garnish:
½ cup heavy cream
Ground cinnamon
⅓ cup finely chopped pecans, lightly toasted

In a saucepan large enough to hold the finished soup, melt the butter and cook the onions until they are soft. Add the squash and cook for an additional 5 minutes. Add the stock, orange rind and juice, pears, salt and pepper to taste, nutmeg and allspice. Bring the soup to a boil; then lower the heat and simmer covered for 30 minutes, or until the squash and orange rind are very soft.

Purée the soup mixture in a blender or processor, and return to pan. Reheat the soup to a boil. (If desired, the soup may be thinned by adding a little water.)

Make the garnish: Beat the cream in a bowl until it holds soft peaks. Ladle the soup into bowls. Top the soup with a spoonful of cream and sprinkle on some cinnamon and the pecans.

Yield: 4 to 6 servings

BOSTON
SYMPHONY
ORCHESTRA
SEIJI OZAWA
*Music
Director*

Occasional letters come from the young listeners attending the youth concerts, and some of them display not only an interest in the music, but an unconscious humor.

*"Dear Mr. Dickson:
I enjoyed the concert very much. I have an ear for music, and it listened to every bit."*
~ from a boy of eleven

New Bedford Kale Soup

*1 pound beef shin bone (lean and meaty)
1 cup coarsely chopped onion
1 ½ teaspoons salt
1 clove garlic, crushed
6 to 8 cups water
1 ½ pounds linguiça, cut into ½-inch slices
1 (10¾-ounce) can tomato soup
1 (10¾-ounce) can pea soup
1 pound fresh kale
2 cups peeled and cubed (1-inch) white potatoes
2 (14-ounce) cans red kidney beans
3 to 4 sprigs fresh mint*

In a kettle simmer the shin bone, onion, salt and garlic in water for about 2 hours. Skim off the residue on the top; then add the linguiça and both soups. Simmer for an additional ½ hour.

Thoroughly wash the kale, remove the stems, and cut it diagonally into wide pieces. Add the kale, potatoes and beans to the soup; continue to simmer until the potatoes are almost tender, about 20 minutes. Add the mint. Cook for another few minutes, or until the potatoes are completely cooked. Remove the soup from the stove and take out the shin bone. Trim the meat from the bone, cutting it into small pieces. Return the meat to the pot.

Yield: 8 servings

Note: The soup is best prepared a day ahead to allow the flavors to blend.

Linguiça can be found in ethnic grocery stores or most markets.

This is a delicious winter soup.

Lentil and Brown Rice Soup

½ cup raw lentils, picked over and washed
⅓ cup raw brown rice
2 tablespoons olive oil
2 cloves garlic, minced
2 tablespoons soy sauce
2 bay leaves
5 cups beef broth, or water, divided
1 small onion, finely chopped
2 medium carrots, thinly sliced
1 large stalk celery, finely chopped
Handful of celery leaves
1 (14-ounce) can plum tomatoes, with their liquid, chopped
½ cup tomato sauce, or tomato juice
¼ cup dry red wine
1 teaspoon dried basil
1 teaspoon paprika
½ teaspoon marjoram
½ teaspoon dried thyme
Salt and pepper

Place the lentils, brown rice, olive oil, garlic, soy sauce and bay leaves in a large pot and cover with 3 cups of the beef broth. Bring to a boil; cover and simmer over low heat for 7 to 8 minutes.

Add the remaining 2 cups of broth along with the onion, carrots, celery, celery leaves, tomatoes, tomato sauce, wine, basil, paprika, marjoram, thyme, and salt and pepper to taste, and bring back to a boil. Cover and simmer over low heat for 25 to 30 minutes, or until the vegetables are cooked to desired doneness.

Yield: 4 servings as a lunch; 6 servings as a first course

Variation: The beef broth provides a heartier taste, but water may be substituted when using the recipe as a vegetarian soup.

BOSTON SYMPHONY ORCHESTRA
SEIJI OZAWA
Music Director

Although the Youth Concerts in their present form were introduced at a later date, the Esplanade Concerts, begun on July 4, 1929, subsequently provided the venue for the first Children's Esplanade Concert. It was normal for 5,000 people to attend each concert - in fact, a crowd of 10,000 from time to time was not unusual!

Isaac Stern
Violin

Isaac Stern needs no introduction to music lovers. He is one of the foremost violinists of the century and, with more than 100 recordings, one of the most recorded artists of our time.

"Of my many favorite dishes, My Favorite Borscht is the one I enjoy preparing most," says Isaac Stern. Mr. Stern is often asked about special dishes or dietary restrictions before he attends a gala dinner. His reply is always the same, and conveys his love of food: "Yes, I like food with my dinner."

My Favorite Borscht

3 pounds beef shinbone
2 pounds beef brisket, cut into 1-inch pieces
4 cups shredded cabbage
2 cups diced beets
2 large onions, chopped
3½ cups canned tomatoes
¾ cup lemon juice
6 cloves garlic, minced
¼ cup chopped parsley
1 small bay leaf, crumbled
1 teaspoon paprika
3 tablespoons sugar
1 teaspoon salt
Freshly ground black pepper
Sour cream, for serving

Cover the shinbone and brisket with 2 quarts of water in a large pan. Bring to a boil, reduce heat, and simmer covered for 1 hour. Add the cabbage, beets, onions, tomatoes, lemon juice, garlic, parsley, bay leaf, paprika, sugar, salt and pepper, and simmer for an additional 2 hours.

Remove the shinbone, trim off the meat, and discard the bone. Cut the meat into 1-inch pieces. Return the meat to the soup and simmer for an additional 10 minutes. Serve with sour cream.

Yield: 6 servings

Elegant Carrot Soup

2 tablespoons vegetable oil
1 cup coarsely chopped onion
1 tablespoon peeled and minced fresh ginger
¼ cup uncooked long grain rice
1 teaspoon curry powder
2 pounds carrots, peeled and sliced ¼-inch-thick
10 cups defatted chicken broth
Salt and black pepper
2 tablespoons chopped fresh mint, for garnish

Heat the oil in a large heavy pot over low heat. Add the onion and ginger; cook for 10 minutes, stirring occasionally. Add the rice and curry powder; cook for 1 minute, stirring constantly. Add the carrots and broth. Raise the heat and bring the soup to a boil. Reduce heat to a simmer and cook covered for 30 minutes, or until the carrots are tender. Cool the soup slightly.

Purée the soup in batches in a blender or food processor until it is very smooth. Return it to the pot and heat it gently. Season the soup with salt and pepper to taste.

Serve garnished with the chopped mint leaves.

Yield: about 8 servings

Note: This is a rich and creamy soup without cholesterol and has a very low calorie count.

Artichoke-Shrimp Bisque

1 ½ (14-ounce) cans artichoke hearts, drained and divided
4 tablespoons (½ stick) butter
¼ cup flour
2 dashes grated nutmeg
1 teaspoon salt
Black pepper
3 cups chicken broth
1 ½ cups milk
8 ounces small shrimp, shelled and deveined
¼ cup heavy cream

In a food processor place one half of the artichokes and process until smooth. Cut the remaining artichokes in quarters and set aside.

Melt the butter in a large saucepan or pot. Whisk in the flour. Add the nutmeg, salt, and pepper to taste. Cook the mixture over medium heat for 3 minutes. Stir in the broth, milk and puréed artichokes. Bring the soup to a boil, stirring frequently. Stir in the reserved artichoke hearts, cream and shrimp. Reduce the heat and simmer for about 5 minutes, or until the shrimp are cooked.

Yield: 6 to 8 servings

Note: The leftover soup freezes well.

Variation: Fish stock may be substituted for the chicken broth and 1% milk may be used in place of regular milk.

This is a great start to a special dinner
and it's easy and quick to make!

Oven Fish Chowder

2 pounds haddock fillets
4 potatoes, peeled and sliced
6 to 8 celery leaves, chopped
1 bay leaf
2½ teaspoons salt
4 whole cloves
1 clove garlic, peeled and crushed
3 onions, sliced
10 tablespoons (1 stick plus 2 tablespoons) butter, divided
¼ teaspoon dried dill seed
¼ teaspoon white pepper
½ cup dry vermouth
2 cups boiling water
2 cups light cream
2 tablespoons flour
Snipped fresh dill or chopped fresh parsley, for garnish

Preheat oven to 375°.

Into a large casserole place the haddock, potatoes, celery leaves, bay leaf, salt, cloves, garlic, onions, 8 tablespoons of the butter (1 stick), dill seed, white pepper, vermouth and the water. Cover and bake for 1 hour.

In a saucepan, heat the cream to scalding. Meanwhile, in another pan over medium heat, make a roux with the remaining 2 tablespoons of butter and the flour, and add to the scalded cream, stirring constantly until smooth. Add the cream mixture to the chowder. Stir the chowder to break up the fish filets.

Serve with a garnish of chopped fresh dill or parsley.

Yield: about 8 to 10 servings

This is possibly the easiest chowder you ever made!

In 1968 Harry Ellis Dickson introduced a young 14-year-old violinist, Peter Zazofsky, at one of the Children's Concerts. Peter, whose father, George, was a violinist with the BSO, played the first movement of Mozart's Violin Concerto No. 4. That evening George Zazofsky was scheduled to perform the same concerto, but just before the concert he injured his finger. Young Peter was summoned, and performed the entire concerto in his father's place!

There are probably not too many recorded instances where a son substituted for his father as soloist.

BOSTON
SYMPHONY
ORCHESTRA
SEIJI OZAWA
*Music
Director*

Despite the Children's Esplanade Concerts in the early years, the Boston Symphony had not had formal youth concerts as part of its Symphony Hall schedule. Harry Ellis Dickson was allowed to organize the concerts, have use of the Hall and the music library, but he would have to engage the musicians individually and could not use the name of the Boston Symphony Orchestra.

A small committee of women and a trio of "angels", civic-minded businessmen, under-wrote the concerts, and the "Youth Concerts at Symphony Hall" began.

Caribbean Peanut Soup

1 medium onion, chopped
2 tablespoons butter, or margarine
2 tablespoons flour
4 cups chicken broth
¾ cup creamy peanut butter
1 fresh jalapeño pepper, seeded and finely chopped
Dash of lemon juice
Dash of hot pepper sauce
Pinch of celery salt,
Pinch of dried tarragon
Pinch of curry powder
Salt and pepper
1 cup cream, or nondairy substitute
Minced green onion, for garnish
Chopped roasted peanuts, for garnish

In a saucepan large enough to hold the finished soup, cook the onion in butter until soft. Stir in the flour for about 3 minutes. Stir constantly. Gradually stir in the broth, then the peanut butter. Cook and stir the soup until it is smooth and slightly thickened.

Stir in the jalapeño pepper and then the lemon juice, hot pepper sauce, celery salt, tarragon, curry powder, and salt and pepper to taste. Gradually add and stir in the cream. Simmer the soup for about 30 minutes. Correct the seasonings to taste. (It is advisable to use very small amounts when making your seasoning mix.)

Garnish with the green onion and peanuts.

Yield: 6 servings

Note: Gloves should be worn when handling jalapeño peppers.

This is an unusual, but tasty soup.

Summer Cucumber Soup

3 tablespoons canola oil
1 large onion, chopped
2 cloves garlic, minced
3 (14½-ounce) cans chicken broth
4 large English cucumbers, unpeeled and cut into chunks
1 potato, peeled and thinly sliced
16 ounces yogurt
Snipped dill
Salt and pepper

Heat the oil in a pan. Add the onion and garlic, and cook until the onion is wilted. Add the chicken broth, cucumber, and the potato slices. Cook the soup mixture until the potato is soft. Remove the pan from the heat and allow it to cool.

When it is cooled, purée the soup in batches in a processor. (For a "crunchier" soup, reduce the processing time.) Add the yogurt and dill to the last batch to be puréed. (A large quantity of dill is desired, but you may adjust the amount to personal taste.) Add salt and pepper, also to taste. Refrigerate the soup until cold.

Yield: 6 or more servings

Note: More chicken broth may be added to increase the amount of soup.

This is a wonderful soup for the summer!

BOSTON
SYMPHONY
ORCHESTRA
SEIJI OZAWA
*Music
Director*

DARTS
(Days in the Arts)

"Ten years ago, I was a clumsy, gawky sixth-grader whose somber view of himself was changed in the magical week I spent at Tanglewood. A new world of the arts opened up for me, and every day was a wonderful experience. I look back on DARTS as a turning point in my young life. Thanks."

~ A letter from a former DARTS camper

Summer Soup

⅓ cup sugar
¾ cup water
1 firm ripe peach (about ½ pound), peeled and thinly sliced
2 cups blueberries, rinsed
3 cups strawberries, hulled and rinsed, divided
1 cup raspberries, rinsed, divided
3 tablespoons lemon juice
2 tablespoons raspberry liqueur,
or raspberry-flavored syrup (optional)
2 to 2½ cups lemon sorbet

In a 2½ to 3-quart pan, mix the sugar and water. Bring it to a rolling boil over high heat. Place the peach slices in the boiling syrup and cook for 1 minute. Add the blueberries and cook for 1 additional minute. Remove the mixture from the heat and let it cool.

In a blender or food processor, smoothly purée one half of the peach-blueberry mixture, one half of the strawberries, and one half of the raspberries. Pour the puréed mixture into a bowl along with the peach-blueberry mixture. Add the lemon juice and liqueur (if used). Cover and chill until cold, at least 2 hours, or up to 1 day.

Slice the remaining strawberries, and add them to the soup along with the remaining raspberries. Ladle the soup into shallow bowls; add 1 scoop sorbet to each bowl.

Yield: 6 servings

Variation: Convert the recipe into a slightly different dessert by using the soup as a sauce over a large scoop of lemon sherbet or sorbet.

Black Bean and Salsa Soup

1 (15-ounce) can black beans, drained and rinsed
1 cup beef broth
½ cup thick 'n' chunky-style tomato salsa
½ teaspoon cumin
2 tablespoons sour cream
1 tablespoon sliced green onions

In a food processor bowl with a metal blade, or in a blender container, combine the beans, broth, salsa and cumin. Process for 1 minute or until smooth.

Heat the bean mixture in a medium size saucepan over medium heat until thoroughly heated.

To serve: Ladle the soup into 2 individual soup bowls. Spoon 1 tablespoon sour cream on top of each serving. Swirl the sour cream gently into the soup. Sprinkle the onion slices on top.

Yield: 2 (1 cup) servings

This is a simple recipe for an elegant soup, hot or cold.

BOSTON
SYMPHONY
ORCHESTRA
SEIJI OZAWA
*Music
Director*

Youth Concerts

"Dear Mrs. Volunteer: Thank you for letting us come to Symphony Hall and hear the orchestra. It was awesome. I think the violinists must have very tired arms when they go home. I think I would like to sit behind the big drum and play it. Thank you again, Joseph"

~ Letter from a fourth-grade student (the word "awesome" appears in many students' thank-you letters).

BOSTON
SYMPHONY
ORCHESTRA
SEIJI OZAWA
*Music
Director*

**Serge Koussevitzky
by Olga Koussevitzky**

Vegetable Stew

*2 tablespoons olive oil
2 tablespoons extra-virgin olive oil
4 medium onions, chopped
4 medium carrots, peeled, cut into ½-inch pieces
2 tablespoons minced garlic
2 tablespoons chili powder
2 tablespoons ground cumin
½ pound red potatoes, cut into bite-size pieces and parboiled
1 red bell pepper, cored, seeded and cut into ½-inch pieces
1 green bell pepper, cored, seeded and cut into ½-inch pieces
1 yellow bell pepper, cored, seeded and cut into ½-inch pieces
2 (28-ounce) cans plum tomatoes, chopped, with juices
1 tablespoon tomato paste
1 tablespoon brown sugar
2 teaspoons dried oregano
1 teaspoon fennel seeds
2 yellow squash, halved lengthwise,
seeded and cut into ½-inch pieces
2 medium zucchini, trimmed and cut into ½-inch pieces
½ cup Italian flat-leaf parsley, chopped
Salt and coarsely ground pepper
1 (15½-ounce) can garbanzo beans
2 tablespoons fresh lemon juice*

Place the two oils in a heavy pot over medium heat. Add the onions and carrots, and cook, stirring, for 10 minutes, adding the garlic in the last 2 minutes. Reduce heat to low; stir in the chili powder and cumin. Cook for 1 additional minute.

Stir in the potatoes, peppers, tomatoes, tomato paste, brown sugar, oregano, and fennel. Bring to a boil; then reduce the heat and simmer, partially covered, for 25 minutes, stirring occasionally.

Add the squash, zucchini and parsley. Season with salt and pepper to taste, and adjust the other seasonings, as desired. Stir in the garbanzo beans. Simmer, uncovered, for 20 minutes longer, or until the vegetables are tender, stirring occasionally. Stir in the lemon juice. Cool to room temperature before storing in the refrigerator. Reheat before serving.

Yield: 8 to 10 servings

Note: If stew appears to be too thick, add more tomato juice.

Winter Stew

2 pounds chuck beef, cubed
3 tablespoons flour
2 teaspoons salt
½ teaspoon black pepper
¼ teaspoon ground ginger
3 tablespoons oil
1 cup chopped onion
2 cloves garlic, minced
4 cups multi-vegetable juice
1 stick cinnamon
1 medium eggplant, peeled, cut into cubes
4 carrots, quartered
4 stalks celery, cut into pieces
8 large dried prunes, pitted
1 (5-ounce) can water chestnuts
8 dried apricots

Shake the meat cubes in a mixture of the flour, salt, pepper and ginger. Coat evenly, shake off excess, and brown in the oil in a large, deep frying pan. Stir in onion, garlic and the vegetable juice, mixed with the cinnamon stick. Arrange the eggplant, carrots and celery around meat.

Bring the stew to a boil, reduce heat and simmer, covered for 1 hour. Add the prunes, water chestnuts and apricots. Simmer for an additional 1 hour.

Yield: 4 to 6 servings

This is a lovely dish for a cold winter day.

BOSTON
SYMPHONY
ORCHESTRA
SEIJI OZAWA
*Music
Director*

Over the years thousands of letters have come to Symphony Hall after the youngsters have attended the Youth Concerts.

"I didn't want to go, but my teacher made me. But I liked it!"

~ from a fourth-grade boy

"I felt like crying in 'Clair de Lune' but I was too ashamed."

~ from a young girl

*"Dear Mr. Dickson:
It was a wonderful concert. I couldn't go because I was sick, but my sister told me."*

*~ from a young boy
(evidently a class assignment)*

Seiji Ozawa
BSO Music Director
Boston Symphony Orchestra

"Garlic-gate"

A few years ago, as part of a benefit for the BSO, Seiji was asked to be one of several "celebrity chefs" at the Four Seasons Hotel in Boston. Each chef was to prepare a dish that would then be served to the guests, each of whom had made a substantial contribution to the orchestra.

Seiji was working on a pasta recipe that called for garlic. The hotel had prepared the key ingredients in advance and the garlic they had supplied was crushed, not diced as he was used to. Seiji started heaping spoonfuls of the concoction into the sauce, not realizing that it was exponentially more potent than it should have been.

As a result, the dish was so thick with garlic that those who partook were banned from their homes for days as garlic oozed from their pores.

~ as told to Kim Smedvig

Yosenabe

(Seiji's Fish Stew)

½ to 1 pound fresh scallops
½ to 1 pound red snapper, cut into 1-inch pieces
8 to 10 large shrimp, shelled, tails intact
4 to 6 clams, soaked in water for 2 to 3 hours
6 to 8 Chinese cabbages, cut into bite-size pieces
½ carrot, sliced ¼ inch lengthwise
10 to 12 snow pea pods
3 to 4 scallions, cut into 1-inch lengths
4 fresh shiitake mushrooms, criss-cross pattern cut on tops
½ (16-ounce) package tofu, quartered
1 bunch shirataki, boiled, drained, cut into 2 to 3-inch lengths
6 to 8 cups dashi (water mixed with konbu seaweed,
4 to 5-inches long)
½ cup sake

Sauce:
Ponzu sauce (see note)
Daikon-oroshi (grated daikon)
Sarashi negi (finely chopped scallions)
Shichimi togarashi (red pepper seasoning)

Arrange on a large platter: scallops, fish, shrimp, clams, cabbage, carrots, peas, scallions, mushrooms, tofu and shirataki.

Place a donabe (earthenware casserole) on a portable table cooker, and fill it with the dashi and sake. Bring the mixture to a boil and add half of the ingredients on the seafood/vegetable platter. Simmer for 10 to 15 minutes, or until done.

Meanwhile, place the ponzu sauce, daikon-oroshi, sarashi negi and shichimi togarashi in separate small bowls or dishes.

Serve the cooked portion in individual bowls and pass the sauce ingredients separately. The other half of the seafood/vegetable platter can now be added to the remaining dashi and sake for cooking. This will provide a second helping for the guests!

Yield: 4 to 6 servings

Note: Striped bass, halibut or any other white meat fish may be substituted for the red snapper.

You may make your own ponzu sauce by combining citrus juice, soy sauce and mirin in a 4:1:1 ratio, with vinegar to taste.

Shirataki (devil's tongue starch noodles), ponzu sauce, mirin and daikon may be found in Oriental markets and food stores.

Boston Symphony Chamber Players

The Boston Symphony Chamber Players

Members of the Boston Symphony Chamber Players

BOSTON SYMPHONY CHAMBER PLAYERS

Each spring as the BSO musicians prepare for the Boston Pops season, twelve of the orchestra's first-chair players combine their talents into the intimate ensemble and musical treasure known as the Boston Symphony Chamber Players.

Like the Pops and the Tanglewood Festival Chorus, the Chamber Players speak to the Boston Symphony Orchestra's diverse talents. The ensemble was founded in 1964 during Erich Leinsdorf's tenure as BSO music director. It is the only chamber group in the world made up of the principal players from a major orchestra. The Chamber Players have recorded with Deutsche Grammophon, Nonesuch, RCA and CBS labels. Their first album was awarded a Grammy in 1965. They also perform an annual series of three concerts on Sunday afternoons at the New England Conservatory's Jordan Hall, as well as several concerts each summer at Tanglewood. They have also toured extensively both nationally and in Europe, Japan, and South America.

The musicians' year-round ensemble experience in the orchestra gives them a head start in achieving a polished performance. Performing with the Chamber Players also allows the first-chair string, woodwind, brass, and percussion members the opportunity to make artistic decisions communally. Throughout their history, the Chamber Players have investigated the great masterpieces of the chamber repertory as well

Photo by: © Michael Lutch

as some seldom explored byways. The group regularly introduces new music and frequently expands its repertory by collaborating with BSO colleagues and distinguished guest artists, including Claude Frank, Peter Serkin, and André Previn. Their masterful performances have been described as a "bit of heaven on earth."

The ensemble's leader is Malcolm Lowe, who has served as BSO concertmaster since 1984. He is well known to Boston and Tanglewood audiences as a distinguished violinist and soloist.

Photo by: © Michael Lutch

Members of the Boston Symphony Chamber Players in Concert

BREADS ~ MUFFINS ~ EGGS

The music library of the BSO on the second floor of Symphony Hall is the busiest and probably most important room in the building. It is the nerve center of all musical activity.

The shelves are from floor to ceiling, all containing the orchestra's scores. On the left are thousands of scores of works performed during the more than one hundred years of the orchestra's existence. On the right wall are the players' parts. Throughout the room, in seeming disarray, there are piles of music – music for next week, music for last week, music just arrived from the publisher, music about to be shipped back to the publisher, and music for the current week.

Yet, in all this confusion, nothing ever gets lost; the players always find the right music on their stands at rehearsals and concerts.

Grandmother's Homemade Biscuits

2 cups self-rising flour
⅓ cup shortening
½ teaspoon salt
½ cup milk

Preheat the oven to 400°.

Sift the flour into a mixing bowl. Cut the shortening into the flour with a pastry blender, or by rubbing your hands together as if "dusting sand particles off", until blended. Add the salt. Add the milk and stir only until mixed.

Turn out the mixture onto a floured board, and knead the dough lightly. Roll it out, cut into circles and place on a greased cookie sheet. Bake in the oven for 8 to 10 minutes, or until browned.

Yield: 12 biscuits

Variation: In place of the self-rising flour, 2 cups all-purpose flour plus 2 teaspoons baking powder may be used.

Bran Muffins

2 cups all-bran flakes
1 cup 100% bran flakes
1½ cups sugar
½ cup salad oil
2 eggs, beaten
2½ cups all-purpose flour
2½ teaspoons baking soda
½ teaspoon salt
2 cups buttermilk
1½ cups white or brown raisins, soaked in hot water

Preheat oven to 375°. Grease and flour muffin pans for 24 muffins.

In a bowl, pour 1 cup of boiling water over the two kinds of bran flakes.

In another bowl, blend the sugar, oil and beaten eggs. Mix together the flour, baking soda and salt. Then add the flour mixture to the sugar mixture, alternating it with the buttermilk.

Add the soaked bran and drained raisins to the combined mixtures. Mix well. Grease and flour muffin pans. Fill the muffin pans three-fourths full. Bake for 30 minutes. Check the muffins and, if necessary, bake 5 additional minutes.

Yield: 2 dozen muffins

Note: The recipe may be mixed ahead. Dough may be kept 3 to 4 weeks in refrigerator in covered containers and baked as needed. Do not freeze unbaked.

BOSTON
SYMPHONY
ORCHESTRA
SEIJI OZAWA
*Music
Director*

On one of Harry Ellis Dickson's early tours with the BSO, he discovered that he had left his white bow ties at home. A colleague loaned him one, the kind that you have to tie yourself, which Harry could not do. When he asked the colleague to tie it for him, he said, "Sure, but you'll have to lie down on the floor".

"Why?" Harry asked.

"Well," he said, "I used to help my father, who is an undertaker, and this is the only way I know how."

"No, thanks," said Harry, and that night he learned how to make a bow tie!

BOSTON
SYMPHONY
ORCHESTRA
SEIJI OZAWA
*Music
Director*

Apple Muffins with Brown Sugar Sauce

1 tablespoon butter, softened
1 egg, lightly beaten
1 cup brown sugar
1 cup flour
2 tablespoons hot apple juice, or boiling water
1 teaspoon baking soda
1 teaspoon vanilla extract
1 cup peeled, cored and chopped tart apples
½ cup chopped walnuts or pecans

Sauce:
1 cup brown sugar
2 tablespoons flour
½ cup hot apple juice, or boiling water
4 tablespoons butter
1 teaspoon vanilla extract

Preheat oven to 350°. Grease muffin cups.

In a bowl, combine the butter, egg, brown sugar, flour, apple juice, baking soda, vanilla, apple, and walnuts in the order given. Fill the muffin cups three-fourths full. Bake for 20 to 25 minutes.

Make the sauce: In a sauce pan, combine the brown sugar, flour, hot apple juice, butter and vanilla, and cook over medium heat until thick. Pour the sauce over the muffins and serve immediately.

Yield: about 12 muffins

Variation: For those who prefer their muffins without a sauce, these are still terrific!

Jordan Marsh's Blueberry Muffins

2 tablespoons butter, very soft or melted
2 tablespoons sugar
1 egg
2 cups flour
4 teaspoons baking powder
½ teaspoon salt
1 cup milk
1 cup blueberries, lightly floured
Extra sugar (for topping)

Preheat oven to 400°.

In a mixing bowl, cream the butter and the sugar together. Add in the egg and beat well.

In a bowl, stir flour, baking powder and salt together; then add, alternately with the milk, to the sugar mixture. Gently stir in the blueberries.

Drop the batter by spoonfuls into buttered muffin tins. To recapture the crunchy crust of Jordan Marsh's muffins, sprinkle liberally with extra sugar.

Bake for 25 minutes.

Yield: 1 dozen muffins

This is a great old favorite!

BOSTON
SYMPHONY
ORCHESTRA
SEIJI OZAWA
Music Director

During the 1979 visit to China the BSO players gained an insight into the appalling conditions under which their Chinese colleagues had tried to make music. Western music was prohibited, and the musicians played and practiced surreptitiously, always terrified that they would be caught and punished.

The concertmaster of the Beijing Orchestra, who had been imprisoned for eleven years for advocating Western music, was engaged in a heated discussion during one intermission with Eugene Lehner, a BSO violist. Closer examination of the discussion revealed that they were speaking to each other in Lehner's native Hungarian. The concertmaster had been a student in Budapest!

Joseph Hearne
Bass

Jan Brett
Author and Illustrator

BSO member Joe Hearne joined the orchestra in 1962, and when not making music he collaborates with his wife on her children's books. Listening to Joe play the double-bass with the Boston Symphony has created many inspiring moments for Jan. In fact, the bass-playing bear in her book, "Berlioz the Bear," bears a certain resemblance to Joe.

Jan's recipe for Annie's Corn Cakes was inspired by her young daughter's desire for a pet. Jan turned her daughter's wish into a whimsical children's book about Annie, a young girl who places corn cakes in the snow to attract wild animals, with the hope that one of them might become a pet.

Annie's Corn Cakes

1 ¼ cups flour
¾ cup corn meal
¼ cup sugar
2 teaspoons baking powder
¼ teaspoon salt
1 cup milk
¼ cup olive oil
1 egg, beaten

Preheat oven to 400°. Grease an 8 or 9-inch baking pan.

Mix together the flour, corn meal, sugar, baking powder, and salt. Then stir in the milk, olive oil and egg. Pour the batter into the baking pan; bake for 25 minutes.

Yield: 8 corn cakes

Variation: Try baking the cakes in a pan with corn cob shapes!

Annie placed more corn cakes at the edge of the wood.

Banana Bread

1 egg, beaten
1 cup sugar
¼ cup melted butter
3 medium ripe bananas, thoroughly mashed
½ teaspoon salt (optional)
1 teaspoon baking soda
1½ cups all-purpose flour

Preheat oven to 350°. Lightly grease a regular size loaf pan.

In a bowl, place the beaten egg; add sugar, melted butter, and then the mashed bananas. Add the dry ingredients in the following order: salt, baking soda, and then flour. Mix by hand thoroughly.

Place the mixture evenly in the greased loaf pan. Bake for 50 to 60 minutes.

Yield: 12 servings

Note: This is a very moist banana bread recipe, and may be easily doubled.

The contributor stated that this recipe had been in her mother-in-law's family for over one hundred years!

Before the present method of auditioning for the BSO was adopted (where the applicant is not seen by the jury), a clarinetist named Gino Cioffi, who had performed under many famous conductors, was convinced that the BSO needed him more than he needed the orchestra. Cioffi came to the center of the stage and said, "Good morning, gentlemen, what do ya wanna hear?"

Charles Munch asked, "What have you prepared?"

"Anything you want - concerto, symphony, opera - anything!"

Munch asked, "Do you play the Mozart Concerto?"

"Ma sure!" answered Cioffi, and gave a brilliant performance of the first movement. Finishing with a flourish, Cioffi walked to the edge of the stage and said, "Pretty good, uh?"

Munch turned to Richard Burgin, the concertmaster, and said, "Such confidence! We must have this man!" and Cioffi was hired.

Sarah Chang
Violin

Violinist Sarah Chang contributed this family recipe. She is a gifted young soloist and a favorite with BSO and Pops audiences.

"Being only seventeen, my skills in the kitchen are very limited," says Sarah. "But this bread recipe is a favorite with my family. In fact, I have grown up with it."

Honey-Banana Wheat Bread with Peanuts

⅔ *cup warm water*
1 envelope (1 tablespoon) dry yeast
2 teaspoons sugar
1½ tablespoons melted butter or vegetable oil
¼ cup honey
1 ripe banana, sliced
½ teaspoon vanilla extract
1 teaspoon salt
1½ cups whole wheat flour
1½ cups bread flour
½ cup peanuts, coarsely chopped

In the bowl of a food processor, dissolve the yeast in the warm water (100° to 115°). Stir in the sugar. After a few minutes the fermentation of the yeast should become apparent, as the mixture swells and small bubbles appear on the surface. Add the butter (or vegetable oil), honey, banana slices, vanilla, salt and both flours to the bowl. Pulse the processor on and off until the dough forms into a ball. Remove the dough to a floured counter and roll it out. Sprinkle the peanuts onto the dough; then roll it up jelly roll style. Knead the dough to further mix in the peanuts. Cover and let rest for 20 minutes.

Form into a loaf and place in a buttered or sprayed 9 by 5 by 3-inch loaf pan. Let dough rise in a draft-free place until doubled in size - about 40 minutes. Preheat oven to 350°.

Bake the bread for 50 to 60 minutes. Remove when done and place on a rack for 15 minutes before serving.

Yield: about 10 to 12 servings

Note: This bread freezes well.

Michael's Pumpkin Bread

2 eggs
1 scant cup honey
1 scant cup vegetable oil
1 cup pumpkin
⅓ cup water
2 cups whole wheat flour
1 teaspoon baking soda
¼ teaspoon baking powder
¼ teaspoon allspice
¼ teaspoon cinnamon
¼ teaspoon cloves
¼ teaspoon nutmeg
½ cup raisins and/or chopped walnuts (optional)

Preheat the oven to 350°. Grease a 9 by 5-inch loaf pan.

Beat the eggs and mix in honey, oil, pumpkin, and water. Mix together in a bowl the flour, soda, baking powder, and spices. Gently blend the pumpkin and flour mixes together. Add the raisins, if desired, and mix well.

Bake approximately one hour, or until a toothpick comes out clean.

Yield: 10 servings

*This bread is wonderful by itself, or
topped with vanilla ice cream.*

Leone Buyse
Flute

Leone Buyse joined the Boston Symphony Orchestra in 1983 as assistant principal flute. An active chamber musician, she performed frequently with the Boston Symphony Chamber Players.

She served as acting principal flute for three seasons, before retiring from the orchestra after the 1991 Tanglewood season to assume the position of Professor of Flute at the University of Michigan. She is currently Professor of Chamber Music at Rice University in Texas.

Regarding the Pumpkin Bread recipe, Ms. Buyse says: "My husband, Michael Webster, is a great baker. This is one of our family favorites. We often make triple or quadruple recipes at holiday time, or if we are giving a post-concert reception."

During a rehearsal of the Schumann "Spring" Symphony, Koussevitzky turned to the violins and said, "Gentlemen, be happy. Be gay!" Violinist Joseph Leibovici immediately answered, under his breath, "What's the occasion?"

Watch Hill Maple Walnut Scones

3½ cups unbleached all-purpose flour
1 cup finely chopped walnuts
4 teaspoons baking powder
1 teaspoon salt
⅔ cup butter or margarine
1 cup milk
½ cup maple syrup, divided
½ teaspoon maple flavoring

Preheat oven to 425°. Grease a large baking sheet.

In a large bowl, combine flour, chopped walnuts, baking powder and salt. With a pastry blender or two knives, cut in the butter until the mixture resembles coarse crumbs.

Add milk, ⅓ cup of the maple syrup, and the maple flavoring to the dry ingredients, and mix lightly with a fork until the mixture clings together and forms a soft dough.

Turn the dough out onto a lightly floured surface and knead gently 5 or 6 times. Divide the dough in half. With a lightly floured rolling pin, roll one half of the dough into a 7-inch round. Cut the round into 8 wedges. Repeat with the remaining one half of the dough.

Place the scones on the greased baking sheet. Pierce the tops with the tines of a fork. Brush the scone tops with some of the remaining maple syrup.

Bake the scones 15 to 18 minutes until golden brown. Brush again with any remaining maple syrup. Serve warm with maple butter, if desired. Best served warm.

Yield:16 scones

Note:The scones may be frozen.

Bruschetta with Herbs

¼ cup extra-virgin olive oil
1 tablespoon chopped Italian flat-leaf parsley
1 tablespoon chopped fresh basil
Pinch of dried marjoram
Freshly ground black pepper
8 slices Tuscan, or peasant-style bread,
cut into ¾-inch-thick slices
2 large cloves garlic, peeled

In a small bowl, combine the oil, parsley, basil, marjoram and pepper to taste.

Preheat the broiler, or prepare the grill.

Toast the bread until lightly browned on both sides, turning once. Immediately remove from the heat and rub one side with the garlic. Brush the same side with the herb mixture.

Serve immediately.

Yield: 8 bruschetta

Lavender Butter

8 tablespoons (1 stick) butter, softened
1 teaspoon finely chopped lavender leaves

Stir the lavender pieces into the butter with a fork. Pack the mixture into a small china bowl and refrigerate.

Yield: 8 tablespoons flavored butter

Note: The lavender butter may be spread on rolls, or used as a spread for vegetables (summer squash, zucchini, green beans, etc.) It is excellent for use in a salt-free diet.

John Williams
Boston Pops
Laureate Conductor

We welcome Samantha and John Williams back for the second edition of our cookbook.

John is widely known to audiences around the world for his film scores and as the former conductor of the Boston Pops. His association with the BSO and Pops remains close, and he returns each year as a guest conductor for several concerts. The Boston Symphony Orchestra recorded the score he composed for the movie "Saving Private Ryan" in Symphony Hall under his direction.

John has won five Oscars for his film scores and is the most-nominated individual in Oscar history, but he remains modest: "When people congratulate me on winning the Oscars, I like to remind them of the 34 I have lost."

Whole Wheat Pancakes

1 egg
1 cup non-fat plain yogurt
1 tablespoon butter
1 tablespoon maple syrup
1 teaspoon vanilla extract
1 cup whole wheat pastry flour
1 teaspoon baking powder
¼ to ½ teaspoon salt
Grated nutmeg (optional)
Non-fat milk, for thinning batter

In a bowl, beat together the egg, yogurt, butter, maple syrup and vanilla. Add the flour, baking powder, and salt, whisking until just blended. If desired, grated nutmeg to taste, may be added and blended in. If necessary, non-fat milk may be added to obtain desired batter consistency.

Pour the batter onto a hot nonstick griddle, making pancakes of desired size.

Yield: 2 generous servings

Bridget's Non-Dairy Oatmeal Pancakes

1⅛ cups Edensoy Extra (vanilla flavor)
1 cup oats
2 tablespoons safflower oil
2 eggs, beaten
½ cup flour
1 tablespoon brown sugar
1 teaspoon baking powder
¼ teaspoon salt

In a bowl, combine the Edensoy and the oats, and let stand for 5 minutes.

Add to the oat mixture the oil, eggs, flour, brown sugar, baking powder and salt; mix well. Ladle the mixture onto hot griddle, making 4-inch pancakes.

Yield: Twelve 4-inch pancakes

Note: If Edensoy is not available, and dairy products are not a problem, use regular milk plus a drop of vanilla extract.

*This recipe is particularly good
for those allergic to dairy products.*

BOSTON SYMPHONY ORCHESTRA
SEIJI OZAWA
Music Director

Jonathan Menkis
Horn

Originally from West Orange, New Jersey, and now living in Lincoln, Johathan Menkis received his bachelor's degree from Ithaca College in 1981, then joined the Sacramento Symphony Orchestra as its associate principal horn. He became assistant principal horn with the New Orleans Phiharmonic the following season and was appointed to the Boston Symphony's horn section in 1984. Jonathan is also on the faculty of the New England Conservatory of Music.

French horn player Jonathan Menkis and his wife Ann gave us this recipe. Jonathan loves the outdoors and whenever possible escapes from the city for mountain hikes.

The Inn at Stockbridge

The Inn is a New England-style bed and breakfast set in a 1906 Georgian mansion. Owner Len Schiller provides these lemon cottage cheese pancakes as a special treat for the Inn's guests who came to enjoy Tanglewood.

Lemon Cottage Cheese Pancakes

3 eggs, separated
¼ cup all-purpose flour
¾ cup cottage cheese
4 tablespoons (½ stick) butter, melted
2 tablespoons sugar
¼ teaspoon salt
1 tablespoon grated lemon zest

Beat the egg whites until they hold stiff peaks. In another bowl, beat together the egg yolks, flour, cottage cheese, butter, sugar, salt and lemon zest until well-blended.

With a large spatula, fold the egg whites into yolk mixture. Gently fold until well blended.

Heat a pancake griddle or skillet over medium heat. Pour the batter onto the surface, making small pancake disks, and cook them slowly for about 1 ½ minutes, then turn.

Yield: 12 small pancakes

Cheese Soufflé

2 eggs, beaten
2 cups milk
¼ teaspoon dry mustard
½ teaspoon salt
½ teaspoon pepper
Dash of Worcestershire sauce
1 cup shredded extra sharp cheddar cheese (about ¼ pound)
4 ounces processed cheese, cut into chunks
3 thin slices of bread

Preheat oven to 350°. Butter a baking dish.

In the baking dish, mix together the eggs, milk, dry mustard, salt, pepper, Worcestershire sauce, and both cheeses. Lightly butter the bread slices and press them down into the mixture.

Set the baking dish in a pan of very hot water that comes halfway up the sides of the dish. Bake for 1 hour.

Yield: 2 servings

Variation: Try using French bread as a substitute.

Brunch Eggs with Spanish Sauce

1 (1-pound) loaf white toasting bread
½ cup butter
6 eggs
3 cups milk
¾ teaspoon dry mustard
¾ teaspoon white pepper
1 pound cheddar cheese, grated
Spanish Sauce (recipe follows)

Butter both sides of bread and cut into cubes. Set aside.

In a bowl, combine the eggs, milk, mustard, and white pepper. Layer the cheese and bread cubes in a buttered 13 by 9-inch casserole dish. Pour the egg mixture over all, cover, and refrigerate 8 to 12 hours, or overnight.

When ready to serve, preheat oven to 350°. Bake, uncovered, for 30 to 45 minutes, or until eggs are set.

Yield: 8 servings

Variation: For a heartier brunch dish, place sautéed and crumbled sausage on the bottom of the casserole before adding the cheese and bread.

Spanish Sauce

⅓ cup chopped onion
¼ cup chopped green pepper (optional)
3 ounces fresh mushrooms, sliced (about ¾ cup)
3 tablespoons oil
1 tablespoon cornstarch
1 (16-ounce) can tomatoes, with liquid
1 teaspoon salt
Dash of black pepper
2 teaspoons sugar
Dash of cayenne

In a sauce pan, brown the onion, green pepper (if used), and mushrooms in oil. Combine the cornstarch with 2 tablespoons of the canned tomato liquid, and add to vegetable mixture. Add the tomatoes and its remaining liquid, salt, black pepper, sugar and cayenne. Cook over low heat, stirring often, until vegetables are tender and sauce is slightly thickened, about 15 to 20 minutes.

Yield: about 2½ cups of sauce

Serve the Spanish Sauce with the Brunch Eggs.

Pierre Monteux's memory was legendary. He could detect wrong notes in the most complicated score, and his remarkable memory enabled him to bring back to mind scores he had not conducted in years. Once at his school for conductors in Maine, he was prevailed upon to conduct part of a program - and he chose to do an orchestral version of the Beethoven Septet. Before the rehearsal his wife said, "But, Pierre, I never heard you conduct that piece."

And he answered, "Oh, yes, I conducted it thirty-seven years ago in Paris."

"But have you studied it for the rehearsal?" she asked.

"No", he answered, "I couldn't find the score. But I remember it." And he did at the rehearsal - every note of it.

Cheese and Scallion Puff

3 cups 1% milk
1 ¼ cups finely chopped scallions
¾ cup yellow cornmeal
2 large egg yolks
½ cup freshly grated Parmesan cheese
½ cup grated extra sharp cheddar cheese
1 teaspoon salt, divided
¼ teaspoon freshly grated pepper
7 large egg whites

In a heavy medium saucepan over medium heat, bring the milk and scallions to a simmer. Whisking constantly, slowly sprinkle in the cornmeal. Cook, whisking constantly, until the mixture has thickened, about 5 minutes. Remove from heat and cool for 10 minutes.

Whisk in the egg yolks, Parmesan cheese, cheddar cheese, ½ teaspoon of the salt and the pepper. (The recipe can be made to this point and kept in the refrigerator for 2 days. Prior to continuing, return it to room temperature.)

About 45 minutes before serving, preheat oven to 375°. Lightly oil a 3-quart baking dish.

Beat the egg whites with the remaining ½ teaspoon of salt until they form soft peaks. Whisk one quarter of the beaten egg whites into the puff base, then fold in remaining egg whites.

Spoon the batter into the prepared baking dish, smooth the top and bake for 30 to 40 minutes, or until puffed and golden.

Yield: 6 servings

This is a very light dish, and well worth the work involved.

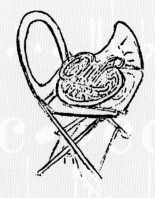

Mushroom Quiche

1 prepared pie crust ("Best Pie Crust Ever", p. 251)
1 teaspoon butter
1 shallot, minced
6 ounces Portobello mushrooms, chopped
4 ounces Gruyère cheese, grated
3 medium eggs
1 cup whipping cream
Nutmeg

Preheat oven to 425°.

Place the prepared pie crust in a 9-inch pie plate. (If a frozen pie crust is used, defrost it first.) Prick it lightly with a fork, making sure that there are no air pockets between the crust and the plate. Flute the edges. Bake the crust in the oven for 15 minutes; remove and reduce heat to 375°.

Prepare the filling: Melt the butter in a saucepan; add the shallots and sauté until golden brown (about 4 to 5 minutes). Add the mushrooms and cook until they are tender. Spread the mushroom mixture evenly in the baked crust.

In a bowl, mix the cheese, eggs and cream; then pour on top of the mushroom mixture. Sprinkle on nutmeg. Bake about 35 minutes, or until set.

Yield: about 4 to 6 servings

Variation: For variety, try using different kinds of cheeses and mushrooms.

BOSTON SYMPHONY ORCHESTRA
SEIJI OZAWA
Music Director

Elita Kang
Violin

Mushroom quiche is a favorite of Elita Kang, a young member of the BSO, who joined the orchestra in 1997 and contributed this recipe.

She is a graduate of the Curtis Institute, where she served as principal second violin and concertmaster as well as substitute with the Philadelphia Orchestra. She is also a two-time winner of the Juilliard Concerto Competition.

Keith Lockhart
Conductor, Boston Pops Orchestra

Lucia Lin
Violin

BSO violinist Lucia Lin and her husband, BSO Pops Conductor Keith Lockhart, are one of the BSO's best-known couples.

Violinist Lucia Lin made her debut as soloist with the Chicago Symphony Orchestra at age eleven. She has been a member of the BSO since 1985, serving as its assistant concertmaster from 1985 to 1991.

"This was the recipe for the main course at our post-wedding brunch," writes Lucy. "Because we were married in Maine, we wanted a touch of Maine in the quiche, therefore the crabmeat."

Crabmeat Quiche with Mushroom Crust

6 tablespoons (¾ stick) butter, divided
11 ounces mushrooms, chopped
⅔ cup finely crushed saltine crackers
1 cup chopped green onions
1 cup shredded mozzarella cheese
½ cup grated Swiss cheese
1 cup half-and-half cream
4 eggs
¼ teaspoon plus a pinch paprika
¼ teaspoon plus a pinch cayenne
½ pound crabmeat

In a large skillet melt 3 to 4 tablespoons of the butter over medium heat. Add the mushrooms and cook until limp. Stir in the crushed crackers, and remove from the heat. Press the mixture evenly over the bottom of a well-greased 9-inch square pan. (Alternatively, a 9-inch quiche pan may be used.)

Melt the remaining butter in a skillet over medium heat. Add the onion and cook until soft. Remove the onions from the skillet and spread over the mushroom-cracker crust.

Preheat the oven to 350°.

In a bowl mix the cheeses with the half-and-half. Beat the eggs; add to the cheese mixture. Add the spices and crabmeat. Pour the mixture over the mushroom-cracker crust.

Bake for approximately 40 minutes. Remove from the oven and allow the quiche to stand for 10 to 15 minutes before cutting.

Yield: 6 servings

BSO On Tour

*The BSO's gala joint concert in
Beijing during its historic 1979 tour to China.*

Osaka, Japan (1999 Tour)

Street scene, Osaka, Japan (1999 Tour)

BSO on Tour

The BSO's national and international tours are filled with magical moments for orchestra members and the Friends who accompany them. The orchestra ventured on its first tour in 1915 and has been traveling ever since. In 1998, Seiji Ozawa and the BSO criss-crossed Europe with sold-out performances in London, Paris, Vienna, and Athens. The two-week tour gave orchestra members the opportunity to meet American and European dignitaries and to visit private homes and museums.

Over the years, the orchestra's international tours have provided dramatic memories. The BSO's triumphant 1979 tour of Shanghai and Beijing made headlines all over the world. In December 1993, when the BSO played in Smetana Hall in Prague, Czech Republic President Vaclav Havel came on stage at the concert's end to congratulate Seiji Ozawa and the orchestra, as well as guest artists Frederica von Stade, Yo-Yo Ma, Itzhak Perlman, and Rudolph Firkuŝný. In Salzburg, Austria, the audience in the Festspielhaus jumped to its feet for an ovation.

Photo by: Thomas Gauger

Afterward the orchestra threw Ozawa a birthday party in a lovely biergarten, where everyone danced to the music of an oom-pah-pah band.

The BSO's tours to Greece are testament to the range of adventures the orchestra encounters in its travels. On one trip, the group had the good fortune to enjoy the run of a cruise ship for a day, including a tour of a nearby island and generous buffets. On a subsequent visit, the tour landed amid blizzard and flood conditions and a power outage in Athens. The show, and the electricity, went on—eventually. When the BSO performed on another Grecian visit at the Herodes Atticus Odeum (the second-century A.D. amphitheater on the Acropolis), the orchestra played to the backdrop of a full moon shining over the Parthenon and the audience.

In May 1999, the orchestra returned to the Far East, with several stops in Japan.

The United States tours are equally rewarding, with the concerts always resulting in rave reviews as they do wherever the BSO goes, whether Europe, Asia, or South America. The BSO on tour is indeed a special part of the orchestra's musical life.

Lending a hand in Leeds, England (1956)

The BSO in performance in Athens, Greece (1991)

BEANS ~ LENTILS ~ PASTA ~ RICE

Richard Svoboda
Principal Bassoon

BSO principal bassoonist Richard Svoboda says he has been perfecting his recipe for vegetarian chili for ten years. "My wife Liz and our kids love it, so I must have finally got it right," Richard says. "I think it tastes better if given a day to rest. The other members of my family disagree: they want to eat it as soon as it's ready."

Vegetarian Chili

1 large onion, chopped
5 cloves garlic, minced
2 teaspoons canola oil
1½ cups diced carrots
1 cup diced celery
1½ cups diced zucchini
1 (28-ounce) can crushed tomatoes
1 (48-ounce) can tomato juice
3 tablespoons molasses
5 tablespoons chili powder
1 tablespoon ground cumin
1 tablespoon crumbled dried oregano leaves
½ teaspoon coriander
¼ teaspoon ground cloves
¼ teaspoon ground allspice
3 cups cooked kidney beans
3 cups cooked garbanzo beans
1 cup diced green pepper
2 cups frozen corn kernels
Finely chopped jalapeño peppers, for passing

In a large stockpot, sauté the onion and garlic in the oil until softened. Add the carrots, celery, and zucchini. Partially cook.

Add the crushed tomatoes, tomato juice, molasses, chili powder, cumin, oregano, coriander, cloves and allspice. Bring to a boil; then add both beans, green peppers and corn. Simmer for 10 minutes.

Serve with the jalapeño peppers passed at the table for individual tastes.

Yield: about 8 servings

Note: It is advisable to wear gloves when handling jalapeño peppers.

White Bean Chili

1 onion, diced
2 cloves garlic, minced
2 tablespoons olive oil
3 (14½-ounce) cans low-fat chicken broth
1 (14-ounce) can chick peas
1 (14-ounce) can cannellini beans
1 (8-ounce) can corn
1 (4-ounce) can green chiles, diced
1 pound cooked chicken breast, cubed
Chopped cilantro, for garnish
Low-fat sour cream, for garnish
Low-fat Monterey Jack cheese, shredded, for garnish

Sauté the onion and garlic in olive oil in a large pot. Add the chicken broth, chick peas, cannellini beans, corn and chiles, along with the chicken, and bring to a boil. Lower heat and simmer, covered, for 45 minutes.

When serving, sprinkle on some chopped cilantro, a dollop of sour cream, and some cheese.

Yield: 4 to 6 servings

Note: It is advisable to wear gloves when handling chili peppers.

Bonnie Bewick
Violin

Bonnie Bewick says this White Bean Chili is a deliciously easy dish to put together. Bonnie, a BSO violinist since 1987, says it's perfect for cool nights. "It hits the spot in winter or early spring when there is a chill in the air and you want something zesty. I'll eat it anytime. I even made it on a hot summer day at Tanglewood for my second date with my husband. It's really wonderful chili!"

Pasta

Touring with the BSO demands impeccable logistical arrangements.

During the 1998 European tour, 201 people (staff, orchestra members and their families) traveled on nine flights, climbed on board 101 buses, and booked 712 hotel rooms!

Packing instruments and equipment is no less a daunting task. When the orchestra departed for Japan in May 1999, they were accompanied by 141 cases weighing 26,000 pounds!

Pasta all'Amatriciana
(Pasta with Bacon-Tomato Sauce)

*8 slices lightly-smoked lean bacon,
cut into ¼-inch pieces crosswise
6 tablespoons olive oil
½ cup chopped onion
1 (28-ounce) can crushed Italian-style tomatoes
Pinch crushed dried red pepper, plus additional, if desired
Salt
1 pound penne pasta
¾ cup freshly grated Romano or Pecorino cheese,
plus additional for serving*

Cook the bacon in a large skillet over low-medium heat until lightly browned. Drain off all the fat. Add the olive oil. Sauté the onion in the oil over low heat until golden, about 8 minutes. Add the tomatoes and cook, stirring occasionally, over medium heat until the sauce is thickened, about 15 minutes. Add the red pepper and salt to taste.

Meanwhile, cook the penne in plenty of boiling water until "al dente", or firm to the bite, about 8 to 10 minutes. Drain well. Add the pasta to the mixture in the skillet. Stir in the Romano cheese.

Serve in the skillet, or turn the pasta out into a warm bowl. Pass additional cheese, if desired.

Yield: 6 first course servings

Bombolini alla Moda Mia
(Pasta with Sausage and Cream)

1 pound rigatoni, or similar bulky pasta
2 tablespoons olive oil
1 pound Italian sausage, bulk or links with casings removed
1 cup heavy cream
1 cup freshly grated Parmesan cheese
Salt and pepper

Cook the pasta in a pot with plenty of boiling water, until it is "al dente", or firm to the bite. Do not overcook the pasta.

While the pasta is cooking, heat the oil in a large skillet. When the oil is hot, break off small pieces of the sausage and add them to the skillet. (You may cook the sausage in larger pieces, if desired, and then break them up during the cooking.) When the sausage is cooked through, remove it from the skillet with a slotted spoon and set it aside.

Heat the cream in a small pan until very warm. (This is done to avoid cooling down the pasta when it is added in at the end.)

When the pasta is cooked, drain it and return it to the empty pot. Over low- medium heat, add the sausage, cream and Parmesan cheese to the pasta. Add salt and pepper to taste. Stir the pasta, mixing the ingredients, and bring it back to a fully-heated condition, and the cheese is starting to melt.

Serve immediately.

Yield: 6 servings

Variation: Add 2 ounces of Gorgonzola cheese to the heated cream and stir until melted.

BOSTON
SYMPHONY
ORCHESTRA
SEIJI OZAWA
*Music
Director*

There are many logistical problems connected with a tour by the Boston Symphony Orchestra in this country and abroad. In addition to plans for shipping all the stands, instruments, wardrobe trunks and music required for the trip, emergencies must also be anticipated. Once in Japan, when almost fifty percent of the orchestra became ill, Charles Munch had to change the program and conduct a chamber orchestra.

BOSTON
SYMPHONY
ORCHESTRA
SEIJI OZAWA
*Music
Director*

The Beethoven "Eroica" symphony was always carried
automatically on all tours of
the orchestra, to be played in
case of the death of a famous
person.

When Franklin Delano Roosevelt
died in April 1945, the orchestra was on the train to Philadelphia, and that night played a
memorial concert for the late
President, including, of course,
the Funeral March of the
"Eroica."

The day JFK was assassinated
the orchestra heard just before
the Friday afternoon concert
that he had been shot. After the
first piece on the program the
two librarians appeared with
the music for the "Eroica;" the
players then knew that the
President was dead.

Pasta de Carnevale
(Sicilian Festival Pasta)

*2 large carrots, diced very small
1 medium onion, finely chopped
½ cup olive oil
2 cloves garlic, crushed
1 to 1½ pounds boneless pork loin, cut into 7 or 8 slices, or
boneless pork loin cutlets, fat removed
¼ cup dry white wine
1 (28-ounce) can crushed Italian-style tomatoes
1 (8-ounce) can tomato sauce
1 teaspoon salt
12 ounces penne or ziti pasta
¾ cup almond pieces, toasted and crushed coarsely (see note)
1 teaspoon ground cinnamon
1 teaspoon freshly ground black pepper
1 cup freshly grated Pecorino Romano cheese, divided*

In a large skillet over medium-high heat, cook the carrots and onion in
the olive oil. After 2 or 3 minutes, add the garlic. Continue cooking the
vegetables until aromatic - about 5 minutes more. Increase the heat to
high and add the pork slices. Sear the meat on both sides.

Add the wine and cook for 30 seconds; then add the tomatoes, tomato
sauce and salt. Stir well. Bring to a boil, lower heat, cover and simmer
until the pork can be shredded by pulling it apart with a fork - about 1½
to 2 hours. Shred the pork by pulling it apart with a fork. Return it to
the sauce and set the pan aside.

Preheat the oven to 375°. Coat a 12 by 9 by 3-inch baking dish (or
circular equivalent) with some oil. Cook the pasta until it is "al dente",
and still firm to the bite. Do not overcook. Drain the pasta well.

Return the pasta to the pot and toss it with the almonds, cinnamon, black
pepper, meat sauce and ½ cup of the Romano cheese. Pack the mixture
into the baking dish, and top with the remaining ½ cup of the cheese.

Bake in the oven for 15 minutes. Turn off the oven and allow the pasta
to rest in it for an additional 15 minutes before serving.

Yield: 6 to 8 servings

Note: Almonds may be toasted dry over medium heat in a skillet,
stirring constantly so not to burn them. Or, alternatively, you may stir
the almonds with some olive oil in a heavy skillet over medium heat
until they "crackle". Remove from heat and blot dry. Cool.

*This is a very festive Sicilian dish. The addition of almonds and
cinnamon reflects the Arab influence on Sicilian cooking as a
result of the several centuries of Moorish occupation.*

Carbonara "Light"

½ pound imported linguine fini
2 tablespoons extra-virgin olive oil
1 clove garlic, minced
¼ pound prosciutto, chopped
¼ cup dry white wine
¾ cup egg substitute
½ cup fresh chopped parsley
½ cup freshly grated Parmesan cheese
Freshly ground pepper
Additional grated Parmesan cheese, for passing

Bring a large pot of salted water to a boil and cook the pasta per package instructions, until it is "al dente", or firm to the bite.

While the pasta is cooking, heat the oil in a pan and sauté the garlic, taking care not to brown the garlic. Add the prosciutto and sauté until it is crispy brown. Add the wine and boil it down, taking care not to allow all the wine to be absorbed.

In a bowl, beat the egg substitute until foamy. Add the parsley and cheese, and mix well. Add pepper to taste.

When the pasta is cooked and drained, place it in a serving bowl. Pour the egg mixture over it and toss. Top with the prosciutto and its garlic sauce from the pan. Pass the additional cheese and, if desired, a black pepper mill.

Yield: 3 to 4 servings

BOSTON
SYMPHONY
ORCHESTRA
SEIJI OZAWA
*Music
Director*

Fredy Ostrovsky
Violin

Katherine Ostrovsky is the wife of retired BSO violinist Fredy Ostrovsky. She enjoyed a long career teaching ballet, and music has always been a large part of their life.

Fredy began learning classical violin as a young boy. During an Army hitch in World War II, he became a member of Glenn Miller's Army Air Force Orchestra. After the war, he became concertmaster of Paul Whiteman's Orchestra. In 1952, he joined the BSO and enjoyed 40 years of music-making with the orchestra until his retirement.

The Ostrovskys are still very much a part of the BSO family. Healthy, delicious cooking is one of Katherine's hobbies.

During their many trips to New York each season (each one almost a mini-tour), many orchestra members have eaten regularly at the Carnegie Delicatessen, which is located near the concert venue at Carnegie Hall.

The proprietor, a kindly and congenial person, has always greeted them with a "Hello, Boston! Welcome to New York!" He is acquainted with the faces but not the names nor the instruments that go with them.

After a heart attack he missed the BSO for a season, but the following year he greeted them once again and informed them how much he enjoyed seeing them on television when he was sick. "I recognized all of you," he said. "There was the lean corned beef, there was the double pastrami, there was the matzo-ball soup!"

Shrimp Marinara with Vermicelli

Garlic Paste:
3 large cloves garlic, finely minced
¾ teaspoon salt
¼ teaspoon freshly ground pepper

Sauce:
½ cup olive oil
1 (28-ounce) can crushed tomatoes
1 (28-ounce) can Italian-style plum tomatoes, juices reserved
½ cup chopped Italian flat-leaf parsley
4 to 5 fresh basil leaves, or a pinch of dried basil
Pinch of red pepper flakes

1 pound vermicelli pasta (or similar pasta of your choice)
1 pound medium-size shrimp, peeled, deveined, cut in half lengthwise

Make the paste: Mix together the garlic, salt and pepper. Using the back of a knife, blend the mixture into a fine paste. Set aside.

Make the sauce: In a large, heavy-bottomed skillet, heat the olive oil over medium-low heat, and add the garlic paste. Sauté for about 1 minute. Add the crushed tomatoes along with their juices. Rinse the can with ½ cup water and add to the skillet. Break up the plum tomatoes in a bowl and add to the skillet along with their juices. Add the chopped parsley, basil and red pepper flakes. Cook over medium-low heat for 30 minutes, until the liquid begins to evaporate. Lower the heat to simmer and cook for an additional 30 minutes.

Bring several quarts of water to a boil in a large pot. Cook the pasta until "al dente" - tender, but firm to the bite. At the same moment that you place the pasta in the boiling water, place the shrimp in the sauce. As soon as the shrimp turn pink, about 1 to 2 minutes, remove the skillet from the heat.

Drain the pasta well, put in pasta bowls and pour the hot shrimp sauce over the pasta. Serve immediately.

Yield: 4 to 6 servings

Shrimp and Lobster "Ravel-ioli" with Cream Sauce

1 ½ pounds fresh egg pasta dough
1 pound shrimp, cooked, peeled, deveined, and finely chopped
½ pound cooked lobster meat, finely chopped
4 tablespoons finely chopped fresh basil
1 teaspoon finely chopped fresh thyme
4 ounces ricotta cheese
Salt and pepper
Hot pepper flakes (optional)

Cream Sauce:
3 cups heavy cream
6 ounces (1 ½ sticks) butter
½ cup freshly grated Parmesan cheese
Chopped fresh basil, for garnish

Make the pasta dough (if not purchased); cover and let rest while you make the filling.

Mix together in a bowl the chopped shrimp, chopped lobster meat, basil, thyme, ricotta, and salt and pepper (and hot pepper flakes, if desired) to taste. Roll out the pasta dough as thinly as possible into two sheets. Set spoonfuls of filling on the dough, about 1 ½ inches apart. Lay a second thin sheet of dough on top. With a fluted pastry cutter, cut the pasta into ravioli shapes. Crimp the edges of each piece with the tines of a fork.

In a large pot of boiling salted water cook the ravioli until "al dente", or firm to the bite. Do not overcook the ravioli. Drain and keep warm.

Make the sauce: In a saucepan, bring the cream to a boil with the butter and simmer until reduced to almost 2 cups. Remove from heat. Add the Parmesan cheese and whisk until smooth. Gently toss the ravioli with the sauce. Garnish with the chopped basil, if desired.

Yield: 4 servings (6 ravioli per person)

Note: Fresh pasta cooks very quickly. After the ravioli have returned to the surface of the boiling water for a minute or two, check for doneness.

Laura Carlo
Radio Host - WCRB

Laura Carlo, is Morning Program Host for WCRB 102.5 FM, Boston, the nation's highest-rated major market classical music station. Since 1998, her program has also been beamed via satellite from Maine to California on WCRB's World Classical Network. WCRB began live stereo broadcasts of Saturday evening BSO concerts in the fall of 1957.

Laura is married to lyric baritone James Coelho, whom BSO and Pops audiences will remember for his stirring performances.

This recipe stems from the couple's collaboration on the BSO fund-raiser "CEO Chefs' Night." Laura prepared this dish for the event, and Jim entertained guests with songs by Gershwin and Porter.

The recipe is named in honor of famous composer Maurice Ravel.

Harry Ellis Dickson
Associate Conductor Laureate
Boston Pops Orchestra

Harry Ellis Dickson is a beloved figure in Boston's musical community. He is Associate Conductor Laureate of the Boston Pops and founder of the BSO's renowned Youth Concerts. He joined the violin section of the BSO in 1938 under the baton of Serge Koussevitzky.

During his 60-plus years with the BSO, he has received awards and honors—but culinary honors are not among them. When asked to share a recipe, Harry asked his son-in-law, former Massachusetts governor Michael Dukakis, to lend us his secret for linguine and scallops, a favorite of Harry's. "Harry is an eater, but not a cook," says the former governor. "This recipe is really his. He loves to have me serve it when he comes for dinner with Kitty and me."

Linguine with Scallops in Cream Sauce

1 ¼ pounds sea scallops
12 ounces linguine
3 tablespoons butter or margarine, divided
10 ounces mushrooms, sliced
1 small onion, finely chopped
1 teaspoon salt, divided
1 tablespoon flour
1 cup half-and-half
¾ cup chicken broth
1 tablespoon dry sherry
½ teaspoon black pepper
1 small bunch spinach (about 8 ounces),
stemmed and thinly sliced
1 pint cherry tomatoes, each cut in half

Rinse the scallops with cold water. Pat dry with paper towels and set aside.

In a pot of boiling water, cook the linguine until "al dente", or firm to the bite. Drain and return to the pot. Keep warm.

Meanwhile, in a 12-inch skillet in 2 tablespoons of the butter, sauté the mushrooms, onions and ¼ teaspoon of the salt. When cooked, remove the mushroom mixture with a slotted spoon into a bowl.

Add the remaining 1 tablespoon of butter to the skillet over high heat and cook the scallops until golden on both sides, turning once. Remove the scallops to a bowl. Add the flour to the skillet and make a roux with the residual butter, stirring constantly until it is thoroughly blended and golden in color, about 3 to 4 minutes. (Do not brown the roux.) Slowly stir in the half-and-half, chicken broth, sherry, pepper and the remaining ¾ teaspoon of salt.

Return the mushroom mixture and scallops to the skillet. Heat to boiling. Stir in spinach and tomatoes. Heat through. Toss the seafood mixture with the linguine, and serve.

Yield: 6 servings

Anna's Pasta e Fagioli
(Anna's Pasta and Beans)

2 tablespoons canola oil
1 medium onion, finely chopped
1 carrot, finely chopped
1 stalk celery, with leaves, finely chopped
2 tablespoons finely chopped parsley
2 cloves garlic, minced
1 (28-ounce) can whole tomatoes, with juice
1 (28-ounce) can crushed tomatoes
1 (15-ounce) can cannellini beans, drained and rinsed
1 (15-ounce) can garbanzo beans
3 cups vegetable broth
1 cup cut-up green beans, 1-inch long
1 cup frozen small lima beans
2 cups escarole, stemmed and cut into 1-inch pieces
1½ cups elbow macaroni
Salt

In a large saucepan, sauté in the oil the onion, carrot, celery and parsley until the onions are golden. Add the garlic and cook for about 1 minute more. Crush the tomatoes between your fingers as you add them to the pan. Stir in the tomatoes and mix well. Cook until the mixture is slightly thickened.

Stir in the cannellini and garbanzo beans, the stock, green beans and lima beans. Return the mixture to a boil. Stir in the escarole; simmer for about 5 minutes. Add the macaroni, and salt to taste. Cook until the pasta is "al dente", or firm to the bite. Serve hot.

Yield: 6 to 8 servings

Note: More stock may be added if the mixture appears to be too thick.

BOSTON
SYMPHONY
ORCHESTRA
SEIJI OZAWA
*Music
Director*

One stormy, miserable night in South Bend, Indiana, the orchestra was awaiting the train for Chicago. Card games, horseplay and other shenanigans followed during the long wait, and the few other passengers seem slightly frightened by these lunatics.

Boaz Piller, a bassoonist, sat next to a young lady in a corner who, it turned out, had missed her train earlier and was obviously disturbed by these antics. He said, "Don't be 'fraid, ve are all nice pipple."

He then sought out Pat Cardillo, an unmarried member of the orchestra. An introduction and short conversation followed, then a separation on the train. Cardillo decided he wanted to get her name, toured the train, found her and got it. A whirlwind courtship followed and they were married the following fall - all this because of a snowstorm, a missed train and a few other imponderables!

Pasta Primavera

1 pound fettuccine or linguine pasta
8 tablespoons (1 stick) unsalted butter
1 medium onion, minced
1 large clove garlic, minced
1 pound thin asparagus, tough ends trimmed,
cut diagonally into ¼-inch slices, tips left intact
½ pound mushrooms, thinly sliced
6 ounces broccoli, broken into small florets
1 medium zucchini, cut into ¼-inch rounds
1 small carrot, peeled, halved lengthwise,
then cut diagonally into ⅛-inch slices
½ cup heavy or whipping cream
½ cup chicken broth
3 tablespoons chopped fresh basil
1 cup frozen peas, thawed
2 ounces prosciutto, chopped
5 scallions, chopped
Salt and freshly ground pepper
1 cup freshly grated Parmesan cheese

Add the fettuccine to a pot of boiling water, and immediately begin the following:

Heat a deep large skillet over medium-high heat. (If using an electric frying pan, set the heat to medium-high.) Add the butter, onion and garlic, and sauté until the onion is softened - about 2 minutes. Add the asparagus, mushrooms, broccoli florets, zucchini and carrot to the skillet, and stir-fry for 2 minutes more. (At this point you may set aside a few pieces of the asparagus or broccoli for garnish later.)

Increase the heat to high and add the cream, stock and basil, and allow the mixture to boil until the liquid is slightly reduced - about 3 minutes. Stir in the peas, prosciutto and scallions, and cook for 1 minute more. Season with salt and pepper to taste.

The pasta should now be cooked "al dente", or firm to the bite. Drain well, and add the pasta, followed by the cheese, to the vegetables in the skillet. (Note that this is the reverse of most pasta cooking.) The pasta will now "finish" in the skillet, absorbing the mixture's flavors. Toss only until thoroughly combined and heated through.

You may serve this in the skillet, or turn the pasta mixture into a warm serving bowl. Garnish with the reserved asparagus or broccoli pieces, and serve immediately.

Yield: 6 to 8 servings as a first course

Pasta Primavera continued

Note: It is important that all the vegetables be cut up ahead, and put in small bowls or piles ready to be used. The pasta water should be boiling, ready for the pasta when the cooking of the vegetables begins. The cooking time for the pasta and the vegetables is identical to the point where they are combined into the final dish. It will help if the dish is prepared in a large skillet, or in an electric frying pan, which can hold the finished dish and be taken to the table for serving.

It may seem with the reduced cooking times of the vegetables that they will not be cooked enough. In fact, the vegetables will end up cooked and firm to the bite, and not mushy.

Don't let the length of the ingredients list alarm you - this is really a quick and easy recipe to prepare, with a variety of textures and tastes that make it delectable. And, just as in a good flower arrangement, the variety of textures and tastes gives this pasta recipe a beautiful presentation and is delectable!

BOSTON SYMPHONY ORCHESTRA
SEIJI OZAWA
Music Director

Serge Koussevitzky always had the dream to take his orchestra to Europe. But it was not to be. Not until 1952, in Charles Munch's second year, did the orchestra tour Europe for the first time, with Munch and Pierre Monteux conducting.

The concert in Paris on May 8, 1952 was a memorable one. Pierre Monteux conducted, and his program concluded with Stravinsky's "Rite of Spring," the same piece he had conducted here at its premiere in 1913.

On that night, almost 40 years earlier, the result was disastrous - hisses, catcalls and even a fist fight at the end. Diaghilev, the director of the great Ballets Russes, was in tears; Stravinsky fled the hall in terror. On this night in 1952, with Stravinsky again in the hall, there was an outburst of applause and bravos. Stravinsky ran up the aisle to the stage, embraced Monteux, and shouted, "Enfin après quarante ans!" ("At last, after forty years!")

Rachel Fagerburg
Viola

Rachel Fagerburg joined the viola section of the BSO in late 1989, having been a Tanglewood Fellow several years earlier and a member of the Boston Pops Esplanade Orchestra.

Rachel is one of five sisters, and all but one are professional musicians playing with symphony orchestras. When growing up, they formed their own quartet. The fifth sister is a well-known marathon runner.

This recipe is one of Rachel's favorites.

Lasagna

¾ pound ground beef or turkey
1 cup chopped onion
3 cloves garlic, minced
¼ cup chopped fresh parsley, divided
2 teaspoons dried oregano
1 teaspoon dried basil
¼ teaspoon black pepper
1 (28-ounce) can whole tomatoes, undrained, chopped
1 (14½-ounce) can Italian stewed tomatoes, undrained, chopped
1 (8-ounce) can tomato sauce
1 (6-ounce) can tomato paste
2 cups nonfat cottage cheese
½ cup freshly grated Parmesan cheese
15 ounces nonfat ricotta cheese
1 egg white, lightly beaten
12 cooked lasagna noodles, divided
2 cups shredded provolone cheese (about 8 ounces), divided

Cook the ground beef or turkey in a large saucepan over medium heat until browned, stirring and crumbling the meat. Drain the meat and set aside. Wipe the pan clean, coat it with cooking spray; add the onion and garlic, and sauté for 5 minutes. Return the meat to the pan. Add 2 tablespoons of the parsley, along with the oregano, basil, pepper, whole tomatoes, stewed tomatoes, tomato sauce and tomato paste. Bring the mixture to a boil. Cover; reduce heat and simmer for 15 minutes. Uncover and simmer an additional 20 minutes. Remove from heat.

Preheat oven to 350°. Coat a 13 by 9 by 2-inch baking dish with a nonstick spray.

Combine the remaining 2 tablespoons parsley, cottage cheese, Parmesan cheese, ricotta cheese and egg white. Stir well and set aside.

Spread ¾ cup of the tomato mixture over the bottom of the prepared baking dish. Arrange 4 noodles over the tomato mixture, top with one half of the cottage cheese mixture, 2 ¼ cups of the tomato mixture, and ⅔ cup of the provolone cheese. Repeat assembling the layers, ending with a noodle layer. Spread the remaining tomato mixture over noodles.

Cover and bake for 1 hour. Sprinkle with the remaining ⅔ cup provolone cheese. Bake uncovered for an additional 10 minutes. Remove from the oven and let stand for 10 minutes before serving.

Yield: 8 servings

Low-Fat Vegetable Lasagna

9 strips (about ½ pound) spinach or regular lasagna, divided
2 (10-ounce) packages frozen chopped spinach
1 cup low-fat ricotta cheese
⅓ cup freshly grated Parmesan cheese, divided
Salt and freshly ground black pepper
½ cup chopped fresh basil
3 ounces soft chèvre cheese
1 quart low-fat spaghetti sauce
4 portobello mushrooms, cut into 1-inch strips
2 cloves garlic, minced
1 tablespoon olive oil
12 ounces shredded low-fat mozzarella cheese

Preheat oven to 375°.

If the pasta is fresh, it does not need precooking. If it is dried, cook it according to package instructions. Do not overcook the noodles. Drain and place the noodles in bowl of cold water.

Cook the spinach in 2 quarts of boiling salted water for 1 minute. Drain. When the spinach is cooled, squeeze the water out of it with your hands.

Mix the ricotta and 2 tablespoons of the Parmesan cheese together in a bowl. Season with some salt and black pepper to taste. Set aside.

Mix the basil, chèvre and spaghetti sauce. Stir the spinach into the ricotta mixture.

Sauté the mushroom strips and garlic in the olive oil in a skillet over medium heat, until the mushrooms give up their liquid.

Spread one third of the sauce mix over the bottom of a 13 by 9-inch baking dish. Arrange the pasta strips over the sauce to make an exact fit. Spread all the spinach-ricotta mix evenly over the pasta. Arrange a second layer of pasta strips over the spinach. Spread one half of the remaining sauce mix over the pasta and spread all the mushrooms over the sauce. Top with final layer of pasta. Spread with the remaining sauce mix. Top with mozzarella and the remaining Parmesan cheese. Bake for 15 minutes covered; then bake uncovered for an additional 15 minutes.

Yield: 6 to 8 servings

Phyllis Walt

Phyllis Walt is the widow of the legendary BSO principal bassoonist Sherman Walt. She says: "Walt had an enormous enthusiasm for food, often declaring, 'This the best food I've ever tasted!'

"He had several dishes that he loved to cook, but Vegetable Lasagna was not one of them. Well, we've all learned to adjust our passion for food to a healthier lifestyle."

Stefan Asbury
Conductor

This recipe was given to us by Stefan Asbury. He originated it during one of the rare weekends spent in his kitchen at home in Oxford, England.

Stefan received a Bernstein Conducting Fellowship at the Tanglewood Music Center in 1990. He now maintains a busy schedule in Europe and keeps close ties to the BSO. He returns to the Tanglewood Music Center every summer to teach, conduct, and organize the Contemporary Music Festival in August.

Pasta with Leeks and Pesto Sauce

2 leeks
2 teaspoons honey
2 to 3 tablespoons pesto sauce (recipe follows)
3 slices cooked bacon, finely chopped
12 ounces linguine (or similar pasta)
Black pepper

Thoroughly rinse the leeks and finely chop them. (Use only the white and nearest portion of the green part.) Steam or boil them until tender. (If the leeks were boiled, drain them before proceeding.) Place the leeks in a bowl and add the honey.

Add the bacon pieces and pesto sauce to the leeks; mix well and set aside.

Cook the pasta until it is "al dente", or firm to the bite. Drain well and place it in a bowl. Add the pesto mixture and mix well. Add a generous grinding of black pepper.

Yield: 4 to 6 servings

Pesto Sauce

2 cloves garlic
1 teaspoon salt
3 cups basil leaves, packed
2 tablespoons chopped parsley (optional)
2 tablespoons pine nuts (pignoli)
½ cup olive oil
½ cup freshly grated Parmesan cheese

Combine the garlic, salt, basil, parsley (if used), pine nuts, and olive oil in the bowl of a processor. Purée the mixture. Stir in the Parmesan cheese.

Yield: about 1 ½ cups of pesto sauce

Note: If the pesto sauce is not used immediately, it may be stored in the refrigerator for several days in a tightly-closed container. For longer storage, drop the pesto by heaping tablespoons onto waxed paper-lined trays and freeze. Once the pesto is frozen, remove it from the paper and place the dollops in a plastic freezer bag. Return to the freezer, and use the dollops as needed to flavor sauces, soups or salad dressings.

Pinci di Montepulciano
(Spaghetti Montepulciano-Style)

6 tablespoons extra-virgin olive oil
½ red onion, finely chopped
2 stalks celery, finely chopped
2 cloves garlic, finely chopped
1 pound chopped beef
4 ounces prosciutto, chopped
¼ cup dry red wine
3 tablespoons tomato paste
Salt and freshly ground pepper
2 cups chicken or beef broth, divided
16 ounces spaghetti
Freshly ground Parmesan or Romano cheese (optional)

Heat the oil in a saucepan and add the onion, celery, and garlic together. Sauté for 5 minutes; then add the ground beef and prosciutto. Sauté for an additional 10 minutes.

Add the wine to the pan, and cook for 2 minutes. Add the tomato paste and season with salt and pepper to taste. Add ½ cup of the broth to the pan, mixing it in very well, and continue cooking the sauce. As the sauce thickens, add another ½ cup of the broth. Repeat the procedure until all the broth has been added and the sauce reaches a nice consistency - about 1 hour.

Cook the pasta according to the package instructions until it is "al dente", or firm to the bite. (Do not overcook the pasta.) Drain it well, and transfer it to a large serving bowl. Pour the sauce over the pasta and mix well. Sprinkle with the cheese, if you desire.

Yield: 6 to 8 servings

BOSTON
SYMPHONY
ORCHESTRA
SEIJI OZAWA
Music
Director

In 1956 the BSO made its second tour of Europe, which included the then-Soviet Union. They were the first American orchestra to play in the Soviet Union and were given a state banquet following their last concert in Moscow.

Many illustrious composers and artists were present, and particular praise came from the great composer Aram Khachaturian: "Today I heard sounds from an orchestra that I never thought possible, and now that I have heard you and what you can do, I must write something especially for you."

BSO on Tour

Most orchestra members feel a bit claustrophobic on tour. There is constant travel and a new city nearly every day.

To invigorate themselves and escape the pollution of Madrid, Malcolm Lowe, Jonathan Menkis, Rick Ranti, and Gus Sebring secured a detailed hiking map of the Guaderrama mountains north of the city. On their one free day, the four set out for a hiking adventure.

Jonathan says the hike was just what the four musicians needed. In addition to the spectacular scenery, there was an exciting slide down a snow-covered mountain and a dip in a mountain stream. "We returned refreshed and recharged for the rest of the trip," he says. "We were even able to enjoy the urban sights of Madrid and the wonderful Prado museum the next morning."

Spaghetti with Pine Nuts and Broccoli

1 pound spaghetti
¾ cup olive oil
3 cloves garlic, minced
¾ cup freshly grated Parmesan cheese
4 tablespoons chopped basil
½ cup pine nuts (pignoli)
6 cups broccoli florets, lightly steamed

Cook the pasta according to instructions until "al dente" - tender, but firm to the bite. Strain and place in a serving bowl.

Add the olive oil, garlic, Parmesan cheese, basil, pine nuts and broccoli. Mix and toss.

Yield: 4 to 6 servings

Serving Suggestion: Additional Parmesan cheese may be passed.

Risotto alla Milanese

4 tablespoons (½ stick) butter
⅓ cup minced onion
1½ cups Italian Arborio rice
2 (14½-ounce) cans chicken broth, heated
⅛ teaspoon saffron
Salt and black pepper
⅓ cup freshly grated Parmesan cheese

Preheat oven to 350°.

In a 3-quart, oven-safe saucepan, heat the butter and onion; cook until the onions are golden. Add the rice, stirring until the butter is absorbed. Stir in the heated broth, saffron, salt and pepper to taste, and heat until boiling.

Bake in the oven for 25 to 30 minutes, or until the liquid is absorbed, and the rice is tender. Stir in the Parmesan cheese and serve.

Yield: 6 servings

Note: Italian risottos have a much creamier consistency than American rices.

Sweet Potato Gnocchi

4 sweet potatoes, peeled and quartered (about 1 ½ pounds)
1 cup ricotta cheese
½ teaspoon salt
½ teaspoon grated nutmeg
2 cups all-purpose flour, divided
Melted butter (optional)
Freshly grated Parmesan cheese (optional)
Freshly ground black pepper

In a large covered saucepan, cook the sweet potatoes in enough boiling water to cover for 25 minutes, or until tender. Drain well; return to the same pan. Over low heat mash the potatoes until smooth, allowing any extra moisture to evaporate.

Transfer the potatoes to large bowl. Stir in the ricotta cheese, salt, nutmeg, and 1 ½ cups of the flour. On a well-floured surface, knead in the remaining ½ cup of flour, kneading for 2 to 3 minutes, or until the dough forms a soft ball. Divide the dough into 8 pieces. With well-floured hands, roll each piece of dough into a 12-inch-long log, about 1 inch in diameter. Cut logs cross-wise into ½-inch pieces. With floured finger, make a dimple in the center of each piece. (If the gnocchi are too sticky to work with in this step, add more flour.)

Cook the gnocchi, several at a time, in a large pot of boiling salted water for 3 to 4 minutes, or until gnocchi rise to surface of the water. (Do not overcook.) Remove with a slotted spoon; drain on paper towels. If desired, top the gnocchi with melted butter, grated Parmesan cheese and black pepper to taste.

Yield: 96 gnocchi

Note: If you do not wish to serve all of this recipe at one time, cool the cooked gnocchi. Place them in a single layer on a baking sheet and freeze until firm. They may be stored in a freezer bag for up to 2 months.

Note: Gnocchi may be used in most dishes that call for a short, bulky form of pasta.

Variation: Flavored gnocchi may be made in a manner similar to that used in making flavored pastas.

In 1979, some seven years after President Nixon's visit there, the BSO went to China. They were the first orchestra to be invited to China from the United States after the establishment of improved relations between the two countries.

This was an exciting trip for Seiji Ozawa for, although Japanese, he was born in Manchuria and had lived in Shanghai, where his father was a dentist and officer in the occupation army.

Wendy Putnam
Violin

Wendy Putnam is not only one of the BSO's youngest members but also holder of the title for the earliest career start: she took her first music lesson at age two. That set a standard. Wendy entered college at 16 and received both bachelor's and master's degrees at Louisiana State University at Baton Rouge.

"While living in Louisiana, I became devoted to New Orleans' recipes like this one," she says. She has also kept up the pace set in her early years. "I love to hike and ride my mountain bike. When I have time away from playing in the violin section, I like to read science fiction and study mathematics plus quantum physics."

New Orleans Sunday Brunch Rice

1 ¼ cups jasmine rice
2 tablespoons olive oil
1 (14½-ounce) can chicken broth,
with added water to equal 2½ cups
1 pound bulk sage sausage
6 minced scallions or green onions
2 cloves garlic, minced
½ teaspoon cayenne
Salt and pepper
¼ cup dry white wine

Sauté the jasmine rice in olive oil over high heat for 1 to 2 minutes while constantly stirring, until the rice is golden in color. Add chicken broth and water, and reduce the heat to simmer. Cover and cook the rice for 15 minutes.

Sauté the sausage until browned; then add the scallions. Mix well, remove from the heat and let rest until the rice is cooked. Combine the rice and sausage mixture in the pan over medium-high heat until ingredients are heated through.

Add the garlic, cayenne, and salt and pepper to taste shortly before serving. At that point, add the white wine, mix thoroughly, and let entire mixture sit over low heat for a few minutes before serving.

Yield: 4 servings

THE BOSTON SYMPHONY ORCHESTRA

The Boston Symphony Orchestra

THE BOSTON SYMPHONY ORCHESTRA

The Boston Symphony Orchestra's more than 100 years of music-making have produced a body of work that rank it as one of the world's most influential orchestras.

Its legacy is awe-inspiring—it has commissioned works from Stravinsky, Bartók, and Copland—and so is its modern musical life. The BSO performs in Boston, at Tanglewood, and on tour around the globe. More than a million people attend its concerts every year. It records regularly and performs dozens of concerts for youth, families, and new audiences. As a tireless advocate for classical music, it has formed partnerships and collaboratives with schools and cultural institutions to build a broader community for the musical arts.

Photo by: © Marc Glassman

Energy has always been the BSO's hallmark. The Boston Symphony Orchestra sprang to life on the stage of the Music Hall on October 22, 1881. The BSO was the brainchild of Henry Lee Higginson. A successful businessman and Civil War veteran, Higginson dreamed of bringing Europe's rich musical culture to his home town. On that night in 1881, he succeeded. He had brought many members of the distinguished cast of musicians from Europe, including the 31-year-old German conductor, Georg Henschel.

Higginson's ambitious vision for the BSO attracted conductors and instrumentalists of international stature from the start. The first four conductors had distinguished themselves in Europe's best concert halls. They were unafraid to perform new music of the day—even when not all Bostonians (particularly music critics) approved of what they heard. In the *Evening Transcript's* October 22, 1882, edition, the newspaper likened the ending of Tchaikovsky's Fifth Symphony to "hordes of demons struggling in a torrent of brandy". The following week, the premiere of a Brahms Symphony inspired the *Boston Advertiser* critic to write, "The audience must have given a sigh of relief when the final chord was played and the agony was over." Despite the critics, Bostonians flocked to the orchestra's performances, lining up by the hundreds each week to buy tickets.

The Victorian-era programming was different from today's symphony performances. The conductors favored opening with a long piece, such as a symphony or concerto, while the players and the audience were fresh. After intermission, they played a series of short pieces, often ending with a flashy composition designed to send the audience off with a rousing flourish.

The first conductors established the tradition the BSO maintains today of performing a range of contemporary and classical music. The musical programs in 1900 included Boston composer Amy Beach, Alexander Glazunov, and the then-alarming Richard Strauss. Over the years, the BSO developed the distinctively rich, voluptuous sound it produces today.

When Karl Muck took over the orchestra in 1906, he continued the tradition by playing such new composers as Debussy, Ravel, and Stravinsky. Muck stayed with the orchestra for most of the next twelve years, including the difficult years of World War I. He took the BSO on its first transcontinental tour in 1915. Two years later, the orchestra made its first recording for RCA. But the war and anti-German sentiment took a toll on Muck, and he left the BSO in 1918.

Beginning in 1920, the orchestra played under the prestigious baton of music director Pierre Monteux. Richard Burgin joined that same year as concertmaster, a post he held for 42 years. In 1924, Serge Koussevitzky was appointed music director, a position he would command for 25 illustrious years. His name became synonymous with the orchestra and Tanglewood, where the Music Shed now bears his name.

Charles Munch succeeded Koussevitzky in 1949 and brought a distinctively "French sound" to the orchestra. Erich Leinsdorf and William Steinberg followed, bringing their own strengths to the music they played and to the orchestra.

A new era began in 1974 when 38-year-old Seiji Ozawa became BSO Music Director. Born in Manchuria of Japanese parents, Ozawa grew up in Japan and was not always on a direct path toward a life in music. After his piano career was cut short when he broke two fingers playing rugby, he was far from certain that music would win out over his other career options. "I studied hard in high school and might have become a businessman," he recalls. "My decision to follow a career in music was slow and difficult. One of my teachers said to me, 'If you want to become a musician, then go ahead and shoot for the top.'"

The BSO played an important part in Ozawa's life even before he became music director. When he left Japan for France in 1959, he was 24 and spoke no English. But he could make music. He won the international conducting competition in Besançon, France, where BSO conductor Charles Munch had an opportunity to hear him. "I went up to him and asked if he would teach me," Ozawa recalls. "He arranged for me to come to Tanglewood. That was the first time I had been to America. I didn't expect this kind of life, and I wanted to stay."

Ozawa's career flowered after the season at Tanglewood. He won a scholarship to study with Herbert von Karajan in Berlin and was invited by Leonard Bernstein to join the New York Philharmonic as assistant conductor. He later moved west to conduct the San Francisco Orchestra.

Ozawa recently marked his 25th year as BSO Music Director. He has brought to Boston and Tanglewood his superb musicianship, commanding technique, and electric energy. As Boston composer Leon Kirchner says, "He has an extraordinary physical gift. He can communicate musical ideas through his body." To see him conduct an orchestra, it is hard to imagine he ever doubted a career in music.

Photo by: © Marc Glassman

POULTRY ~ GAME ~ MEATS

Richard Westerfield
Conductor

Several years ago, Richard Westerfield took a detour in his successful musical career and went to work on Wall Street. Fortunately for concert-goers, he soon returned to investing in music.

Richard was appointed BSO assistant conductor by Seiji Ozawa in 1995 and associate conductor two years later. He first came to Seiji's attention when he won the Min-On Conducting Competition in Tokyo, where Seiji was a juror. He was immediately invited to Tanglewood as a conducting fellow to study under such luminaries as Kurt Masur and Leonard Bernstein, who invited him to be his assistant with the New York Philharmonic.

Richard and his wife Helen have provided us with this wonderful chicken casserole recipe.

Almond Chicken Casserole

Cheese Sauce:

3 tablespoons butter
3 tablespoons flour
½ teaspoon salt
¾ cup chicken broth
1 cup milk
2 tablespoons white wine
⅓ cup freshly grated Parmesan or Romano cheese
½ cup sour cream

1 cup brown rice
3 tablespoons butter, divided
½ pound mushrooms, sliced
½ red bell pepper, seeded and chopped
3 tablespoons chopped yellow onion
¼ cup chopped parsley
2 tablespoons chopped fresh basil
⅓ cup slivered almonds
1 tablespoon almond liqueur or extract (optional)
4 cups cooked chicken, cubed (about 3 boneless breasts)
Salt and freshly ground pepper

Make the cheese sauce: In a saucepan over medium heat melt the 3 tablespoons butter; then add the flour and salt, stirring until blended. Add the broth and stir over heat until slightly thickened. Add the milk, wine, cheese, and stir until smooth - about 2 minutes. Remove the pan from the heat and whisk in the sour cream. Set aside.

Cook the rice per instructions and set aside. Preheat the oven to 350°.

In 2 tablespoons of the butter sauté the mushrooms, red bell pepper and yellow onion until the vegetables are soft, about 5 minutes. Stir in the parsley and basil.

Separately sauté the almonds in the remaining 1 tablespoon butter. Add the almond liqueur (if used) and cook for 30 seconds. Add the almond mixture to the rice, along with the chicken, mushroom mixture and cheese sauce, and mix well. Place in a lightly oiled 4-quart casserole. Season with salt and pepper to taste. Bake covered for 45 minutes, or until bubbly.

Yield: 6 to 8 servings

Chicken and Pears with Port and Stilton Cream

6 boneless chicken breast halves, skins removed
Flour, for dusting
6 tablespoons clarified butter, divided (see note)
Salt and pepper
¾ cup salt-free chicken broth
¾ cup port
1 ½ cups heavy or whipping cream
3 pears, peeled, cored and cut into 6 wedges each
2 tablespoons crumbled Stilton cheese
2 tablespoons minced fresh parsley

Flatten each chicken breast slightly; them sprinkle lightly with the flour.

In a large skillet, heat 4 tablespoons of the butter over medium-high heat. When the butter begins to color, add the chicken breasts. Cook the chicken for about 4 minutes, then turn them and cook the other side until it is springy to the touch. Remove the breasts to a warm platter. Season them with salt and pepper to taste, then tent and place the chicken platter in a 200° oven to keep warm. (A hot tray may be used in place of the oven.)

Add the stock and port to the same skillet and boil until it is reduced by one half. Add the cream and boil until the mixture is reduced to a sauce-like consistency.

Meanwhile, in a small skillet, sauté the pear slices for 5 minutes in the remaining 2 tablespoons of butter. Set aside.

Add 1 tablespoon of the Stilton to the port sauce and stir until melted. Taste the sauce and use the additional 1 tablespoon Stilton, if desired.

Place one chicken breast half on each dinner plate and top with 3 pear slices, some of the sauce, and some minced parsley.

Yield: 6 servings

Note: Clarified butter can be heated, without burning, to a higher temperature than regular butter. To make about ⅓ cup of clarified butter, melt 8 tablespoons (1 stick) butter in a small, heavy saucepan over low heat. Remove pan from heat and set aside for 5 minutes. Using a spoon, carefully remove and discard the foamy white butterfat that has risen to the top. Spoon or pour off the clear liquid. This is the clarified butter. Discard the solids that remain on the bottom of the pan. Allow clarified butter to cool; then cover and refrigerate. (The butter will keep for several weeks.)

BOSTON SYMPHONY ORCHESTRA
SEIJI OZAWA
Music Director

Seiji the Sports Fan

Seiji Ozawa is as well known in Boston's sports arenas as he is within the great music halls of the world. He can discuss batting averages and rushing yardage as easily as he can a Mahler symphony.

On a fall Sunday, he can often be seen at Foxboro Stadium, enthusiastically cheering on the Patriots. And, whenever possible, he will be in the front row at Fenway Park to watch the Red Sox. In fact, if a Red Sox night game goes into extra innings, and he can leave the Hall in time, it is not unusual for him to swing by Fenway Park for the final inning.

Seiji is also an accomplished sportsman who plays a tough game of tennis and is an excellent skier. At the 1998 Winter Olympics in Nagano, he took the first run down the giant slalom course, skiing it with grace and what looked like ease. He never missed a gate!

BOSTON
SYMPHONY
ORCHESTRA
SEIJI OZAWA
*Music
Director*

*Joseph Leibovici sat directly
behind Harry Ellis Dickson in
the BSO violin section and was
noted for his mutterings during
rehearsals and concerts. One
day after the orchestra had
labored through the long
Schubert C Major Symphony on
an unbearably hot day, he said,
"Damn Schubert! He wrote two
symphonies, one unfinished
and the other endless!"*

Chicken Breasts with Pear and Cider Cream Sauce

*6 boneless chicken breast halves, skins removed
Flour
6 tablespoons (¾ stick) butter, divided
4 ripe pears, peeled, cored and quartered
1 ½ cups apple cider
⅓ cup scallions, white part only, sliced
⅓ cup applejack brandy
2 cups light cream
½ teaspoon salt
White pepper*

Flatten the chicken breasts slightly. Sprinkle lightly with flour. In a large skillet, heat 4 tablespoons of the butter over moderately high heat. Add the chicken breasts and sauté for 4 minutes on one side. Turn and cook the other side until the chicken is springy to the touch. Remove to a warm platter. Tent with foil, and set it in a 200° oven, or on a hot tray.

Poach the pear wedges with the cider in a sauce pan for 10 to 20 minutes until they are soft, but not mushy. Remove the pears; reserve the liquid.

Add the remaining 2 tablespoons of the butter to the sauté pan and sauté the scallions over medium heat for 1 minute. Remove the pan from the burner and add the brandy; then replace it on the burner, and deglaze the pan. Add the cream, salt, white pepper to taste, and the pear poaching liquid. Bring it to a gentle boil, reducing the liquid by one half. Strain, and adjust the seasonings, if necessary.

Arrange the chicken breasts on an ovenproof platter or pan. Arrange the pear slices on and around the chicken, and pour the sauce over all. Place the platter under the broiler for 1 minute.

Yield: 6 servings

Note: Always remove the pan from an open flame when adding any liquor or liqueur. The fumes could ignite.

Chicken Breasts with Green Peppercorn Sauce

6 to 8 boneless chicken breast halves
5 tablespoons flour
1 teaspoon salt
2 cloves garlic, minced
2 medium onions, peeled and cut into wedges
4 tablespoons olive oil, divided
1 cup dry white wine
1 cup light cream
2 tablespoons green peppercorns, rinsed and drained
1 (14½-ounce) can chicken broth

Preheat the oven to 200°.

Pound the chicken breasts until ½-inch-thick. Coat with a mixture of flour and salt. (Save the remaining flour mixture.) In a skillet, sauté the chicken in 2 tablespoons of the oil over medium heat 5 minutes per side. Remove the chicken and place it in a pan in the oven to keep warm.

In the same skillet, sauté the onion and garlic in the remaining 2 tablespoons of oil, until they are golden. Add the wine and peppercorns, smashing the peppercorns with the back of a wooden spoon and stirring them into the mixture. Boil until the sauce is reduced slightly. Add the cream and bring all to a boil.

In a separate pan make a roux with the remaining flour mixture and some of the boiling sauce. Add the chicken broth and roux gradually and alternately until desired consistency and quantity of sauce is reached.

Check seasonings, adding some garlic salt, if desired. Remove chicken from oven. Place it on serving dish and pour the sauce over it.

Yield: 4 to 6 servings

Carol Procter
Cello

Carol Procter is one of the many Tanglewood Music Center graduates to go on to a career with the BSO. Since joining the BSO in 1965, she has been a frequent performer of chamber music and a soloist with the Boston Pops.

Carol shares this delicious chicken recipe with us.

BOSTON
SYMPHONY
ORCHESTRA
SEIJI OZAWA
*Music
Director*

Such praise was heaped upon Koussevitzky during his years with the BSO, that he quite humanly was influenced by all of it. A story is told that after a concert a friend said, "You know, Serge Alexandrovitch, you are not only the greatest conductor; you are the only conductor!"

Koussey, pulling himself up, said, "Come now, there are other fine conductors in the world."

"Who?" asked the friend.

"Well..." And he turned to his wife: "Natasha, who?"

Quick Chicken Cacciatore

2 tablespoons olive oil
1 cup sliced onions
3 to 4 cloves garlic, finely chopped
2 tablespoons flour
4 boneless and skinless chicken breast halves (about 2 pounds)
1 (28-ounce) can chopped tomatoes ("kitchen-ready" style)
½ cup sliced carrots
1 teaspoon dried basil
1 teaspoon dried oregano
½ cup dry white or red wine
Salt and pepper

In a large heavy pot, sauté the onions and garlic in the oil.

Sprinkle the flour on the chicken and sauté it with the onions and garlic until the chicken is browned on both sides. Add the tomatoes, carrots, basil, oregano, wine, and salt and pepper to taste. Simmer, covered, for 30 minutes, or until juices run clear from the chicken.

Yield: 4 servings

Variation: The chicken may be cut up into bite-size pieces before cooking. (Flouring procedure: Put chicken into bag with the flour; shake to coat the chicken.)

Serving Suggestion: The chicken cacciatore goes well with buttered broad noodles or pasta of choice, and a green salad.

Lucille's Chicken Marengo

4 pounds boneless chicken breasts, cut into pieces
Salt and pepper
½ cup flour, for dredging
4 tablespoons (½ stick) butter
2 tablespoons olive oil
2 pounds trimmed mushrooms (small caps left whole,
but sliced if regular-sized mushrooms)
4 cups seeded and chopped tomatoes (about 8 medium)
3 cups dry white wine
1 ½ pounds pearl onions, blanched and peeled
Chopped fresh parsley, for garnish

Sprinkle the chicken with some of the salt and pepper, and dredge in the flour. Shake off any excess flour.

Melt the butter in a large heavy pan over medium-high heat. Cook the chicken in batches, until it is golden on all sides. Remove the chicken and juices from the pan and set aside.

Add the mushrooms and olive oil to the same pan and sauté until the mushrooms are golden. Stir in the tomatoes, wine and onions. Reduce the heat to medium and return the chicken and juices to the pan. Stir, cover, and simmer for 20 minutes. Uncover the pan and simmer until the chicken is cooked through, approximately 20 minutes more. Season with salt and pepper to taste.

Transfer to serving bowl and garnish with parsley.

Yield: 6 to 8 servings

Note: If pearl onions are not available, small onions may be used. Slice them in half after blanching and peeling them.

Lawrence Wolfe
Assistant Principal Bass

Larry Wolfe joined the bass section in 1970, becoming the youngest member of the orchestra. He is also musical director for the James Library and Arts Center in Norwell, Mass., and regularly invites fellow BSO members to play at the center.

"My BSO colleagues love to come to Norwell to play chamber music in an intimate setting and to a perennially sold-out house," *he says. "What better way to celebrate a successful concert than with good food?"*

Larry's post-concert dinners are famous thanks to the culinary artistry of longtime friend and chef extraordinaire Lucille Butler. This recipe is one of her favorites.

BOSTON
SYMPHONY
ORCHESTRA
SEIJI OZAWA
*Music
Director*

Chicken with Artichokes and Wine

4 boneless chicken breast halves (about 2 pounds)
Salt and pepper
2 tablespoons olive oil
½ cup dry white wine
1 (8½-ounce) can artichoke hearts, drained and quartered; or
1 (10-ounce) package of frozen artichoke hearts, thawed
½ cup sour cream
4 strips bacon, cooked and crumbled
¼ cup chopped fresh parsley

Sprinkle the chicken with some salt and pepper. In a large skillet heat the oil over medium-high heat. Add the chicken, and brown lightly on both sides. Add the wine, stirring to loosen any brown particles from the skillet. Add the artichokes, cover and simmer for 10 to 12 minutes, or until the chicken is firm and white throughout. Remove the chicken to a warm platter and cover with foil to keep warm.

Add the sour cream to the artichoke mixture in the skillet; heat over low heat for 1 minute. Do not boil. Stir in the crumbled bacon and parsley.

Pour the sauce over the chicken.

Yield: 4 servings

Serving Suggestion: The chicken may be served over white or wild rice, or over angel hair pasta.

Party Chicken

4 ounces dried beef
8 boneless chicken breast halves (about 4 pounds)
8 thin slices bacon
1 (10¾-ounce) can cream of mushroom soup
8 ounces sour cream
2 cups sliced fresh mushrooms, lightly sautéed (optional)
Paprika

Preheat oven to 350°.

Layer the dried beef on the bottom of a 13 by 9-inch pan. Roll each breast half and wrap a slice of bacon around it. Place the rolled chicken on the dried beef bed.

Mix the cream of mushroom soup with the sour cream and pour over all.

(If mushrooms are being used, add them here.)

Sprinkle with paprika and bake for 1 ½ hours.

Yield: 8 servings

This is an old recipe, but still a very good one.

BOSTON
SYMPHONY
ORCHESTRA
SEIJI OZAWA
Music Director

During the Koussevitzky era there was considerable discussion about his "beat". His arms would come down so slowly, especially beginning a slow piece, that it was difficult to determine exactly when the musicians should begin playing.

When Alfred Krips, a violinist and later assistant concertmaster, was asked, "How do you start?" He answered, "I'm not quite sure. When the stick starts coming down, I shut my eyes, and when I open them, everybody is playing, so I sneak in quietly."

Renowned conductor Sir Thomas Beecham was not fully acquainted with the BSO's rehearsal and performance schedule during his first visit with the orchestra. He was unaware that after the Tuesday performance there was a Wednesday morning rehearsal for the same program, which was repeated on Thursday. After he failed to show at ten o'clock, the manager reached him at the hotel, and finally urged him to come to the Hall.

At about noon he shuffled to the podium and asked if anyone could tell him the reason for this meeting. There was silence. "I thought the concert went quite well last night," he went on. "is there someone here not satisfied? Come now, speak up!"

Boaz Pillar, the contrabassist did speak up: "Everything was fine!"

"Well, that's good enough for me! Good day, gentlemen!" And rehearsal was over.

Orange-Coconut Chicken

1 (3½ to 4-pound) frying chicken, cut into serving pieces
½ teaspoon salt
¼ cup butter
3 ounces frozen orange juice concentrate
1½ cups water
½ cup raisins
2 tablespoons flour
2 tablespoons sugar
½ teaspoon cinnamon
1 tablespoon freshly grated ginger
½ cup shredded coconut

Season the chicken with the salt. In a large skillet, brown the chicken in the butter. Remove the chicken from the pan with a slotted spoon and set aside.

In a bowl, mix the orange juice concentrate with the water. Add the raisins to soak, and set aside.

Add the flour, sugar, cinnamon, and ginger to the large skillet, stirring to make a smooth paste. Gradually add in the orange juice with the raisins, and stir until the mixture comes to a boil. Return the chicken to the skillet; reduce the heat, and simmer for 45 minutes. Remove it from the heat and allow it to cool. Place the chicken in the refrigerator for a few hours to mellow.

Reheat prior to use. Just before serving, sprinkle the chicken with the coconut.

Yield: 4 servings

Serving suggestion: Serve the chicken over buttered rice.

This dish both looks and tastes great!

Curried Chicken

2 medium onions, chopped
6 garlic cloves, crushed
1 (1½-inch) piece gingerroot, minced
1¼ cups water, divided
¼ cup vegetable oil
2 tablespoons salt
1 teaspoon ground cumin
1 teaspoon turmeric
1 teaspoon ground coriander
½ teaspoon crushed red pepper
1 (16-ounce) can tomatoes
½ teaspoon cinnamon
½ teaspoon ground cloves
2 tablespoons tomato paste
1 (3½ pound) chicken, skinned, cut into serving pieces

Mix the onion, garlic, ginger and ¼ cup of the water. Simmer in oil for 8 minutes.

Add the salt, cumin, turmeric, coriander, red pepper, tomatoes, cinnamon, cloves, and tomato paste. Simmer for an additional 10 minutes. Add the chicken; cover and simmer for 30 minutes.

Yield: 4 to 6 servings

Serving Suggestion: Serve the chicken with chutney and rice.

This is a nice do-ahead recipe which freezes very well.

BOSTON
SYMPHONY
ORCHESTRA
SEIJI OZAWA
Music
Director

When Danny Kaye, the great entertainer, was engaged to conduct the BSO in a pension-fund benefit concert, it was discovered that he had only about ten minutes experience in conducting a symphony orchestra!

After three weeks of daily "conducting" lessons with Harry Ellis Dickson in a hotel suite, he made a successful appearance with the BSO. He was a great natural talent and had a fantastic ear and musical memory.

At a rehearsal for the New York Philharmonic's pension concert, Dimitri Mitropoulos said, "You know, this isn't funny. This man is a great conductor!"

In December 1944, Béla Bartók came to Symphony Hall to hear the first performance of his Concerto for Orchestra, which had been commissioned by Koussevitzky.

He sat in the first balcony, and almost immediately began to cry out: "No, no! It is too fast!" Koussevitzky reddened a bit, stopped, and started again. Another cry: "No, no! It is too loud!" Another stop and start. The contest continued until Koussevitzky asked, "Please, Mr. Bartók, you vill take a pincil and paper and write it your observations and ve vill talk during di intermission."

Remembering that Koussevitzky would never take orders from anyone, it is no surprise that after the intermission he returned to say, "Gentlemen, I have it a talk with Bartók, and he say 'Everything is fine!'"

Pan-Seared Chicken

2 boneless chicken breast halves (about 1 pound)
Salt and pepper
4 ounces (1 stick) butter, divided
1 tablespoon olive oil
6 small red bliss potatoes, halved
4 whole shallots
1 large sprig rosemary
1 large sprig thyme
2 to 3 whole cloves garlic
1 Granny Smith apple, peeled, quartered and cored
½ cup apple cider

Preheat oven to 450°. Season both sides of the chicken breasts with some salt and pepper.

Put 2 tablespoons of the butter and the olive oil in a large sauté pan over high heat. When the butter starts foaming, add the chicken, potatoes, apples and shallots. Cook the chicken until it is golden brown on one side. Turn it over, add the rosemary, thyme and garlic, and place it in the oven. (If an ovenproof sauté pan is not available, transfer the chicken and other ingredients at this point to an oblong casserole.)

Stir the chicken occasionally. When the chicken is firm and the potatoes are fork tender (about 20 to 30 minutes), remove the pan from the oven. Place the chicken mixture on a large plate and cover to keep warm.

Deglaze the sauté pan or casserole with the apple cider, and reduce it slightly over medium-high to medium heat. Add the remaining butter, and salt and pepper to taste. Drizzle the cider sauce over the chicken.

Yield: 2 servings

Note: The recipe may be multiplied for additional servings.

Indonesian Chicken Kabobs

⅓ cup chunky-style peanut butter
¼ cup light soy sauce
¼ cup lemon juice
¼ cup sesame oil
2 tablespoons Hoisin sauce
2 teaspoons ground ginger
2 teaspoons freshly chopped basil
2 cloves fresh garlic, minced
Black pepper
Cayenne
1½ pounds boneless, skinless chicken breasts

In a bowl, combine the peanut butter, soy sauce, lemon juice, sesame oil, Hoisin sauce, ginger, basil, garlic, and the black pepper and cayenne to taste. Mix well and set aside.

Cut up the chicken breasts into chunks approximately 1½-inches in size. Thread the pieces of chicken onto skewers. Place the skewers of chicken in a container with a cover.

Pour the marinade over all and refrigerate covered. Marinate for 4 hours, turning the skewers occasionally.

Prepare the broiler or grill. Cook the chicken and serve immediately.

Yield: 4 to 6 servings

Note: Hoisin sauce is available in many supermarkets and in Asian food stores.

In the early days of recording, only about five minutes of music could fit on the wax-acetate records. No splicing was available; mistakes meant a complete repeat.

In recording Debussy's "La Mer" with Koussevitzky, the timing required a high trumpet note to be included at the end of the record side. The note kept cracking and repeats were made. Finally, the note came out beautifully, the trumpeter beamed, and Koussevitzky, with great exuberance, blurted out: "Thanks to God!" The red light went out and the producer, tears in his eyes, came out to request another take.

"Thanks to God!" was on the recording.

Roast Chicken with Olives and Potatoes

*1 (6 to 7-pound) chicken
5 tablespoons olive paste (olivada), divided
2 bay leaves
Olive oil, for rubbing
Salt and black pepper
4 tablespoons fresh thyme, or 4 teaspoons dried, divided
4 medium russet potatoes, peeled and cut into 1½-inch pieces
2 tablespoons olive oil
½ cup kalamata olives*

Preheat oven to 450°.

Slide your hand between the chicken skin and meat on the breast and legs to form pockets, being careful not to tear the skin. Spread 3 tablespoons of the olive paste into these pockets over the breast and leg meat. Spread the remaining 2 tablespoons of the olive paste in the cavity of the chicken. Place the bay leaves in the cavity. Tie the legs together to hold shape. Rub olive oil into the chicken skin, and sprinkle with salt and pepper to taste, and one half of the thyme. Place the chicken in a large roasting pan, and roast it for 15 minutes.

During this cooking time, place the potatoes in a large bowl with the 2 tablespoons of olive oil, along with some salt and pepper to taste, and the other half of the thyme. Mix well.

After the chicken has cooked for 15 minutes, add the potatoes to the pan, and cook for an additional 15 minutes. Reduce the oven temperature to 375°, and roast for 1 hour longer, basting occasionally with pan juices, and turning the potatoes so that they brown on all sides. Add the olives to the pan. Continue roasting until the juices run clear when the chicken is pierced in the thickest part of the thigh, about 10 minutes.

Transfer the chicken to a platter, and let it "rest" for about 10 minutes. Then cut it into serving pieces. Pour the chicken juices into a large cup and degrease.

Serve the chicken pieces on a platter, surrounded by the potatoes and olives, passing pan juices separately.

Yield: 4 to 6 servings

Note: Olivada is available in gourmet and food specialty stores.

Chicken Enchiladas

Filling:
1¾ pounds boneless chicken (breast and/or thigh)
¾ cup grated Monterey Jack cheese
⅓ cup chopped green onion
½ cup plus 2 tablespoons sour cream, or plain yogurt
½ teaspoon salt
¼ teaspoon pepper
10 medium (6-inch) flour tortilla shells

Sauce:
1 (14-ounce) can tomato sauce
½ green bell pepper, seeded and chopped
2 teaspoons chili powder

½ cup grated Monterey Jack cheese

Preheat the oven to 350°.

Cube the chicken and cook it in a frying pan coated with a nonstick spray, until any pink color disappears; drain off any liquid. Remove from the heat and stir in the Monterey Jack cheese, green onion, sour cream (or yogurt), salt and pepper. Divide the mixture evenly between the 10 tortilla shells and roll each up.

Place each rolled tortilla in a 13 by 9-inch baking dish that has been coated with a nonstick spray, with the roll seam side down. Set aside.

In a saucepan combine the tomato sauce, green pepper and chili powder; bring to a boil and simmer uncovered for 5 minutes. Pour the sauce over the enchiladas in the baking dish. Top with the grated cheese. Bake in the oven for 20 minutes.

Yield: 5 servings (2 enchiladas per person)

Variation: For spicier enchiladas, use Monterey Pepper Jack cheese.

BOSTON
SYMPHONY
ORCHESTRA
SEIJI OZAWA
*Music
Director*

With all his fame and glory, the great pianist Artur Rubinstein remained a modest man, almost self-deprecating.

Once at a recording session after the first "take" of the Tchaikovsky Concerto he said, "I played enough wrong notes to write a whole new concerto! Now let us do it again!" The recording session lasted over five hours - until one o'clock in the morning. Then Rubinstein said, "Now I could begin all over again".

He was then eighty years old.

BOSTON
SYMPHONY
ORCHESTRA
SEIJI OZAWA
Music Director

Chicken Rice Burritos

⅓ cup sliced green onion
1 garlic clove, crushed
2 teaspoons butter or margarine
7 cups shredded cooked chicken
1 teaspoon chili powder
2½ cups chicken broth, divided
1 (16-ounce) jar picante sauce, divided
1 cup long grain rice
½ cup sliced ripe black olives
3 cups shredded cheddar cheese, divided
12 (10-inch) flour tortillas, warmed
Additional picante sauce, for garnish (optional)
Additional cheddar cheese, for garnish (optional)

In a skillet, sauté the onion and garlic in the butter until tender. Stir in the chicken, chili powder, ¼ cup of the broth and ¾ cup of the picante sauce. Heat through; then set aside.

In a medium saucepan, bring the rice and remaining broth to a boil. Reduce the heat, cover and simmer for 20 minutes. Drain off any remaining liquid. Stir in the remaining picante sauce; cover, and simmer for 5 to 10 minutes, or until the rice is tender. Stir the rice into the chicken mixture. Add the olives and 2 cups of the cheese.

Preheat the oven to 375°.

Make the burrito by spooning 1 cup of the filling, off center, on each tortilla. Fold the sides and ends over the filling, then roll up the tortilla. Arrange the burritos in 2 ungreased 13 by 9 by 2-inch baking dishes. Sprinkle with the remaining cheese. Cover and bake for 10 to 15 minutes, or until heated through. Garnish with additional picante sauce and cheese, if desired.

The burritos may be made ahead and frozen, if desired.

Yield: 6 servings

Variation: This recipe is equally delicious cold as a burrito sandwich.

Tummy Ticklin' Turkey

4 tablespoons olive oil
1 medium onion, chopped
1 clove garlic, minced
6 turkey cutlets (about 1½ pounds)
1 cup burgundy cooking wine
1 (10¾-ounce) can condensed cream of mushroom soup
8 ounces chopped mushrooms
¼ teaspoon black pepper

In a large skillet, sauté the onion and garlic in the olive oil until the onion turns translucent.

Add the turkey cutlets and brown them on both sides. Add the wine and cream of mushroom soup. Stir well; bring just to a boil.

Add the chopped mushrooms and black pepper. Reduce the heat and simmer covered at least 1 hour, or until done; stirring occasionally.

Yield: 4 to 6 servings

Serving Suggestion: Serve the turkey over rice.

BOSTON
SYMPHONY
ORCHESTRA
SEIJI OZAWA
Music Director

Scott Andrews
Clarinet

Scott Andrews joined the orchestra in 1996 as the BSO's second clarinet. A Tanglewood Music Center Fellow in 1991 and 1994, Scott has also been principal clarinet of the New England Chamber Orchestra and the Toho Gakuen Symphony Orchestra. In 1999 he was selected as the Chair of the BSO Players Committee.

Scott and his wife Nina gave us this "tummy ticklin' recipe."

Matthew Ruggiero
Bassoon

Turkey involtini is a favorite of the Ruggiero family. "It is a great alternative to the traditional Thanksgiving turkey," says Matthew, "and our eight grandchildren love it because they don't have to wait while the bird is being carved in front of them."

Matthew retired from the bassoon section of the orchestra in 1990 and now travels in Asia teaching and training young musicians of the Youth Orchestra of Asia.

Roast Breast of Turkey Involtini
(with Apple, Apricot and Currant Stuffing)

7 tablespoons diced dried apricots
3½ tablespoons currants
4 tablespoons (½ stick) butter, at room temperature, divided
½ medium onion, chopped
2 medium tart green apples, peeled, cored, and diced
6 tablespoons slivered almonds
2 cups dry breadcrumbs
½ teaspoon salt
¼ teaspoon dried sage, crumbled
3 to 4 tablespoons chicken stock
1 (5 to 5½-pound) fresh whole turkey breast, boned and trimmed, skin retained
3 cups apple cider
½ cup applejack or cognac
Sprigs of fresh parsley and sage, for garnish

Soak the apricots and currants in a bowl of boiling water to cover until plump and soft - about 15 minutes. Drain.

Melt 1 tablespoon of the butter in a heavy, medium skillet over medium heat. Add the onion and cook until slightly softened, stirring occasionally - about 6 minutes. Remove the onion and drain on paper towels.

Melt 1 tablespoon of the remaining butter in same skillet over medium heat. Add the apples and cook until slightly softened, tossing occasionally - about 5 minutes. Drain the apples on paper towels.

Combine the apricots, currants, onion, apples, almonds, breadcrumbs, salt and sage in a bowl. Blend in the chicken stock. If the stuffing is too dry, add another tablespoon of stock. Adjust seasoning with salt. Cool completely. (At this point, the recipe can be prepared one day ahead and refrigerated.)

Butterfly the turkey by laying the meat with skin side down in front of you. Starting at the center, hold the knife parallel to the meat with the blade facing the left, and make a lengthwise cut through the meat on the left side. Do not cut through to the edge. Open the flap. Turn the meat and repeat on the right side. Spread the meat out flat; and cover with waxed paper. Gently pound it into a thickness of ½ to ¾ inch. Season generously with salt.

Spread the stuffing on the turkey breast, leaving a ½-inch border. Starting with the long edge, roll the meat into a 16 by 3-inch cylinder. Tie at 1 to 2-inch intervals with kitchen twine. Secure the ends with toothpicks.

Preheat the oven to 350°.

Roast Breast of Turkey Involtini *continued*

Mix the cider and applejack. Rub the turkey with the remaining 2 tablespoons of butter. Set the turkey on the rack in a roasting pan. Roast until the skin is browned, and juices run clear when the meat is pierced with a knife - about 1 hour, basting every 15 minutes with ½ cup of the cider mixture. Remove the turkey from the oven and let stand for 15 minutes.

Degrease the basting liquid in the pan. Pour the remaining cider mixture to obtain 1 ½ cups liquid total. Stir the cider mixture back into the roasting pan over high heat, scraping up browned bits.

Slice the rolled turkey into ½-inch-thick slices and carefully arrange on a large serving tray. Spoon cider mixture over the slices and garnish with sprigs of fresh parsley and sage.

Yield: 8 servings

BOSTON
SYMPHONY
ORCHESTRA
SEIJI OZAWA
*Music
Director*

In the twenties and thirties the names of Fritz Kreisler, Mischa Elman, and Jascha Heifetz dominated the field of violinists. There is an apocryphal story that Elman and Heifetz were eating lunch together when the headwaiter brought an envelope addressed to "the world's greatest violinist." Heifetz read the envelope and said, "This is for you, Mischa."

Elman read it and handed it back, insisting it was for Heifetz. Heifetz passed it back and said, "Well, open it anyway." Elman did and his face fell. Heifetz said, "What does it say?"

"It says", said Elman, "Dear Fritz!"

Pamela Frank
Violin

Pamela Frank is a world renowned violinist and self-proclaimed recipe author.

In reflecting on her BSO memories, Pam provided the following comments:

"Quite literally, I owe my life (or rather, my existence) to Tanglewood, since that is where my parents (Claude Frank and Lillian Kallir) first met in 1947! My post-womb association with the BSO also began there during my first summers—in fact, I was introduced to orchestral music while sitting (and probably screaming) on the lawn outside the Shed! What a thrill it is for all of us that now I am lucky enough to enjoy a relationship with the BSO both in Symphony Hall and at Tanglewood (the scene of the crime) from the other side of the stage!"

About the recipe, Pam says, "It's just a way of emptying out the refrigerator!"

Thanksgiving Stuffing from Hell

1 to 3 heads garlic, minced, plus additional, if desired
6 onions, chopped
1 cup chopped carrot
1 cup chopped celery
2 bunches scallions, minced
Oil for frying
"Many" packages of stuffing, cubed and grain-style
12 ounces (3 sticks) butter more than required by stuffing package instructions
"Tons" of currants and yellow raisins
"Lots" of pecans
"Lots" of slivered almonds
"Lots" of chopped walnuts
Pitchers of apple cider
6 eggs

In a pan, sauté the garlic, onions, carrot, celery, and scallions in the hot oil. Add more garlic!

Prepare the stuffing by following the instructions on the bags of stuffing, but adding more water and butter than indicated. Add the currants, raisins, pecans, almonds, walnuts, apple cider and eggs (going heavy on the apple cider and raw eggs for added moisture).

Stuff your face and the bird - in that order!

(Ed. Note: As the above ingredients list indicates, Pamela Frank possesses not only world-class talent as a violinist, but also a matching sense of humor. If you feel adventurous, follow the above ingredients list; if you prefer a more detailed one, use the following measurements and procedure for the stuffing.)

Thanksgiving Stuffing from Hell continued

1 clove garlic, minced (plus additional if desired)
1 small onion, chopped
½ cup chopped carrot
½ cup chopped celery
2 scallions, minced
Oil for frying
¼ cup currants and yellow raisins
¼ cup pecans
¼ cup slivered almonds
¼ cup chopped walnuts
½ cup plus additional apple cider
2 eggs
1 (16-ounce) package stuffing, cubed or grain-style

Sauté the garlic, onion, carrot, celery and scallions in the oil. (Add more garlic if desired.) Set aside.

Follow directions on package to make the stuffing, adding more cider and butter than indicated. Add the currants, raisins, pecans, almonds, walnuts and sautéed mixture. More apple cider and eggs should be added for moisture, if needed. Stuff the turkey prior to roasting.

Yield: Stuffing for a 12 to 14 pound turkey

BOSTON
SYMPHONY
ORCHESTRA
SEIJI OZAWA
*Music
Director*

Pierre Monteux on music critics: "When I started my career I was a violinist. When that became too difficult, I became a viola player. When that became too difficult, I became a conductor. And when I can no longer do that, I will become a critic."

Duck Breasts with Cranberries

1 cup dry red wine
½ cup dried cranberries
1 tablespoon extra-virgin olive oil
6 skinless duck breast halves (about 5 ounces each)
Salt and freshly ground pepper
10 ounces shiitake mushrooms, stems removed, thinly sliced
4 shallots, thinly sliced
½ cup water
3 teaspoons honey mustard

Preheat oven to 250°.

Combine the wine and dried cranberries in a small saucepan, and simmer them over low heat for 3 minutes. Set aside.

Heat the oil in a large skillet. Season the duck breasts on both sides with salt and pepper. Add the duck breasts to the skillet and cook over moderately high heat until well-browned and medium rare - about 3 minutes per side. Transfer the duck pieces to a baking sheet, cover with foil, and keep warm in the oven.

Add the mushrooms and shallots to the skillet, cover and cook over low heat, stirring once, until they are browned, about 4 minutes. Uncover and add ½ cup water into the skillet. Cook over moderately high heat scraping all the browned bits from the sides and until the water has reduced by one half. Add the cranberry mixture, and cook until it is reduced by one third. Stir in the honey mustard and season well with salt and pepper to taste.

Remove the duck breasts from the oven and pour any accumulated juices into the sauce. The duck breasts can be left whole or cut into ¼-inch-thick slices and arranged on a warm platter. Reheat the sauce again and pour over the duck.

Yield: 3 to 6 servings

Variation: Sour cherries may be substituted for the cranberries.

Serving Suggestion: For an extra treat try serving this dish over saffron rice pilaf!

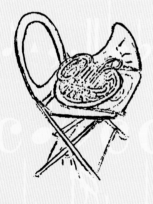

Duck with Apricot-Mustard Sauce

2 duck breasts (about 8 to 10 ounces each), skins removed

Sauce:
1 cup apricot preserves
¼ cup cider vinegar
3 tablespoons coarse-grained mustard

Preheat the oven to 375°.

Bake the duck breasts for 20 minutes. While the duck is baking, make the sauce.

In a small saucepan, combine the apricot preserves, vinegar and mustard. Bring the mixture to a boil over medium heat, stirring constantly. Reduce the heat to low and simmer, continuing to stir constantly for 5 minutes. Remove from the heat and cool to room temperature. (The sauce can be slowly reheated at serving time, if necessary.) You should have about 1 ¼ cups of sauce.

Remove the duck from oven and lower temperature to 350°. Spread the duck with the apricot-mustard sauce. Bake the duck for an additional 30 to 40 minutes.

Yield: 2 servings

Note: The sauce will keep in the refrigerator for up to 2 weeks.

Note: If duck breasts are not readily available, a whole duck may be used. Quarter the duck, remove the skin and cut away the excess fat. Cook the four pieces as above. There is sufficient sauce for the additional duck.

Serving Suggestion: Rice makes a nice accompaniment for this dish.

BOSTON SYMPHONY ORCHESTRA
SEIJI OZAWA
Music Director

Arthur Fiedler started his BSO career in 1915, but he was not the first Fiedler in the orchestra. His father Emmanuel joined the symphony in 1885 at age 26. His uncle Benny joined the orchestra in 1898 and stayed for 45 years until his death in 1942. A younger uncle, Gustave, joined after World War I and stayed only a few years. With Arthur's entrance into the BSO in 1915 and tenure until his death in 1979, the Fiedlers established a record for one family's continuous association with just one orchestra - 94 years!

Blantyre

The Scottish-style manor house in Lenox is a country resort within easy distance of Tanglewood.

Chef Michael Roller at Blantyre shares this favorite duck recipe with us.

Breast of Duck with Lentils and Tart Apple Vinaigrette

Vinaigrette:
1 Golden Delicious apple, peeled, seeded, and diced small
½ cup fresh apple juice
¼ cup lemon juice
½ cup extra-virgin olive oil
2 teaspoons fresh thyme leaves
Salt and pepper

4 (8-ounce) duck breasts, skin on, fat thinly trimmed to less than ⅛ inch
2 large shallots, diced
1 stalk celery, diced
1 carrot, diced
½ cup diced leek
3 cups lentils du pay, cooked "al dente"
2 tablespoons finely chopped basil leaves
2 tablespoons cider vinegar
¼ cup olive oil
5 sprigs fresh thyme, for garnish

Make the vinaigrette by combining the apple, apple juice, lemon juice, ½ cup of olive oil, thyme leaves, and salt and pepper to taste.

Season the duck and sauté to rare, or desired doneness. Let the duck "rest" while finishing the remaining steps. Sauté the shallots, celery, carrot and leek very briefly. Combine them in a bowl with the lentils and basil. Add the vinegar and the ¼ cup of olive oil, and season to taste.

Spread the lentils over a large serving plate. Slice the duck breast on the bias and arrange in a star pattern atop the lentils. Sprinkle apple vinaigrette around the duck. Garnish with thyme sprigs.

Yield: 6 servings

Bulgogi
(Korean Beef)

1 to 1½ pounds boneless shell sirloin steak
Scant ¼ cup soy sauce
2 tablespoons sesame oil
2 tablespoons sesame seeds
2 tablespoons chopped garlic
4 tablespoons sugar
⅓ teaspoon black pepper
3 tablespoons sake wine
4 tablespoons chopped scallions

Trim the steak and cut it into ½-inch strips.

In a bowl or dish, combine the sliced beef with the soy sauce, sesame oil, sesame seeds, garlic, sugar, black pepper, wine and scallions. Marinate for at least 20 minutes.

Cook the beef over a grill for best results, turning only once. Do not overcook. The beef may also be cooked under a broiler on high heat.

Yields 4 to 6 servings

Note: Any tender cut of beef may be used in this recipe.

Variation: Make enough beef to refrigerate leftovers; then cut up for use in a dinner salad.

BOSTON SYMPHONY ORCHESTRA
SEIJI OZAWA
Music Director

Bo Youp Hwang
Violin

Bo Youp Hwang gave his first solo violin performance with an orchestra when he was 12 years old in his native Korea. By the time he was 18, Mr. Hwang had won two prestigious prizes leading to study with the Fine Arts String Quartet at the University of Wisconsin. He was later appointed assistant concertmaster of the Milwaukee Symphony Orchestra. He joined the Boston Symphony Orchestra in 1973. Mr. Hwang has performed on several occasions with the Boston Pops and was active as first violinist with the Francesco String Quartet.

Over the past few years, he has returned to Korea several times to perform. A dedicated teacher, he has taught many successful young musicians in Boston and served on the faculty of the Boston University Tanglewood Institute and the New England Conservatory of Music.

BOSTON SYMPHONY ORCHESTRA
SEIJI OZAWA
Music Director

Ron Barron
Principal Trombone

Ron Barron joined the BSO trombone section in 1970 and became principal in 1975.

During the Tanglewood season, Sunday evenings are reserved for Ron's barbecue when he puts away his trombone to cook for his family and BSO colleagues.

Ron is also an avid wine collector. He suggests a hearty red, such as a California Syrah, to accompany this flank steak.

Flank Steak Barbecue

1 medium to large flank steak, about 2 to 3 pounds
Soy sauce
Finely chopped or crushed fresh garlic
Finely chopped fresh ginger
Finely chopped onion (optional)

In a marinade dish or pan cover the steak with soy sauce, along with as much garlic and ginger as you have time and patience to finely chop. (Add the onion also, if used.)

Cover, and allow the steak to marinate for several hours. Grill over a hot fire to sear the outside, and then move the steak to a reduced heat source until medium done, using the marinade to baste while grilling.

Serve the steak hot or cold, slicing it perpendicular to the meat grain into thin strips.

Yield: 4 to 6 servings

Festive Tamale Pie

1 cup chopped onion
1 cup chopped green pepper
1 tablespoon butter or margarine
¾ pound ground beef
2 (8-ounce) cans seasoned tomato sauce (about 2 cups)
1 (12-ounce) can whole kernel corn, drained
or 1 (10-ounce) package frozen, thawed
1 cup chopped ripe black olives
1 clove garlic, minced
1 tablespoon sugar
1 teaspoon salt
⅔ teaspoon chili powder
Dash of pepper
1 ½ cups shredded sharp cheddar cheese

Cornmeal Topping;
¾ cup yellow cornmeal
½ teaspoon salt
2 cups water
1 tablespoon butter or margarine

Preheat the oven to 375°. Grease a 10 by 6 by 1 ½-inch baking dish.

Cook the onion and green pepper in hot butter or margarine until tender, but not brown. Add the meat and brown lightly. Add the tomato sauce, corn, olives, garlic, sugar, salt, chili powder, and black pepper. Simmer 20 to 25 minutes, or until thick. Add the cheese; stir until it is melted.

Pour the mixture into a baking dish. Set aside.

Make the topping: Stir the yellow cornmeal with the salt and cold water. Cook over medium-high heat, stirring until thick. Add butter or margarine. Mix well.

Top the casserole with the cornmeal topping, making 3 lengthwise stripes. Bake the casserole for 40 minutes, or until top is lightly browned.

Yield: 6 servings

This is definitely a party pleaser!

BOSTON
SYMPHONY
ORCHESTRA
SEIJI OZAWA
*Music
Director*

Honoring Seiji

Two of the most renowned composers of the twentieth century's second half– Olivier Messaien and John Williams–are among the numerous composers who have honored Seiji Ozawa.

After Messaien heard the young Seiji Ozawa conduct his "Turangalila-Symphonie," he presented him with the score, which he had inscribed: "To the great Seiji Ozawa, his symphony!!, January 15-16-17-18, 1975."

To honor Seiji Ozawa on his 25th Anniversary Season as The BSO's Music Director, John Williams composed an orchestral piece, entitled "for Seiji" for him as a gift. The Maestro gave the world premiere to open the BSO's final concerts of the 1998-99 subscription season, and John Williams gave the Tanglewood premiere during the BSO's opening weekend that summer.

Maestro Williams observed that his new piece was intended to demonstrate the extraordinary sound and flexibility of the Boston Symphony Orchestra under Seiji's baton.

BOSTON SYMPHONY ORCHESTRA
SEIJI OZAWA
Music Director

Hollywood comes to Symphony Hall

The musical score written by John Williams for the Steven Spielberg movie "Saving Private Ryan," was recorded in Symphony Hall by the BSO. The orchestra is world renowned, but why did Hollywood decide to travel across the country to record one movie score?

Steven Spielberg is a fan of the Boston Pops, and often plays their recordings in his car while driving around Los Angeles, and portions of his Academy Award-winning "Schindler's List" were recorded by the BSO. So, when he was discussing the recording of the "Saving Private Ryan" movie score with John, he said, "Let's go to Boston and record with the best orchestra."

So Hollywood came to Symphony Hall, and it was a splendid week for everyone. Even the star of the movie, Tom Hanks, was on hand for some of the recording sessions. It was especially gratifying for John Williams, who has spent so many years making music in the Hall, and for Steven Spielberg, whose enthusiasm for the orchestra and Hall knew no bounds.

Hungarian Goulash from Transylvania

2 large yellow onions, roughly chopped
4 tablespoons vegetable oil, divided
1 teaspoon caraway seed
1 large clove garlic, crushed
2 tablespoons hot paprika
1 cup unbleached flour (for dredging)
2 tablespoons sweet paprika
2 pounds top round beef, cut into 1-inch cubes
2 to 3 cups water
Kosher salt
1 tablespoon tomato paste
½ pint sour cream, for garnish
1 bunch scallions, finely chopped, for garnish

In a heavy skillet sauté the onions in 1 tablespoon of the oil until golden brown. Add the caraway seeds and crushed garlic; sauté for 1 to 2 minutes. (Be careful not to burn the seeds.) Add the hot paprika and stir until the onions are coated. Remove the onions and set aside in a heavy pot or Dutch oven.

Mix the flour and sweet paprika on a board or large plate. Dredge the beef in the flour mixture, shake off any excess flour, and sauté the beef in batches in the remaining 3 tablespoons of oil until browned. Remove the beef and add it to the reserved onions in the pot. Mix the beef and onions together.

Scrape the skillet and add 1 cup of the water. Heat until blended. Add the water and its scrapings to the pot. Add the remaining water until the beef is covered. Cover the pot and simmer at least 2 hours, adding water as needed. (If made ahead of time for later use, allow the goulash to cool; then skim any oil off the surface.)

Before serving, add salt to taste. Blend in the tomato paste and heat through on the stove or in the oven. Garnish each serving with a dollop of the sour cream and some of the scallions.

Yield: 6 to 8 servings

Note: The recipe calls for both hot and sweet paprika.

Serving Suggestion: Serve with egg noodles.

18th Century Pot Roast

3 to 5 pounds rolled, boneless pot roast (chuck or rump cut)
4 to 6 ounces finely ground veal, mixed with 1 egg white
4 to 6 slices medium to thick bacon
3 tablespoons flour, divided
1 teaspoon salt
½ teaspoon pepper
3 tablespoons cooking oil
1 ½ cups beef broth
1 cup dry red wine
1 or 2 bay leaves
4 to 6 medium mushrooms, sliced

"Lard" the roast by making holes in the beef and filling them with the veal mixture. Tuck the bacon strips under the strings around the rolled roast (or lay them around the roast and retie it with string).

Mix 2 tablespoons of the flour with the salt and pepper, and rub it over the roast..

Heat the oil in a heavy Dutch oven (or a deep pan with a lid) until it is very very hot. Braise the roast on all sides, until the bacon is brown and crisp. Pour the broth and wine over the roast, add the bay leaf or leaves, and simmer for 3 ½ hours.

Remove the roast, cut off the string and remove the bacon, reserving the liquid in the pan. Wrap the roast in foil to keep it warm while making the sauce.

Make the sauce: Remove the bay leaf or leaves from the liquid. Skim off the fat and cook down the liquid to 2 to 2 ½ cups. Add the sliced mushrooms and thicken with the remaining 1 tablespoon of flour, blended with some cold water. Season to taste.

Slice the roast as thinly as possible, and arrange on a warm platter with the sauce on the side.

Yield: 10 to 12 servings

For his inaugural benefit concert with the BSO, Danny Kaye received conducting lessons from Harry Ellis Dickson in a hotel room. Kaye, along with ten minutes of conducting experience, also could not read music! After conducting Rossini's Overture to "La Gazza Ladra," he looked up at the balcony towards Charles Munch, and shouted: "Not bad, eh Chuck?"

Later, Munch sternly inquired of Harry, "What is this Chuck business?"

"It's an affectionate name for Charles," Harry replied.

Later, Danny received an autographed photo that read: "To Danny, from his friend, Chuck."

From the BSO's inception in 1881 until the 1955-56 season, its musicians were all men. During that season Doriot Anthony Dwyer became the first female member of the BSO.

A fine flutist, she had the further distinction of becoming the only female first player of any major symphony orchestra.

As a first player in the BSO, Doriot did not play in the Pops. (The first chair players make up the Boston Symphony Chamber Players during the Pops season.) It was not until the mid-60s that cellist Carol Procter became the first female player of the Pops.

Charcoal-Grilled Butterflied Leg of Lamb

1 cup dry red wine
¾ cup soy sauce
2 to 3 cloves garlic, crushed
1 tablespoon coarse ground black pepper
1 tablespoon fresh tarragon leaves
½ cup fresh mint leaves, chopped
2 tablespoons fresh rosemary
1 leg of lamb, boned and butterflied (about 4 to 6 pounds)

Combine the wine, soy sauce, garlic, black pepper, tarragon, mint, and rosemary in a glass bowl. Place the butterflied lamb in a glass baking dish and pour the marinade over the lamb. Refrigerate, covered, at least 8 hours (or overnight), turning the lamb a few times to thoroughly soak both sides of the meat.

One hour before serving, pour the marinade from the baking dish into a small bowl. When the charcoal fire is hot, and the coals have a white ash on them, place the lamb flattened about 4 to 5 inches above the fire. Grill the first side about 20 minutes and baste several times with the marinade. Turn the meat over for an additional 20 minutes of cooking, again basting the lamb. (For medium rare lamb, check the center of the roast after 30 minutes of total cooking time.)

To serve, cut the lamb into thin slices and arrange on a plate with sprigs of fresh rosemary.

Yield: 6 to 8 servings (4 pounds of lamb), or 8 to 10 servings (6 pounds of lamb)

Indian Lamb

1 tablespoon unsalted butter
1 tablespoon vegetable oil
2 cloves garlic, minced
1 large onion, thinly sliced
1 teaspoon fresh gingerroot, minced
1 teaspoon ground cumin
1 teaspoon ground coriander
1 teaspoon ground cardamom
1 teaspoon ground turmeric
½ teaspoon salt
½ teaspoon pepper
1 teaspoon sugar
2 pounds lean lamb, cut into 1-inch pieces
1 large Granny Smith apple, peeled, cored, and sliced (or cubed)
2 green or unripe bananas, peeled and cut into ½-inch pieces
1½ cups chicken broth
1 tablespoon cider vinegar
Cayenne

In a large, heavy saucepan (or Dutch oven), heat the butter and oil. Add the garlic, onion and ginger. Cook on medium heat for 5 to 7 minutes. Add the cumin, coriander, cardamom, turmeric, salt, pepper and sugar and stir well. Add the lamb and brown evenly on all sides. Add the apple and bananas, and mix well.

Add the broth and vinegar; bring to a boil. Lower the heat and simmer for approximately 1 hour, or until the lamb is tender, and the liquid has thickened to sauce consistency. Add cayenne to taste.

Yield: 6 to 8 servings

Serving Suggestion: The lamb may be served with chutney, chopped peanuts, grated coconut and raisins as condiments, if desired. It may also be served with basmati rice.

Harry Ellis Dickson has a connection with the very first Boston Symphony of 1881. During the sixtieth anniversary in 1941, he met a player, Daniel Kountz, who had played under three of the orchestra's first conductors - Georg Henschel, Wilhelm Gericke, and Arthur Nikisch. Dickson asked him what they played in those early days. Kountz replied, "Oh, the usual - Mozart, Haydn, Beethoven, Schubert and Gluck."

"Did you play any modern music?" asked Dickson.

"Oh yes, especially later under Gericke, there was a modern piece on every program."

"Like what?" he was asked.

"Well, Dvořák, Tchaikovsky, Brahms."

Lamb Medallions in Mushroom Caps

8 lamb rib chops
8 mushrooms (large enough to hold lamb medallions)
2 tablespoons honey
3 tablespoons white vinegar
¼ cup chopped fresh mint leaves, or 2 tablespoons dried
2 to 3 tablespoons oil
1 ounce Boursin, or other flavored, cream cheese spread
2 tablespoons butter

Using a sharp paring knife, cut out the center section of each chop to get a circle of meat (the "medallion"). Cut the caps out of the mushrooms and scoop out enough of the insides to allow enough room to hold the lamb medallions.

Measure out the honey and vinegar into a cup. Add the mint to the mixture.

Heat the oil in a pan over medium-high heat. Add the mushroom caps, top side up. Cook for 3 minutes and turn. Cook for another 3 minutes; then remove from pan to serving plates, stem side up. Cover to keep warm.

Add the medallions to the pan and brown on both sides, then turn heat down to medium and continue cooking for a total of 5 minutes on each side for 2-inch-thick medallions, 4 minutes for 1 ½-inch-thick meat or 3 minutes for 1-inch-thick meat.

While cooking the lamb, spread the inside of the mushroom caps with the cheese spread. Remove the skillet from the heat and place a lamb medallion inside each cap.

Prepare the sauce: In the pan used to cook the lamb, drain the oil and add the butter. Add the mint mixture to the pan. Stir over low heat for 1 minute. Pour the sauce over lamb.

Yields: 4 servings

A very elegant dish to serve on an elegant occasion!

Lamb Curry

1½ pounds lamb, cut into 1-inch cubes
4 tablespoons flour
2 tablespoons curry powder
1 teaspoon salt
¼ teaspoon black pepper
⅓ cup canola oil
1 small onion, chopped
5 cloves garlic, peeled
1 (14½-ounce) can beef or chicken broth
½ cup dried apricots
½ cup dried prunes
½ cup dried raisins
½ cup dry vermouth
¼ cup pine nuts (pignoli)
½ cup ketchup
1 apple, peeled, cored and sliced
1 cup light cream
4 cups cooked rice (about 1¼ cups raw)

Place the lamb pieces, flour, curry, salt and pepper in a plastic bag; shake well to mix. Heat the oil in a large pan and sauté the lightly coated lamb until slightly brown - about 5 minutes. Remove the lamb to a bowl.

In the same pan sauté the onion and garlic about 5 minutes. Return the lamb to the pan, along with the broth and simmer for 25 minutes. Add the apricots, prunes, raisins, vermouth and pignoli nuts and simmer an additional 25 minutes.

Just before serving, add the ketchup, sliced apple and light cream. Bring to a simmer and cook for 5 minutes.

Yield: 4 to 5 servings

Serving Suggestion: Serve the lamb curry over rice.

This is a truly creative lamb meal.

Ralph Gomberg
Oboe

Oboist and recipe author Ralph Gomberg joined the orchestra as principal oboe in 1950 and retired in 1987, after a highly illustrious career with the orchestra and the Chamber Players.

He is one of seven children, five of whom graduated from the Curtis Institute in Philadelphia. At 18, he was appointed principal oboe of the All-American Youth Orchestra under Leopold Stokowski. His career was interrupted by World War II, when he served in the U.S. Navy.

Conductor William Steinberg's years with the BSO were marked with periods of illness.

During the intermission of a Carnegie Hall concert with the BSO, Steinberg came off the stage and announced to the assistant conductor, "You're on, Michael; I cannot continue."

Michael quickly changed into his evening clothes and waited in the wings while the announcement was made to the audience that Steinberg was ill and that Tilson Thomas would replace him.

Thus began the brilliant career of Michael Tilson Thomas.

Pork in Pastry Pockets

4 tablespoons (½ stick) butter, divided
2 pork tenderloins (about 1½ pounds total)
7 or 8 sage leaves
2 large cloves garlic, thinly sliced
1 large yellow onion, thinly sliced
1 large shallot, thinly sliced
6 large white mushrooms, halved, then thinly sliced
1 (17-ounce) package frozen puff pastry sheets
*1 large golden Bartlett pear, peeled, cored,
and cut into ⅛-inch slices, divided*
½ pound Monterey Jack cheese, coarsely grated, divided
2 egg yolks, beaten with 2 teaspoons water

Preheat oven to 400°.

Melt 2 tablespoons of the butter and roll the tenderloins in it. Cut slits in the tenderloins and insert sage leaves. Cook the meat to medium-rare in the oven for about 30 minutes, or until desired doneness. Let the pork sit for 1 minute; then slice it into ¼-inch-thick medallions. Reset the oven temperature to 375°.

Melt the remaining 2 tablespoons of butter in a medium-size sauté pan; add the garlic, onion, shallot and mushrooms, and cook until golden.

Roll out each pastry sheet to a 12 by 10-inch rectangle. Divide each sheet into thirds (10 by 4-inches), and round the corners to make long ovals.

Place the pork medallions, then the vegetables, a slice of pear, and 1 large tablespoon of the grated cheese on one side of each pastry piece. Paint the edges of each piece with water to facilitate sealing. Fold the pastry sheet over, turn up the edges to enclose the filling, and press the edges with a fork to seal. Paint each pocket with the egg wash. Place on greased baking sheets and bake for 30 minutes, or until pastry is golden.

Serve warm or at room temperature.

Yield: 6 large pockets

Note: Pork may be initially cooked in a microwave oven, covered with plastic wrap, on the high setting for 5 minutes.

Texas Spareribs

¾ cup ketchup
¼ cup lemon juice
⅓ cup brown sugar
1 tablespoon Worcestershire sauce
½ teaspoon allspice
1 teaspoon garlic powder (optional)
1 teaspoon salt
1 teaspoon minced green onion
1 teaspoon seasoned pepper
4 to 5 pounds pork spareribs

In a bowl mix the ketchup, lemon juice, brown sugar, Worcestershire sauce, allspice garlic powder (if used), salt, green onion, and seasoned pepper. Spread the mix over the meat. Put the spareribs into a plastic bag in a bowl and refrigerate for 24 hours, turning the bag twice.

Preheat the oven to 350°.

Place the ribs in the oven in a large pan and cook for 1 hour. Then lower the oven temperature to 200° and cook for an additional 3 hours. Turn once and baste the ribs during this period.

Yield: 6 servings

You don't have to go to Texas to enjoy this treat!

BSO Broadcasts

On January 23, 1926, Boston's airwaves reverberated with the opening notes of the BSO's first on-air broadcast. The performance was the first of twelve Saturday night concert transmissions funded by W.S. Quinby, who pledged $1,000 for each concert. Radio station WEEI, the Edison Electrical Illuminating Company, carried the broadcasts. The orchestra's first network broadcast came that fall over the airwaves of WBZ. It was the first network broadcast in New England.

Johanna Hill Simpson
Music Director
Performing Artists at Lincoln School (PALS)

Johanna Hill Simpson, known as Jody, says this dish is so tasty her family learned to prepare it when she's away. "My pork roast is a Sunday dinner favorite with my husband and our three sons. And they now have learned to make it themselves, thereby ensuring a delicious Sunday meal even when I am rehearsing or away at Tanglewood."

Jody is the music director of Performing Artists at Lincoln School. Her outstanding children's chorus performs with the BSO in Boston and at Tanglewood. "The children in PALS love to sing for Seiji. He has a special 'kid' channel that is always tuned into them."

Marinated Charcoal-Grilled Pork Roast

¼ cup soy sauce
¼ cup Hoisin sauce
¼ cup sherry
2 garlic cloves, minced
2 teaspoons chopped fresh ginger
½ cup peanut oil
½ teaspoon hot oil
½ teaspoon sesame oil
½ cup rice vinegar
2 scallions, chopped
1 boneless pork loin roast (about 3 to 4 pounds)

In a bowl, mix the soy sauce, hoisin sauce, sherry, garlic, ginger, peanut oil, hot oil, sesame oil, rice vinegar and scallions.

Lightly score the pork loin around the outside and put it into a glass casserole. Pour the marinade over the pork. Cover and place the dish in the refrigerator for several hours, or overnight. Turn several times.

Grill the pork over hot coals until done. Slice it to desired thickness.

Meanwhile, reduce the marinade on the stove top to one half, and use as a sauce over the sliced pork.

Yield: 6 servings

Note: Hoisin sauce may be found in Asian and food specialty shops.

Try freezing the pork loins or tenderloins with their marinade in freezer bags. When it's time to cook, defrost the appropriate amount of pork and the marinade procedure will be already completed.

Minted Pork Chops

Salt
2 center-cut boneless pork chops
1 ripe mango
2 tablespoons olive oil
1 Granny Smith apple, peeled, cored and chopped
3 sprigs fresh mint
Juice of 1 lime

Lightly salt the pork chops and cut off any extra fat. Set aside.

Peel the mango by cutting vertically through the skin, and then cut out the fruit.

Heat the olive oil in a medium heavy frying pan. Add the apple, mango and mint. Turn down the heat and cook for about 7 minutes, stirring occasionally to prevent burning. Stir in the lime juice and add the pork chops.

Cover the pan and cook the chops for approximately 5 minutes on each side, depending on their thickness. If the fruit appears to be burning, add more lime juice or 2 tablespoons of water.

Yield: 2 servings

BOSTON
SYMPHONY
ORCHESTRA
SEIJI OZAWA
Music Director

Conductor Pierre Monteux was a dear, kind, simple man. He was always calm; nothing seemed to ruffle him, not even his irrepressible third wife, Doris, a Maine Yankee whom he adored and referred to as his "Eroica."

She once burst into the hall during a conducting class and shouted, "Pierre, I'm leaving you and never coming back!"

There was silence in the room as Monteux slowly rose from his seat. "Leave the checkbook," he said.

Red Lion Inn

The famous Red Lion Inn is situated in the heart of Stockbridge, Massachusetts, just a few miles from Tanglewood. Its grand porch, overlooking Main Street, is a favorite lounging spot for concert-goers following an evening of music.

Chef Douglas Luf kindly shares his delicious roasted pork loin recipe with us.

Roasted Coriander and Brown Sugar-Cured Pork Loin

⅛ cup cracked coriander seed
¼ cup kosher salt
⅛ cup freshly ground black pepper
⅛ cup herbes de Provence
1 trimmed center-cut boneless pork loin (about 1½ to 2 pounds)
1 pound brown sugar

Mix the coriander, salt, pepper and herbes de Provence together. Place the pork loin in a shallow container and dust it with the herb mixture, then rub the mixture into the pork. Pack the brown sugar around the pork loin. Let it stand, covered, in the refrigerator for 24 hours.

Preheat oven to 375°.

Remove the pork loin from refrigerator and remove the sugar cure. Place the pork loin in a roasting pan on a rack. Roast in the oven for 35 minutes, or until the internal temperature of the meat reaches 145°.

Cut the pork into slices of desired thickness.

Yield: 4 servings

Piccata di Vitello

8 thin slices veal scaloppine, about 1½ pounds
Salt and pepper
2 tablespoons flour, for dredging
¼ cup olive oil
4 tablespoons butter
⅓ cup dry white wine
½ cup veal or chicken broth
Juice of 1 lemon
2 tablespoons chopped fresh parsley
1 tablespoon capers (optional)

Pound the veal with a flat mallet. Sprinkle with salt and pepper to taste; then dredge in flour. Shake off any excess flour.

Heat the oil in a large skillet. When the oil is hot, add the veal and brown on both sides - about 2 minutes. Remove the meat to a warm platter. Pour off any extra oil; return the skillet to the heat.

Add the butter to the skillet. When the skillet is hot and butter has melted, return the veal to skillet; cook briefly on both sides. Add the wine, broth, lemon juice and parsley. Simmer over low heat, turning the veal slices occasionally, until the sauce has a nice consistency. (If capers are used, they should be added while sauce is simmering.)

Yield: 4 to 6 servings

BOSTON SYMPHONY ORCHESTRA
SEIJI OZAWA
Music Director

At a post-concert celebration for Pierre Monteux's 80th birthday, the distinguished African-American tenor Roland Hayes stood and movingly addressed the group, saying, "It was Pierre Monteux who made me the first of my race to appear with a symphony orchestra."

John Oliver
Director
Tanglewood Festival Chorus

In December 1994, John Oliver proudly displayed the talents of his Tanglewood Festival Chorus to audiences in Japan and Hong Kong, when the group accompanied the Boston Symphony Orchestra on its Far East tour in performances of the Berlioz "Requiem".

It was the first overseas trip for the chorus, whose only other international concert appearance had been an earlier visit to Canada.

Veal and Morels with Cream

4 ounces pappardelle pasta
1 ⅓ cups firm and dry morels
5 tablespoons butter, divided
Salt and pepper
4 veal scaloppine fillets, pounded thin
Flour, for dredging
⅓ to ½ cup Marsala wine
Zest of 1 lemon, finely chopped and lightly salted
Hot pepper flakes (optional)
1 cup heavy cream

Cook the pasta in a large quantity of water. While the noodles are cooking, skim off a cup or so of the pasta water and reserve it. When the pasta is "al dente", drain and return it to the pot. Add some of the reserved water to the pot, cover, and place it on a turned-off burner.

Brush any dirt from the morels, but do not wash them. Cut off the bottom of the stem of each morel, discard it, and then cut the remainder in half lengthwise. Any that are particularly large may be cut into quarters.

In a skillet large enough to eventually hold the veal as well as the mushrooms, melt 2 tablespoons of the butter over a high heat and add the morels when the butter sizzles. Immediately sprinkle with a good amount of salt and pepper, and toss until the morels take on a nice golden brown color. Remove the skillet from the heat and lift the morels out of the skillet with a slotted spoon or tongs and place them in a bowl. Set aside.

Cut the veal into 1-inch-wide strips, and then into 2-inch-long pieces. In the skillet melt the remaining 3 tablespoons of butter. (Olive oil may be substituted for the butter in this step, if desired.) On a layer of waxed paper or foil, toss the veal with salt, pepper and flour to coat them. When the butter (or olive oil) is hot, add the veal strips to the pan. (If the recipe is being doubled or more, cook the veal in batches, or it will not brown properly.) Toss the veal over high heat until it is thoroughly cooked and has taken on a brown crusty exterior. Transfer the veal to a shallow plate in a single layer with a slotted spoon or tongs. To keep the veal warm, replace the cover of the pasta pot with the plate, uncovered (so that the veal does not become steamed).

Veal and Morels with Cream continued

Add the Marsala wine to the skillet, along with the lemon zest and pepper flakes (if being used). Boil down to a syrup-like consistency, scraping up the tasty bits in the pan as you go. Add sufficient cream to give you a good amount of sauce (about ½ cup per serving). Adjust the seasoning, and when cream comes to a boil, add it and the reserved veal to the pasta, and toss thoroughly over a low heat.

Yield: 2 servings

Note: Morels are difficult to obtain except in spring. Shiitake mushrooms may be substituted, if desired.

BOSTON
SYMPHONY
ORCHESTRA
SEIJI OZAWA
*Music
Director*

On the list of prominent conductors who have appeared with the BSO is Sir John Barbirolli. He brought a sense of camaraderie to the orchestra. He treated the players as friends and fellow musicians - he himself had been a cellist in an orchestra.

At one rehearsal he went into the cello section, borrowed Jean Bedetti's instrument, and demonstrated a certain passage, to the applause of the orchestra.

"Do not applaud," he said, "I am out of practice."

BOSTON SYMPHONY ORCHESTRA
SEIJI OZAWA
Music Director

Ron Della Chiesa, WGBH Radio Host

This recipe was received from Ron Della Chiesa and his wife Joyce, who is a restauranteur and chef. Ron is a radio host for WGBH and has had a long association with the BSO. He is the well-known personality and voice behind the Friday after-noon live broadcasts of the BSO from Symphony Hall, and, in the summer, the BSO Sunday after-noon concerts broadcast live from Tanglewood.

The BSO has been part of the legacy of WGBH since day one, when the station signed on the air in October 1951 with a broadcast of the BSO Saturday night concert.

Ossobuco Milanese

Olive oil, for frying
Butter, for frying
3 cups chopped onion
2 cups chopped carrots
2 cups chopped celery
1 head garlic cloves, crushed
Flour, for dredging
Salt and pepper
8 veal shanks, about 2-inches-thick
2 cups dry white wine
3 cups veal or chicken stock
2 cups chopped tomatoes (about 4 medium)
Mixed herbs (thyme, parsley, basil, lemon peel strips, sage and a few bay leaves)

In a large skillet, heat a mixture of olive oil and butter until the butter is melted. Add the onion, carrots, celery and garlic to the skillet, and sauté until the vegetables are softened. Set aside. Preheat the oven to 325°.

In the same skillet heat more olive oil and butter until it is very hot. Dredge the veal shanks in flour seasoned with some salt and pepper to taste, shaking off any excess flour. Brown the shanks on both sides. Remove the veal and place it in a large saucepan with a cover. Pour off most of the fat from the skillet and add the wine to deglaze it, cooking for about 30 seconds. Pour the wine and the collected drippings onto the veal in the saucepan.

In same skillet, bring the stock to a simmer; add the tomatoes and herbs. Pour this mixture, along with the previously sautéed vegetables, over the veal pieces. All should come to the top of the veal pieces. Cover and bake in the oven for 1 ½ to 2 hours. When done, carefully remove veal and strain the sauce, reserving the juices. Boil down the juices until thickened; then pour the sauce over the veal.

Yield: 8 servings

Note: An easy way to dredge the veal is to place the seasoned flour in a large plastic bag. Add the veal shanks and shake the bag well. It will coat the meat more evenly.

Serving Suggestion: Traditionally, this is served with Risotto Milanese (p. 104)

Veal and Shallot Stew

9 tablespoons (1 stick plus 1 tablespoon)
unsalted butter, divided
2 pounds boneless veal, cut into small cubes
5 tablespoons flour, divided
2 teaspoons paprika
1½ teaspoons ground coriander
⅛ teaspoon salt
¼ teaspoon pepper
2½ cups chicken broth
3 cups seeded and diced plum tomatoes
(about 2 pounds), divided
1½ cups sliced yellow onion
12 to 15 whole shallots, peeled
2 cloves garlic, minced
¼ cup chopped Italian flat-leaf parsley
1 tablespoon dried tarragon
Grated zest of 1 orange
½ pound mushrooms, cut into quarters
½ cup heavy cream
Parsley, for garnish

Preheat oven to 350°.

Melt 4 tablespoons of the butter in a large Dutch oven. Add the veal and sauté, but do not brown it, over a low heat, turning frequently. In a small bowl, stir together 2 tablespoons of the flour, the paprika, coriander, salt, and pepper. Sprinkle the mixture over the veal and cook over low heat for an additional 5 minutes. Add the chicken broth, 2 cups of the tomatoes, the onions, shallots, garlic, parsley, tarragon and orange zest. Bring it to a boil on the top of the stove. Transfer the Dutch oven, covered, to the oven and bake for 1 hour and 15 minutes, or until the veal is tender.

While the stew is baking, melt 2 tablespoons of the butter in a skillet. Sauté the mushrooms until golden. Reserve the mushrooms and liquid.

Remove the stew from the oven when it is done, and place it on a stove-top burner at a simmer. In a skillet, melt the remaining 3 tablespoons of butter. Sprinkle in the remaining 3 tablespoons of flour, and cook over low heat, whisking constantly. Stir 1 cup of stew liquid into the flour and butter mixture. Stir constantly for 3 to 5 minutes. Then whisk in the cream. Add this mixture to the stew. Gently stir in the remaining 1 cup of tomatoes and the mushrooms. Simmer for an additional 5 minutes.

Yield: 4 to 6 servings

Serving Suggestion: Serve over broad egg noodles and garnish with parsley.

Soloists are the "spice" added to an orchestral concert, and they are to be admired enormously, not only for their talent but also for their durability. Jascha Heifitz, the great violin virtuoso, once ridiculed the notion that a sensitive musician must be fragile. "The delicate concert artist," he said, "must have the nerves of a bullfighter, the digestion of a peasant, the hide of a politician, and the tact of a nightclub hostess."

Rubira Sauce

*7 pounds large, ripe tomatoes, peeled, seeded, and roughly cut
7 cups sugar (about 3 pounds)
16 ounces (1 pint) cider vinegar
1 (1-ounce) stick cinnamon, broken into pieces
½ ounce whole cloves*

Place the tomatoes, sugar and vinegar in a pot. Put the cinnamon and cloves in a bag and place the bag in the tomato mixture. Bring the liquid to a boil. Reduce the heat and simmer for 6 hours.

Cool and put the tomato sauce in jars and seal.

Serving Suggestion: The sauce may be used for meat or for pasta.

Raisin Sauce for Ham

*1 cup brown sugar
⅓ cup grape juice
⅓ cup pineapple juice
½ cup drained crushed pineapple
½ cup seedless raisins
3 tablespoons lemon juice
4 tablespoons vinegar
½ teaspoon whole cloves*

Combine the brown sugar, grape juice, pineapple juice, pineapple, raisins, lemon juice, vinegar and cloves in a pan and cook for 15 to 20 minutes.

Yield: about 2 cups sauce

Note: For a thicker sauce, add 2 teaspoons of corn starch mixed in water; stir over heat until the desired consistency is attained.

Mustard Sauce for Ham

¼ cup sugar
2 tablespoons dry mustard
1 tablespoon flour
1 cup light cream
2 egg yolks, beaten
½ cup cider vinegar

Mix the sugar, dry mustard and flour together in a bowl. Place the cream and beaten egg yolks in another bowl, and add the flour mixture to it. Cook the mixture in the top of double boiler over (but not touching) boiling water until it thickens, stirring occasionally with a wire whisk. When quite thick, but not stiff, add the vinegar and stir until smooth.

Serve hot.

Yield: 1 pint (about 10 servings)

Note: This is best made at the last minute. However, it may be made ahead of time and kept warm over low heat. (It tends to separate if reheated). It may also be used cold.

Apricot-Cranberry Chutney

½ cup apple juice
½ cup orange juice
1 cup dried apricots
1 large apple, cored and chopped
2 tablespoons grated fresh ginger
2 teaspoons cinnamon
1 teaspoon cardamom
12 ounces cranberries
2 tablespoons brown sugar
3 to 4 tablespoons apple or rice vinegar

In a pan bring the apple and orange juices to a boil. Add the apricots and let mixture stand off the heat, until the apricots are softened. Remove the apricots from the pan and finely chop them..

In a saucepan combine the apricots, apple, ginger, cinnamon, cardamom and cranberries. Cook until the cranberries "pop". Add the sugar and vinegar; cook an additional 5 minutes.

Yield: about 3 cups chutney

Serge Koussevitzky was at one time responsible for introducing more new works by American composers than any other conductor. There were premieres by William Schuman, Roy Harris, Samuel Barber, Howard Hanson, David Diamond, Harold Shapero, Lukas Foss, Irving Fine, and Leonard Bernstein, to name a few.

Koussevitzky used to try to spread his enthusiasm for any new work to the orchestra. More than once he would announce, "Dis is di greatest since Beethoven!"

In the last quarter of the twentieth century, Seiji Ozawa has continued this tradition of introducing and commissioning new music.

Koussevitzky once announced that there would be a special rehearsal of new music (unsolicited scores of which are constantly sent to conductors). There was little time to look at the music, and the compositions were completely unfamiliar to the players. Bedlam reigned, despite Koussevitzky's efforts to control the proceedings.

At one point in the rehearsal, the second oboist, Jean Devergie, turned to Fernand Gillet, the first oboist.

"What are we playing next?" he asked. Gillet pointed to the next piece.

"My God!" Devergie exclaimed, "I just played it!"

Spiced Orange Wedges

4 oranges, unpeeled
½ teaspoon baking soda
2 cups sugar
½ cup vinegar
12 whole cloves
3 pieces stick cinnamon

Cover the oranges with water in a saucepan. Add the baking soda and bring to a boil. Boil for 20 minutes, or until the oranges are easily pierced with a fork. Drain and cut each orange into 8 wedges.

In another sauce pan combine the sugar with 1 ¼ cups of water, the vinegar, cloves and cinnamon. Stir over low heat until the sugar is dissolved. Then boil for 5 minutes.

Add the orange wedges and simmer for 20 minutes. Cool, cover and refrigerate.

Yield: about 2 ¼ cups relish

Note: The recipe keeps almost indefinitely in the refrigerator.

Serving Suggestion: The orange wedges go well with fresh or smoked pork or duck.

TANGLEWOOD
FESTIVAL CHORUS

Photo by: © Chris Lee

The Tanglewood Festival Chorus
at the United Nations (Olympic Opening Ceremonies - February 1998)

TFC members in Puccini's "Madama Butterfly" (February, 1999)

TANGLEWOOD FESTIVAL CHORUS

The Tanglewood Festival Chorus is the official chorus of the Boston Symphony Orchestra. The volunteer group of professionally trained singers is acclaimed for power, beauty of tone, and mastery of many styles. The chorus has been led by John Oliver since its founding in 1970. Oliver's imprimatur on the Tanglewood Festival Chorus is obvious: it is today one of the leading symphony choruses in America and the world.

The group's 150 members donate their time and energy to be part of the BSO family. The TFC's level of professionalism is exemplary, and chorus members commit to a demanding rehearsal and performance schedule in Boston, New York, and at Tanglewood throughout the season.

Over the years, chorus members have included students, home-makers, doctors, lawyers, investment bankers, and the occasional stray musicologist. Members have come from more than a dozen countries. Regardless of their background, the singers are bound by their love of choral music and their loyalty to the TFC. Membership is a prized accomplishment: more than 90 percent of TFC members return each season. Each year only a few spaces open to be earned through a highly competitive audition process.

Courtesy of Tanglewood Festival Chorus

Chorus members after an AIDS walk

In February 1999 the Tanglewood Festival Chorus participated in an historic event. Courtesy of satellite technology, the group performed from the United Nations General Assembly as one of six choruses on five continents that sang Beethoven's *Ode to Joy* as a global grand finale to the opening ceremonies of the 1998 Winter Olympics with Seiji Ozawa conducting.

The chorus' repertory includes baroque masterworks of Bach, romantic French outpourings by Berlioz, and modern tours de force by Stravinsky and Messiaen. Such distinguished composers as Sir Michael Tippett and Donald Martino have written works especially for the chorus. To mark the chorus' twenty-fifth anniversary in 1995, Leon Kirchner composed for them *Of things exactly as they are.*

The Tanglewood Festival Chorus on the Esplanade

SEAFOOD ~ SHELLFISH

BOSTON
SYMPHONY
ORCHESTRA
SEIJI OZAWA
*Music
Director*

Bonnie Bewick
Violin

In addition to performing as a BSO violinist, Bonnie Bewick has soloed with the Boston Pops and numerous other orchestras.

She came across Salmon with Vodka Sauce during her travels. "I ordered this dish, or a version of it, at a trendy restaurant in the Berkshires and was really intrigued by the flavor and delicate pink color of the sauce," Bonnie remembers.

"Often when I taste something I really like, I go home and try to duplicate it. I don't know if this is how the chef made the salmon, but my version turned out just great! It's simple and low fat. What more could you ask?"

Salmon with Vodka Cream Sauce

1 (14½-ounce) can low-sodium chicken broth
¾ pound salmon fillet
2 tablespoons olive oil
7 or 8 plum tomatoes, chopped
¾ cup basil leaves, chopped
1 large clove garlic, minced
4 tablespoons light cream cheese
Salt and pepper
2 ounces vodka
2½ cups cooked farfalle (butterfly) pasta
(about 5 ounces uncooked)
Freshly grated Parmesan cheese (optional)

In a large nonstick pan heat the chicken broth until it approaches boiling. Add the salmon fillet, cover the pan and poach for 10 to 12 minutes, or until firm. Remove the salmon to a plate and flake it. Reserve the chicken broth.

Heat the olive oil in the same skillet and sauté the tomatoes, basil and garlic. When they are cooked through, return the broth to the pan, then add the cream cheese, stirring to blend. Season with salt and pepper to taste; then add the vodka.

Place the salmon back into the pan and combine it with the sauce. If the sauce is too thin, add more cream cheese. If it is too thick, add more chicken broth. Serve over the pasta and garnish with Parmesan cheese, if desired.

Yield: 2 servings

Prentice Pilot's Salmon

2 heaping tablespoons Dijon mustard
4 tablespoons honey
⅓ cup olive oil
Dash of cayenne
1 cup freshly chopped ginger
1 pound salmon fillets, skins removed

In a bowl, thoroughly mix the Dijon mustard and the honey. Add the olive oil to the honey mixture; mix thoroughly. Stir in the cayenne. Add the cup of chopped ginger and again mix thoroughly.

Marinate the salmon in the honey sauce for at least 1 hour before broiling the salmon. Broil on each side for 3 to 4 minutes, or until it becomes slightly charred and opaque in the center.

Yield: 2 servings

BOSTON SYMPHONY ORCHESTRA
SEIJI OZAWA
Music Director

Ann Hobson Pilot
Harp

Principal harp Ann Hobson Pilot gave us this recipe for salmon. She joined the orchestra in 1969 and was named principal harp in 1980. Since then, she has become a well-known soloist with the BSO and the Pops.

She and her husband became fascinated with the origins of the harp and in 1996 took a sabbatical to Africa to study the instrument's origins. Their study led to a television documentary on the harp's evolution.

Roland Small
Bassoon

Roland Small is a member of the bassoon section in the BSO, having joined the orchestra in 1975.

In addition to their salmon recipe, Roland Small and his wife, Kikue, shared the story of their romantic start together. After meeting in Japan when Roland played there with the Yomiuri Symphony, they fell in love, married, and moved to North America. Their two daughters were born during the family's eight-year stay in British Columbia while Roland was a member of the Vancouver Symphony.

The Smalls are now settled in Boston and Tanglewood. Kikue teaches bilingual studies in Belmont public schools and is a fine cook.

Brown Sugar-Marinated Salmon

1 pound salmon fillet
2 tablespoons salt
2 tablespoons brown sugar
4 tablespoons imported sake wine

Sprinkle salt on both sides of the salmon fillet; refrigerate covered for a few hours (preferably overnight). Rinse the salt off the salmon with cold water and pat dry with a paper towel.

Melt the brown sugar in the sake, either in the microwave oven or in a pan on the stove top. After it is cooled, pour it over the salmon. Refrigerate covered again for a few hours, or overnight.

When ready to serve, broil the salmon on a grill.

Yield: 2 servings

Baked Salmon with Lemon-Thyme Crumb Topping and Spiced Parsley Mayonnaise

½ cup chopped fresh Italian flat-leaf parsley
½ cup plus 2 tablespoons freshly grated Parmesan cheese
¼ cup chopped fresh thyme, or 1 tablespoon dried, crumbled
2 teaspoons lemon zest
½ teaspoon salt
4 small whole garlic cloves, peeled
2 cups fresh white breadcrumbs
8 tablespoons (1 stick) butter, melted and divided
1 (3 to 4-pound) salmon fillet

Spiced Parsley Mayonnaise:
⅓ cup minced fresh Italian flat-leaf parsley
⅓ cup minced fresh cilantro
¼ cup minced green onion
2 tablespoons red wine vinegar
1 clove garlic, minced
½ teaspoon minced fresh oregano,
or ¼ teaspoon dried, crumbled
¼ teaspoon freshly ground black pepper
⅛ teaspoon cayenne pepper
1 cup mayonnaise

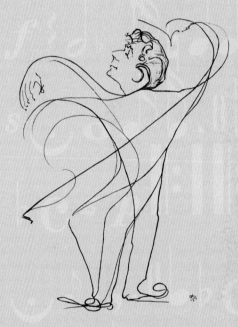

**Leonard Bernstein
by Olga Koussevitzky**

Process the parsley, Parmesan cheese, thyme, lemon zest and salt. With the processor running, drop the garlic into the feed tube; continue processing until finely chopped. Place the mixture into a medium bowl and add breadcrumbs to mixture. Stir to combine well. (Mixture may be prepared to this point 1 day ahead. Cover and refrigerate; bring to room temperature before continuing with recipe preparation.)

Preheat oven to 350°.

Toss the mixture with 6 tablespoons of the butter.

Pat salmon dry. In a well-buttered shallow baking pan, place the salmon fillet skin side down. Brush with the remaining 2 tablespoons melted butter. Cover with the breadcrumb mixture. Bake the fish until opaque in the center, about 15 to 20 minutes.

Make the Spiced Parsley Mayonnaise: Combine the parsley, cilantro, green onion, vinegar, garlic, oregano, black pepper and cayenne in a bowl. Cover, and let stand at room temperature for at least 1 hour (or overnight). When ready to use, stir in the mayonnaise. (If preparing 1 day ahead, cover and refrigerate. Restore to room temperature before serving.) Serve with baked salmon. (Makes about 1 ¾ cups.)

Yield: 6 servings

Dimitri Mitropoulos first conducted the BSO in 1936, and
made a tremendous impression
on the orchestra at the first
rehearsal.

His memory was such that he
had no scores at the rehearsal,
but knew the rehearsal numbers
in the music and what page
each musician was playing on.

He also called each player by
name! He explained afterward:
"It is really nothing at all.
Anyone can learn to do it. As
for the musicians' names, I
consider it the conductor's duty
to know his players, so on the
train I memorized their names.
It is really nothing."

Swordfish with Cilantro Paste

Cilantro Paste:
1 cup fresh cilantro leaves
1 clove garlic, minced
1 tablespoon pine nuts (pignoli)
½ teaspoon salt
Juice of ½ lime
2 tablespoons olive oil

1 teaspoon curry powder
1 teaspoon ground cumin
½ teaspoon ground ginger
½ teaspoon chili powder
½ teaspoon salt
½ teaspoon black pepper
2 tablespoons olive oil
2 pounds fresh swordfish steaks

Make the cilantro paste: Place the cilantro, garlic, pine nuts, salt, lime juice and olive oil in a blender or food processor. Blend until smooth and paste-like.

Combine the curry powder, cumin, ginger, chili powder, salt and pepper in a small bowl, and rub the mixture into the swordfish. Set aside.

Place a large skillet over medium-high heat and, when it is hot, add the oil. Add the swordfish and cook for about 4 to 5 minutes per side, depending on the thickness of the steaks. Transfer to heated plates, and serve with a tablespoon of the cilantro paste on each portion.

Yield: 4 servings

Serving Suggestion: Try serving the swordfish with couscous.

This is a flavorful recipe for company!

Potato-Crusted Cod with Fresh Baby Spinach

8 ounces skinless, boneless codfish
½ cup flour, for dredging
1 egg, whipped (form-whipped to mix white with yolk)
1 cup large potato flakes
2 tablespoons olive oil

Vinaigrette:
2 shallots, thinly sliced
1 vine-ripened tomato, peeled, seeded, cut into large dice
½ cup red wine vinegar
½ cup extra-virgin olive oil
Pinch sugar
Salt and pepper

3 cups fresh baby spinach leaves, cleaned
2 basil leaves, cut julienne, for garnish

Preheat oven to 375°.

Dredge the cod in flour; shake off the excess, then dip it into whipped egg. Dredge the cod in the potato flakes.

In a hot sauté pan, sauté the fish in the olive oil, browning both sides. Place the fish on a baking sheet in the oven for 5 to 8 minutes.

While the fish is in the oven, prepare the vinaigrette: In another pan, combine the shallots, tomato, vinegar, ½ cup of olive oil, sugar, and salt and pepper to taste. Place over low heat to warm through.

When the fish is done, place the spinach in the center of the plates. Fan the fish in front of the spinach; top the greens and fish with the warm vinaigrette. Garnish with a sprinkle of basil, if desired.

Yield: 2 servings

Note: Scrod, cusk, or any other white, flaky fish may be substituted for the cod. Cooking time may vary due to thickness of fish.

BOSTON
SYMPHONY
ORCHESTRA
SEIJI OZAWA
*Music
Director*

Amnon Levy
Violin

Amnon Levy's musical career began in Tel Aviv, Israel, where he was born. After hearing the young musician play, world-renowned violinist Jascha Heifitz urged Amnon's teacher to send him to the United States for advanced training. Soon thereafter he attended the Juilliard School of Music in New York and the Curtis Institute of Music in Philadelphia.

Amnon joined the BSO as a second violinist in 1964, moving to the first violin section of the orchestra in 1972. He says, "To play violin with the BSO and achieve the high level of performance required, I am constantly practicing, much like a professional athlete. The body, as well as the mind, needs to feel in tune."

With regard to his trout recipe he comments, "My family and I particularly enjoy this dish while listening to Schubert's 'Trout Quintet'".

Baked Stuffed Trout

1 whole trout, cleaned
Freshly ground black pepper
1 teaspoon fat-free mayonnaise
1 teaspoon finely chopped garlic
1 teaspoon finely chopped onion
1 teaspoon finely chopped celery
1 tablespoon finely chopped fresh tomato

Preheat oven to 400°.

Sprinkle the inside and outside of the trout with ground black pepper. Rub the fish cavity with the mayonnaise. Arrange the garlic, onion, celery and tomato in the fish cavity.

Oil a sheet of foil. Wrap the entire fish in the foil and place in a pan. Place the pan on an oven rack and bake for 30 minutes.

Remove from the oven. To serve, carefully unwrap the foil and lay the fish onto a plate.

Yield: 1 serving

Variation: Fresh herbs of your choice may be added to the stuffing.

Serving Suggestion: Rice pilaf and steamed vegetables are a recommended accompaniment.

Spring Garden Flounder

Dressing:
1 teaspoon Dijon mustard
Juice of 1 lime
1 tablespoon honey
2 cloves garlic, finely chopped
¼ to ⅓ cup extra-virgin olive oil
Salt and pepper

4 cups spinach leaves, stems removed
4 stalks asparagus, tough ends trimmed
4 fillets of flounder (about 1 ½ pounds)
Salt and pepper

Parchment paper, for baking

Preheat the oven to 450°.

Make the dressing: Whisk together the mustard and lime juice until a liaison is formed. Beat the honey and garlic into the mixture - amounts may be adjusted for personal tastes. Beat in the olive oil and season with salt and pepper to taste. (More or less oil may also be used, as desired.) Set aside.

Cut the asparagus into lengths conforming to the width of the fish fillet, and blanch in boiling water for exactly 2 minutes. (For garden fresh asparagus, reduce the blanching time to 1 ½ minutes.) Drain and immediately place the asparagus in ice water to cool. Drain again and set aside.

Lightly butter an ovenproof casserole. Use a spinner to wash and dry the spinach leaves; then, place them in an even layer in the bottom of the casserole. Pour half of the dressing over the spinach and toss thoroughly with your hands. Redistribute the spinach evenly in the bottom of the casserole.

Gently score each flounder fillet on both sides and season with salt and pepper to taste. Place an asparagus tip and another piece or two from the stem on each fillet and roll it up. Place each fillet roll on the bed of spinach, seam side down. When all are assembled, spoon the remaining dressing over the fish.

Lightly butter the parchment paper and press down lightly over the assembled ingredients. Bake for 15 minutes, and serve.

Yield: 4 servings

Serving Suggestion: A nice cold Sancerre or a Meursault wine makes an excellent accompaniment to this dish.

BOSTON
SYMPHONY
ORCHESTRA
SEIJI OZAWA
Music
Director

John Oliver
Director
Tanglewood Festival Chorus

John Oliver traces his love of food to the age of seven, when his first musical job was to play the organ at the 7 a.m. daily Mass in Janesville, Wisconsin. After Mass, he and his grand-mother would walk to the local soda fountain for a chocolate malted milk.

Since 1970, John has been director of vocal and choral activities at the Tanglewood Music Center; he is the founding conductor of the Tanglewood Festival Chorus.

Mark Volpe
BSO Managing Director

Mark Volpe was appointed Managing Director of the BSO in 1997. In addition to being an accomplished clarinetist, Mark is a graduate of the University of Minnesota Law School. His BSO appointment provided a homecoming for his wife, Martha, who had worked as Seiji Ozawa's assistant before moving to Baltimore where she met her husband.

The Volpes enjoyed this dish at the Vail, Colorado home of Susan and Richard Rogel, supporters of the Vail Bravo Music Festival and the Detroit Symphony. "Rich is a fantastic cook, and after this delicious meal, I asked for the recipe," says Martha.

Peppers Stuffed with Rice and Tuna

4 large red or orange bell peppers
1⅔ cups Italian Arborio rice
Extra-virgin olive oil
¼ cup chopped parsley
12 basil leaves, chopped
½ tablespoon salted capers
1 clove garlic, minced
4 ounces fontina cheese, cut into strips
3 ounces tuna (packed in olive oil)
⅓ cup freshly grated Parmesan cheese
2 egg yolks
Salt
2 tablespoons melted butter
4 anchovies, salted

Cut the peppers in half lengthwise, removing ribs and seeds.

Place the rice in a pan with 3⅓ cups water. Bring to a boil, cover, and simmer for 10 to 15 minutes. Drain the rice; add a tablespoon of the oil. Mix thoroughly and set aside.

In a small saucepan over medium-low heat, sauté the parsley, basil, capers and garlic gently for a few minutes, taking care not to burn the garlic. Mix this sauce with the rice.

Break up the tuna and mix it with the fontina strips; add both to the rice mixture, along with the Parmesan cheese, egg yolks, and salt to taste. Mix well. Stuff the pepper halves with the rice mixture. Place the peppers in a lightly-oiled ovenproof dish.

Preheat the oven to 325°.

Break up the anchovies in a small pan with the melted butter. Pour some of the anchovy butter on top of the rice mixture in each pepper half. Place the dish in the oven and bake for 30 to 40 minutes.

Yield: 4 to 6 servings

BOSTON SYMPHONY ORCHESTRA
SEIJI OZAWA
Music Director

Tuna Barbecue

½ cup olive oil
1 cup white wine
2 tablespoons dill or tarragon
2 tablespoons fresh lemon juice
2 pounds tuna steaks

In a bowl, mix together the olive oil, wine, dill (or tarragon) and lemon juice.

Marinate the fish steaks in the mixture for a few hours, or overnight, in the refrigerator, covered. Turn at least once.

Grill the fish over a cooling fire (not the hottest coals). Cook for 10 minutes per 1 inch of thickness.

Yield: 6 servings

Note: If you prefer a "blackened" fish, you may wish to add more spices to the marinade.

Variation: Tuna and swordfish do best, but mahi-mahi or halibut, or any other firm-fleshed fish steaks, would also work well.

Serving Suggestion: For a wine, a Chardonnay (some oak tones) or a Sauvignon Blanc (some smoke or wood flavors) make a fine accompaniment.

Seiji Ozawa on the tennis court

Photo by: © Lincoln Russell

Spanish Mackerel

1 large or 2 small mackerel fillets (about 1 to 1 ¼ pounds)
Salt and freshly ground black pepper
2 tablespoons olive oil
⅓ cup dry white wine

Sauce:
1 tablespoon olive oil
2 cloves garlic, chopped
1 small onion, chopped
1 rib of celery, chopped
3 small tomatoes, peeled, seeded and chopped
Salt and freshly ground pepper

Season the fish lightly with the salt and pepper, and sauté it, skin side up, in the olive oil for 2 to 3 minutes. Turn the fish over and pour in the wine. Simmer for 2 to 3 minutes longer, or until the fish flakes. Set the fish aside in the pan, covered, to keep hot until the sauce is ready.

Make the sauce: Heat the olive oil in another pan, and add the garlic, onion, celery, and tomatoes. Stir over medium heat for about 10 minutes, or until the vegetables are tender. Season with salt and pepper to taste.

Pour the sauce over the fish, and return the pan to the heat long enough to heat through.

Yield: 2 servings

Serving Suggestion: Serve the Spanish Mackerel with white rice.

BOSTON
SYMPHONY
ORCHESTRA
SEIJI OZAWA
*Music
Director*

Seiji Ozawa
Music Director
Boston Symphony Orchestra

Vera and Seiji Ozawa tell us this recipe is easy to prepare and a family favorite when they gather at their summer house near Tanglewood.

As one might imagine, Seiji is very eclectic in his tastes. He is particularly fond of Japanese specialties such as bee larvae and soup with live minnows. However, he is equally at home with American delicacies—some of his favorites being Fenway franks, Italian sausages at Foxboro Stadium, and barbecue. Woe to anyone who takes him on in the hot sauce arena—he's been known to douse his meal with the infamous "Inner Beauty" hot sauce from the East Coast Grill in Cambridge as if it were ketchup!

During the Tanglewood season, Seiji finds just enough time to indulge in his favorite sport of tennis. If you have seen him on the podium, you can imagine his speed and agility on the tennis court.

The Four Seasons Hotel Boston

The restaurant at the Four Seasons Hotel has been the setting for several Opening Night at Symphony post-concert dinners.

Executive Chef Edward Gannon produced the menu for our cover photo, and has generously provided us with the recipe for its preparation on our own special occasion!

Chef Gannon advises:

"All steps may be done in advance of serving. Prepare all ingredients up to the 'to serve' point. This leaves more time to mingle with guests and leaves a cleaner kitchen while entertaining. It is less stressful and, most importantly, it gives the guests a sense that you 'have it all under control!'"

Roasted Lobster with Crabmeat Wontons, Pineapple Compote, Snow Peas and Fenugreek Broth
(cover recipe)

4 (2-pound) lobsters
¾ cup pineapple compote (see recipe below)
38 snow peas
1 cup fenugreek broth (see recipe below)
12 crabmeat wontons (see recipe below)
2 tablespoons butter
Salt and pepper
3 tablespoons extra-virgin olive oil
1 tablespoon snipped chives

Cook the lobster: Fill a large lobster pot three-fourths full with heavily salted water. Bring to a full, rapid boil and add the lobster, taking care not to overcrowd the pot. Cook for 8 minutes, then shock the lobsters in an ice bath to stop cooking. Remove the meat from claws and knuckles. Split the tails in half lengthwise, leaving the shell on. Reserve the meat and the bodies separately. Make the Crabmeat Wontons.

Crabmeat Wontons
1 egg
Salt and pepper
3 ounces crabmeat, picked through to remove shell particles
1 teaspoon chopped cilantro
12 wontons skins, cut into 2-inch squares
Canola oil, for frying

Whisk the egg together with a little water to create an egg wash.

Toss the crabmeat with the cilantro and season with salt and pepper to taste. Lay out the wonton skins so that they face you as a diamond, and brush the edges with egg wash. Divide the crabmeat into 12 equal portions and place each in the center of a wonton. Fold the bottom corner to the top to create a triangle shape. Pull the two bottom corners together, and seal with egg wash. Refrigerate until ready to serve. Make the Pineapple Compote.

Pineapple Compote
2 cups ¼-inch diced pineapple
1 star anise
¼ of a vanilla bean, split
1 tablespoon honey

Combine the pineapple, star anise, vanilla bean and honey in a saucepan. Bring the mixture to a simmer and cook until all liquid has evaporated. Remove from the heat and reserve for serving.

Roasted Lobster continued

Prepare the snow peas: Trim the snow peas and cut on one tip at an angle. Blanch them in lightly salted water for 1 minute. Plunge them into an ice bath to stop cooking and reserve for serving. Make the Roasted Lobster Stock.

Roasted Lobster Stock
Olive oil, for frying
1 carrot, cut into small dice
1 stalk celery, cut into small dice
1 medium onion, cut into small dice
4 cooked lobster bodies
(reserved from lobster preparation), crushed
¼ cup tomato purée
¼ cup white wine
¼ cup brandy
3 sprigs fresh thyme
1 bay leaf

In a medium saucepan heat the olive oil; then add the carrot, celery and onion, cooking until they are lightly caramelized. Add the lobster bodies and continue to caramelize. Add the tomato purée and cook, stirring frequently.

Add the wine and brandy, bring the mixture back to a simmer. Add enough water to just cover the lobster. Add thyme and bay leaf; simmer for 30 minutes. Strain; return to pan and cook until reduced to 2 cups. Reserve for use in Fenugreek Broth. Make the Fenugreek Broth.

Fenugreek Broth
Olive oil for frying
2 shallots, chopped
3 cloves garlic, chopped
1 lemon grass, chopped
1 tablespoon fenugreek seeds
2 cups roasted lobster stock
1 sprig fresh basil
1 sprig fresh cilantro
1 bay leaf

In a saucepan, heat the olive oil and add the shallot, garlic and lemon grass. Cook over medium heat until tender. Add the fenugreek and lightly toast. (Do not over toast the seeds or they will become bitter.) Add the lobster stock along with the basil, cilantro and bay leaf. Simmer for 15 minutes, then strain. Reserve.

Assemble the dish: In a deep-fryer or deep frying pan, heat the canola oil to 325° for frying.

Arthur Fiedler by
Martha Burnham Humphrey

Roasted Lobster continued

In the early days the soloist would often not rehearse at all. Jacques Thibaud, the French violinist, came to Symphony Hall to play the Beethoven Violin Concerto. He arrived minutes before the concert and proceeded onto the stage.

Unfortunately, the program called for the Mendelssohn Concerto, which calls for the violinist to begin playing almost immediately. Thibaud, waiting for the orchestra to begin the long introduction for the Beethoven concerto, placed the violin at his side. There followed a series of bows and nods between conductor and soloist until the conductor started. Thibaud almost decapitated himself as he realized what happened and swung his violin up to his chin.

"Why didn't you tell me it was Mendelssohn?" he asked.

Back came the reply: "Why didn't you ask?"

Roasted Lobster *continued*

Preheat the oven to 400°.

Reheat the pineapple compote; reserve warm. Bring the broth/sauce to simmer, whisk in butter, season to taste and reserve warm.

Deep-fry the wontons in the oil without overcrowding until golden brown. Drain and reserve warm.

In a large sauté pan, heat the olive oil over high heat, and add the lobster tails shell side down. Cook for 2 minutes on the stove; then place them in the oven for 3 minutes. Add the claws, and cook until they are heated through; reserve.

Toss the snow peas in the hot oil from roasting the lobster.

For each serving: Place some pineapple compote in the center of bowl. Remove the lobster tail from the shell. Arrange snow peas around the bowl and place the tail on the compote. Then add the claws. Spoon the broth/sauce over and around the lobster. Place 3 wontons around the lobster. Sprinkle with chives and serve immediately.

Grilled Scallops with Lemon and Herbs

1 pound sea scallops
Fresh or dried bay leaves
1 small mild onion, cut into 1-inch chunks,
and separated into layers
3 tablespoons extra-virgin olive oil
1½ tablespoons fresh lemon juice
½ teaspoon dried oregano
Salt and freshly ground pepper

Prepare the grill or broiler.

On 8 short skewers, thread the scallops alternately with the bay leaves and the pieces of onion.

In a small bowl, whisk together the oil, lemon juice, oregano, and salt and pepper to taste. Brush the scallops with some of the sauce.

Grill or broil until the scallops are just opaque, about 3 to 4 minutes on each side. Place the skewers on a serving plate and drizzle with the remaining sauce.

Yield: 4 to 6 servings

Creamed Seafood au Gratin

Sauce:
½ cup butter
½ cup flour
4 cups heavy cream
Oyster liquid

3 cups sautéed sliced mushrooms (about ¾ pound)
¾ pound cooked lobster meat
1 cup drained oysters, liquid reserved for sauce
1 cup minced haddock (about 8 ounces)
Bread crumbs for topping
Freshly grated Parmesan cheese

Preheat oven to 350°.

Make the sauce: Melt the butter in a saucepan; add the flour, cream and oyster liquid. Stir to make a smooth cream sauce. Add the mushrooms to the cream sauce.

Gently combine the lobster meat, oysters and haddock with the cream sauce. Place the combined seafood mixture into an ovenproof casserole. Cover with bread crumbs and sprinkle with the Parmesan cheese.

Bake for 30 minutes.

Yield: 4 to 6 six servings

Variation: This dish may also be served over toast points, or in toast cups or puff pastry.

Serving Suggestion: Serve this delicious seafood casserole over rice.

BOSTON
SYMPHONY
ORCHESTRA
SEIJI OZAWA
*Music
Director*

Josef Hofmann, one of the world's greatest pianists, was a curmudgeon of a man, who seemed to hate everybody, but mostly conductors. His favorite pastime when playing with an orchestra was to try to throw the conductor by taking impossibly fast tempos, sudden rubatos, and illogical changes of tempo and dynamics.

He did such a thing with Koussevitzky during the Schumann Piano Concerto, taking off every time the orchestra caught up with him. All the time there was a devilish look of supreme satisfaction on his face.

He once told Richard Burgin, one time concertmaster, that the only conductor he was never able to lose was Karl Muck.

Roulade of Dover Sole with Lobster and Caviar

Lobster Mousse:
1 (1-pound) female lobster
½ pound fillet of Dover sole, or any white fish
½ teaspoon salt
Pinch black pepper
Pinch nutmeg
1 egg white
1 cup heavy cream
¼ cup fresh herbs (parsley, chives, tarragon), minced

Caviar Sauce:
1 medium shallot, minced
½ cup dry vermouth
Juice of ½ lemon
2 tablespoons heavy cream
½ pound butter
Pinch of salt and pepper
2 ounces osetra caviar (see note)

8 fillets of fresh Dover sole (about 3½ to 4 pounds)
1 pound baby spinach leaves, for garnish
1 bunch fresh chervil, for garnish

Note: This recipe requires ½ pound of raw fish. You may use the Dover sole, raw lobster meat, scallops, or any available fish. It is best to make the mousse with a pink color. This can be done by using the roe of the lobster, plus the ½ pound of raw fish; or, use salmon as the raw fish, and fold in diced cooked lobster meat at the end.)

Make the Lobster Mousse: Cook the lobster. Remove the meat and roe. Set the roe aside and finely dice the lobster tail meat. Place the completely dry bowl and steel blade of a food processor in the freezer for at least 30 minutes. (Have all other mousse ingredients chilled before beginning recipe.) Remove the food processor components from the freezer and put in the bowl the raw fish, roe, salt, black pepper, and nutmeg. Begin processing immediately and after 30 seconds, without turning off the processor, add the egg white. After 10 more seconds, slowly begin adding the heavy cream. It should take 30 to 45 seconds to add all the cream. Only at this point should the processor be turned off.

Scrape down the sides and process for another 5 to 10 seconds. The mousse should be smooth. If the lobster roe (or salmon) was used, the color will be pink. Remove the mousse from the bowl and fold in the

Roulade of Dover Sole with Lobster and Caviar continued

chopped herbs and the finely diced lobster meat. Keep well-chilled for a maximum of 24 hours, if not used immediately.

Make the sauce: Combine the shallots, vermouth, and the lemon juice in a heavy-bottomed saucepan. Reduce the mixture over medium heat until almost all the liquid has evaporated. Add the cream and reduce slightly. Add the butter in 1-inch cubes to the reduction, whisking constantly over medium heat until all the butter is incorporated. Adjust the seasoning, if necessary, with salt, pepper, or a few more drops of lemon juice. Strain the sauce and keep in a warm place. Gently stir in the caviar at the last minute.

Prepare the fillets by spreading a thin layer of lobster mousse on the skin side of the 8 fillets. Roll up each fillet and secure with a toothpick. (The sole may be prepared several hours in advance up to this point.) When ready to cook, set the fillets in a steamer, so the rolled sides are facing up, and cook over gentle steam for about 8 minutes. Remove from the steamer and let rest for 1 or 2 minutes, and then slice through the roulade horizontally to check doneness. If it is not completely cooked in the center, return it to the steamer for another minute; otherwise, drain for a second on a paper towel and then arrange on warm plates.

To serve, arrange some baby spinach leaves in the center of the plate. Place 1 roulade, sliced horizontally and shingled, on the spinach. Nap the sauce over the sole. Garnish with a sprig of chervil.

Yield: 8 servings

Note: Osetra is considered the most versatile and popular caviar. It is available in some food specialty shops and in whole food markets.

**Pierre Monteux
by Olga Koussevitzky**

181

BOSTON
SYMPHONY
ORCHESTRA
SEIJI OZAWA
*Music
Director*

*Chilled Maine Lobster
over Rice Noodles with Mango*

Dressing:
½ cup grapefruit juice
¼ cup mirin
1 tablespoon fish sauce
Juice of 1 lime
1 tablespoon minced lemon grass

2 (1½-pound) cooked Maine lobsters, shelled
2 cups cooked rice noodles
1 European cucumber, cut into julienne
1 cup mango, cut into julienne
1 tablespoon basil leaves, stems removed
1 tablespoon mint leaves, stems removed
1 tablespoon cilantro leaves, stems removed
1 cup sweet and sour vegetables
½ cup fried crisp ginger, cut into julienne
12 edible flowers, for garnish

Make the vinaigrette: In a bowl combine the grapefruit juice, mirin, fish sauce, lime juice and lemon grass. Set aside.

Make the salad by dividing the lobster into 4 equal portions. Toss the rice noodles in enough dressing to coat them, and place them on center of plate. Toss the cucumbers with enough dressing to coat them, and place on top of noodles. Arrange the lobster around the noodles and place a claw atop the cucumbers.

Combine the mango, herbs, vegetables and remaining dressing, and place over and around the lobster, spooning the dressing over the top. Sprinkle with the crisp ginger and garnish with the flowers.

Yield: 4 servings

Note: Mirin and fish sauce may be found in oriental markets and in food specialty shops. Packaged sweet and sour vegetables may be used in place of a personal favorite recipe.

Serving Suggestion: This recipe makes a lovely luncheon salad.

Scallops in Green Peppercorn Sauce

1½ pounds sea scallops
2 tablespoons clarified butter (see note)
½ clove French shallot, finely chopped
1 cup fish stock
2 teaspoons green peppercorns
1 cup heavy cream
1 tablespoon cognac
Salt and pepper
4 crawfish, steamed, for garnish (optional)
Chopped parsley, for garnish (optional)

Cut the scallops in half horizontally. In a heavy skillet, add the clarified butter and sauté the scallops over medium heat until lightly golden, about 45 seconds total time. Set them aside.

Add the shallot to the skillet and sauté it lightly, then add the fish stock. Increase the heat to medium-high and let the stock reduce to almost nothing (about ¼ cup of liquid remaining). Add the green peppercorns and cream to the skillet. Bring to a boil; then remove from the heat and add the cognac. (Caution: Do not add cognac to the pan over or near an open flame. The fumes could ignite. Take the pan away from the heat source to add the liqueur, then return it to the stove.)

Reduce the heat to medium-low and adjust the seasoning with salt and pepper to taste. Return the pan to the heat and simmer until the sauce sticks lightly on the back of a spoon. Towards the end of the simmering, add the scallops to the sauce to warm them up; then serve immediately. Add a steamed crawfish and some parsley to each plate as garnish, if desired

Yield: 4 servings

Note: Clarified butter can be heated, without burning, to a higher temperature than regular butter. To make about ⅓ cup of clarified butter, melt 8 tablespoons (1 stick) butter in a small, heavy saucepan over low heat. Remove pan from heat and set aside for 5 minutes. Using a spoon, carefully remove and discard the foamy white butterfat that has risen to the top. Spoon or pour off the clear liquid. This is the clarified butter. Discard the solids that remain on the bottom of the pan. Allow clarified butter to cool; then cover and refrigerate. (The butter will keep for several weeks.)

Serving Suggestion: Serve this elegant dish on a bed of white rice, along with a side dish of asparagus or broccoli.

BOSTON
SYMPHONY
ORCHESTRA
SEIJI OZAWA
Music Director

James DePreist
Conductor

James and Ginette DePreist sent us this recipe with fond memories of James' appearance as a BSO guest conductor. He has led the orchestra at Symphony Hall and Tanglewood.

James has followed in the musical footsteps of his famous aunt, contralto Marian Anderson, and is one of the America's leading conductors. Since 1980, he has served as music director of the Oregon Symphony and the Monte Carlo Symphony, and as principal guest conductor of the Helsinki Philharmonic.

"Madama Butterfly" in Symphony Hall

A highlight of the celebration of Seiji Ozawa's silver anniversary as Music Director was a fully-staged production of Puccini's "Madama Butterfly" in February 1999.

Maestro Ozawa had previously conducted Strauss' "Elektra" and "Salome," Tchaikovsky's "Pique Dame," and Verdi's "Falstaff" with the BSO, and had always wished to perform "Madama Butterfly" at Symphony Hall with the Boston Symphony.

Super Seafood Casserole

⅔ cup dry white wine
⅓ cup water
1 quart scallops
2 tablespoons fresh chopped parsley
Pinch of tarragon
2 cups thick cream sauce (recipe follows)
1 medium onion, chopped and sautéed in butter
½ pound button mushrooms, quartered and sautéed in butter
1 (6-ounce) can crabmeat
Freshly grated Parmesan cheese

Preheat oven to 350°.

In a shallow pan place the wine and water; add the scallops, parsley and tarragon. Bring to a boil; turn off the heat and allow to sit for 2 to 3 minutes. Drain, reserving 1 cup of the liquid for use in cream sauce recipe.

Combine the scallops, onions, mushrooms, crabmeat and the cream sauce. Place the mixture in a casserole and sprinkle the top with the Parmesan cheese. Place in the oven for 10 to 15 minutes, or until the top is lightly browned and the casserole is bubbly.

Yield: 4 to 6 servings

Variation: Any type of quality mushrooms may be used as a substitute.

Cream Sauce

6 tablespoons butter
6 to 8 tablespoons flour
1 cup milk
1 cup reserved liquid from scallop preparation
Salt and pepper

In a medium saucepan, slowly heat the butter just until melted and golden, but not browned, stirring constantly. Remove the pan from the heat. Add the flour, and salt and pepper to taste; stir until smooth. Add the milk and reserved scallop liquid alternately, a little at a time, stirring after each addition. Return the pan to the heat. Over medium heat, bring the sauce to a boil, stirring constantly. Reduce heat; simmer for an additional 1 minute.

Yield: about 2 cups

Crab Cakes with Basil Mayonnaise

Basil Mayonnaise:
36 fresh basil leaves
1 ½ cups mayonnaise
2 teaspoons Dijon mustard
2 teaspoons lemon juice
¼ teaspoon cayenne

2 tablespoons olive oil
2 celery stalks, finely chopped
¼ cup chopped onion
2⅔ cups white breadcrumbs, divided
¼ cup snipped fresh chives
2 tablespoons chopped fresh parsley
6 tablespoons flour
2 eggs
Vegetable oil for frying

Make the Basil Mayonnaise: Blanch the basil leaves in a saucepan of boiling water for 30 seconds. Drain and place in ice water to cool. Drain and pat dry with paper towels. Finely chop the basil. In a bowl mix the mayonnaise, mustard, lemon juice and cayenne. Set aside ½ cup of the mixture for use later with the crab cakes; mix the basil into the remaining mayonnaise.

Make the crab cakes: In a pan, heat the oil over medium heat. Add the celery and onion, and sauté about 5 minutes, until soft. Transfer to a bowl. Stir in the crabmeat, ⅔ cup of the breadcrumbs, chives and parsley, along with the ½ cup reserved mayonnaise mixture. Form into 2 ½-inch diameter cakes. Put the cakes on a baking sheet, cover separately and chill. (Basil mayonnaise and crab cakes can be made one day ahead.)

Place the flour in a small bowl. Whisk the eggs in another small bowl. Place remaining breadcrumbs in another bowl, or on waxed paper on a working surface. Coat each crab cake with flour, then dip the cake first into the egg, then into the breadcrumbs. Heat the vegetable oil in a skillet over medium heat. Add the crab cakes a few at a time; cook until golden and heated through, about 5 minutes. Serve with the basil mayonnaise.

Yield: 8 crab cakes

These crab cakes are surprisingly moist -
and absolutely delicious!

Arthur Fiedler's second opportunity to conduct the full BSO was not as successful as his first. When Serge Koussevitzky found out that Fiedler was to conduct a small group of BSO musicians to accompany the then-popular idol of the teenage set, Frank Sinatra, in Symphony Hall, he became furious.

"Fiedler," he shouted on the telephone, "how you can do such a thing? How you can conduct the Boston Symphony after you perform with this Sinatra?" and he disengaged him. (The concert never came off anyway; Sinatra became ill and canceled.)

Finally, after 25 years at the Pops, Fiedler was once again asked to conduct the BSO, this time by Charles Munch. the reviews were again uniformly good.

Scalloped Oysters

1 cup crumbled dried bread (medium coarseness), or crouton-style unseasoned stuffing mix
2 cups crumbled (medium coarseness) salted crackers
8 ounces (2 sticks) butter, melted
2 pints frying-size oysters
Salt and pepper
8 tablespoons oyster liquid
4 tablespoons milk or cream

Preheat oven to 400°.

In a bowl mix the bread and cracker crumbs, and stir in the butter. Put a thin layer of the mix in the bottom of a shallow 8-inch square pan. Cover with the oysters and sprinkle with salt and pepper to taste. Add one half of each the oyster liquid and the milk or cream. Repeat with another layer and cover the top with the remaining crumb mixture.

Bake for 10 minutes to brown the crumbs, checking frequently to ensure that the crumbs don't burn; then lower the heat to 325° and bake the oysters for an additional 35 minutes.

Yield: 4 servings

Note: Never allow more than two layers of oysters. If three layers are used, the middle layer will be undone, while the other two layers are properly cooked.

If prepared a day ahead, moisten by sprinkling surface with a little milk, as the oyster mixture is parted at intervals with a knife, before reheating.

TANGLEWOOD MUSIC CENTER

Outdoor rehearsal at the Tanglewood Music Center

Photo by: Stu Rossner

Seiji Ozawa Hall at Tanglewood

Photo by: © Walter Scott

Seiji Ozawa with Tanglewood Fellow

TANGLEWOOD MUSIC CENTER

Founded to bring together great musicians and aspiring artists, the Tanglewood Music Center is now the premier summer training program for gifted young musicians.

Inaugurated in 1940 by BSO music director Serge Koussevitzky as the Berkshire Music Center, the TMC provides musical training unlike any other.

Each summer at Tanglewood, the BSO's summer home in the Berkshire hills of Massachusetts, members of the orchestra, additional artist faculty, master teachers, composers, conductors, and students savor Koussevitzky's dream of a permanent home for teaching the arts of musical composition, performance, and leadership. Learning is paramount at the TMC, but so is the prized atmosphere of cooperation and collegiality.

Each year over 1,000 students apply to the Tanglewood summer program. A talented 150 are accepted. Each receives a fellowship covering tuition, room, and board. The intensive eight-week program includes seminars, master classes, and performances in opera, orchestra, and chamber music ensembles.

The TMC's curriculum includes a range of collaborative and musical possibilities, including interdisciplinary programs, coaching sessions with BSO players, and chamber music residencies by eminent artists from around the world. TMC Fellows also participate in each summer's Festival of Contemporary Music, an exploration of the music of our time which attracts the attention of composers, performers, the press, and enthusiastic audiences alike.

The BSO's involvement with the TMC is a close one. Half of the BSO instrumentalists are TMC alumni, as are 20 percent of the members of other major American symphony orchestras.

The 1,200-seat Theatre-Concert Hall, located across the lawn from the Shed, opened in 1941 to house the TMC's concerts and operas. It was at the Theatre-Concert Hall that the TMC opera program staged the American premiere of Benjamin Britten's opera *Peter Grimes,* directed by Boris Goldovsky and conducted by Leonard Bernstein with the composer present.

Photo by: © William Mercer

Yo-Yo Ma with TMC Fellows

Seiji Ozawa Hall

More than four decades later, the BSO's 1986 acquisition of the neighboring 120-acre Highwood estate paved the way for a major expansion of the TMC. The 1,180-seat Seiji Ozawa Hall opened in 1994. It serves as the performance hall for the TMC orchestra, recitals, and chamber ensembles; it also hosts the Prelude concerts given by BSO and Tanglewood Festival Chorus members, and recitals by distinguished visiting artists. Ozawa Hall also houses a recording facility. The grounds of the Highwood estate were named the Leonard Bernstein Campus after the illustrious conductor and composer who was a member of the first TMC class.

From their summer at the TMC, the young performers return to enrich the cultural lives of their communities. Over the last 60 years, the roster of TMC students and faculty has grown to read like a musical "Who's Who." Aaron Copland, Leonard Bernstein, and Lukas Foss have studied, taught, and performed here. Other distinguished artists who have been a part of the TMC experience are Eleazar de Carvalho, Boris Goldovsky, Sarah Caldwell, Zubin Mehta, Lorin Maazel, Michael Tilson Thomas, Gunther Schuller, Robert Spano, Gilbert Kalish, Shirley Verrett, Phyllis Curtin, Yo-Yo Ma, Emanuel Ax, André Previn, Peter Serkin, Wynton Marsalis, Leontyne Price, Dawn Upshaw, and the BSO's own Seiji Ozawa.

At the TMC, the BSO fulfills its dual mission as an artistic and educational resource. It is no exaggeration to say that the convergence of master performers and composers with aspiring students holds the key to the future direction of symphonic and classical music. As a result, the TMC represents both a legacy and a promise.

Tanglewood Fellows off to class

VEGETABLES ~ SALADS

BOSTON
SYMPHONY
ORCHESTRA
SEIJI OZAWA
Music
Director

Roasted Stuffed Artichokes with Pine Nuts and Raisins

1 lemon
4 medium artichokes
½ cup dried bread crumbs
4 anchovy fillets, finely chopped
2 tablespoons chopped drained capers
2 tablespoons toasted pine nuts (pignoli)
2 tablespoons golden raisins
2 tablespoons chopped Italian flat-leaf parsley
1 large clove garlic, finely chopped
Salt and freshly ground pepper
½ cup extra-virgin olive oil, divided
½ cup dry white wine

Fill a large bowl with cold water and squeeze the juice of 1 lemon in it. Using a large knife, trim off the top 1 inch of each artichoke. Rinse the artichokes under cold water. Then cut off the stem of the artichoke even with its base, so that the artichoke will stand upright in the pan. Peel off the rough skin of the stems, reserving the trimmed stems for cooking with the artichokes. The small leaves at the base of the artichoke may be bent back and pulled off . Using a scissors, trim off the pointed tops of the artichoke's leaves. The fuzzy choke in the center may be removed with the tip of a small spoon, or a knife with a rounded tip. Place the trimmed artichoke in the bowl of water.

Preheat the oven to 400°.

In a bowl, combine the bread crumbs, anchovies, capers, pine nuts, raisins, parsley, garlic and salt and pepper to taste. Stir in ¼ cup of the olive oil.

Gently spread open the artichoke leaves. Stuff the artichokes loosely with the bread crumb mixture. Stand the artichokes in a small baking dish just large enough to hold them together. Pour the wine around the artichokes. Drizzle the remaining ¼ cup olive oil over and around the artichokes. Cover with foil and bake for 1 hour.

Uncover the artichokes and bake for an additional 5 to 10 minutes, or until the hearts are tender when pierced in the center with a knife. Check the pan during the cooking period, adding a few tablespoons water if the pan is becoming dry. Cool the artichokes and serve at room temperature.

Yield: 4 servings

Asparagus with Two Cheeses

2 pounds thick asparagus
Salt
¼ cup freshly grated Parmesan cheese
2 ounces imported Italian fontina or Bel Paese cheese,
rind removed and thinly sliced
¼ cup chopped pine nuts (pignoli)
1 tablespoon fine dry bread crumbs

Preheat oven to 450°. Arrange an oven rack on the highest level. Butter a 13 by 9 by 2-inch baking dish.

Soak the asparagus in cold water for 10 minutes. Trim off the tough lower portion of each stalk where the color changes from green to white. Pour about 1 inch of water into a large skillet and bring it to a boil. Add salt to taste and add the asparagus. Cook until the asparagus is partially tender - about 5 minutes. Drain well.

Place a layer of asparagus in the baking dish; add a second layer with the tips overlapping the bottom ends of the first layer. Sprinkle the asparagus with Parmesan cheese, then cover them with the slices of fontina. Sprinkle with the nuts and bread crumbs.

Bake for 15 minutes, or until the cheese is melted and the nuts are browned. Serve hot.

Yield: 4 servings

Green Beans Basque-Style

1 pound small, narrow green beans,
ends trimmed, cut into 1-inch pieces
¼ cup extra-virgin olive oil
1 dried hot chili pepper, halved
6 tomatoes, peeled, seeded and chopped
¼ cup finely minced fresh parsley
3 to 4 large basil leaves, finely minced
2 cloves garlic, minced
1 teaspoon dried thyme
1 teaspoon dried oregano
Salt and freshly ground pepper
Freshly grated Parmesan cheese

Rinse the beans under cold water and drain well. In a medium-sized pot bring salted water to a rolling boil and add the beans. Cook for 5 to 7 minutes, or until crisp-tender. Drain in a colander and immediately plunge the beans into ice water to stop any further cooking. Drain the beans and set aside.

In a medium-size heavy iron skillet, heat the olive oil over high heat. Add the chili pepper and cook until the pepper is darkened. Remove the pepper and discard it.

Into the same oil in the same skillet add the tomatoes, parsley, basil, garlic, thyme, oregano, salt and pepper to taste, and bring to a boil. Reduce the heat, partially cover the pan, and simmer for 25 minutes, or until the sauce is thick.

Stir in the beans, cover and simmer for an additional 10 minutes. Taste and correct the seasonings, if necessary. Serve hot. Pass the Parmesan cheese separately.

Yield: 4 servings

Note: It is advisable to wear gloves when handling hot chili peppers.

Variation: To make this recipe into a main dish, add 2 cups cooked white beans and ½ cup diced smoked ham in the same step where the green beans are stirred into the sauce. Simmer for 15 minutes.

Green Beans with Walnuts

1 tablespoon red wine vinegar
2 large garlic cloves, minced
Salt and pepper
3 tablespoons walnut oil
1 pound fresh green beans, trimmed and cut in half
¼ cup chopped walnuts

In a bowl blend the vinegar, garlic and salt and pepper to taste. Whisk in the oil in a thin stream.

Place the beans in boiling water and cook until just tender - about 5 minutes. Drain and toss with the dressing.

Top each serving with the chopped toasted walnuts.

Yield: 6 servings

Note: If walnut oil is not available, substitute 3 tablespoons olive oil and 1 teaspoon walnut extract.

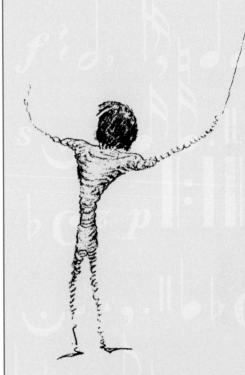

Seiji Ozawa
by Olga Koussevitzky

Roasted Cauliflower

1 medium cauliflower, cut into florets, 1 to 2-inches in size
¼ cup extra-virgin olive oil
Salt and black pepper
Freshly grated Parmesan cheese

Preheat the oven to 350°.

In a small roasting pan toss the cauliflower with the oil and a slight amount of salt and black pepper. Bake in the oven, stirring occasionally, for 40 minutes, or until tender and lightly browned. Sprinkle with the Parmesan cheese and return to the oven for 2 to 3 minutes more.

Remove the cauliflower from the roasting pan with a slotted spoon. Allow it to cool to room temperature before serving.

Yield: 4 servings

BOSTON
SYMPHONY
ORCHESTRA
SEIJI OZAWA
*Music
Director*

I

Adagio molto	C ♪ = 88
Allegro con brio	¢ ♩ = 112
Andante cantabile con moto	3/8 ♪ = 120
Allegro molto e vivace	3/4 ♩ = 108
Adagio	2/4 ♪ = 63
Allegro molto e vivace	2/4 ♩ = 88

II

Adagio molto	3/4 ♪ = 84
Allegro con brio	C ♩ = 100
Larghetto	3/8 ♪ = 92
Allegro	3/4 ♩ = 100
Allegro molto	¢ ♩ = 152

III

Allegro con brio	3/4 ♩ = 60
Adagio assai	2/4 ♪ = 80
Allegro vivace	3/4 ♩ = 116
Allegro molto	2/4 ♩ = 76
Poco andante	2/4 ♪ = 108
Presto	2/4 ♪ = 116

IV

Adagio	¢ ♩ = 66
Allegro vivace	¢ o = 80
Adagio	3/4 ♪ = 84
Allegro vivace	3/4 ♩ = 100
Allegro ma non troppo	2/4 ♩ = 80

Carrots with Capers

1 pound baby carrots, peeled
2 tablespoons butter
2 tablespoons olive oil
1 teaspoon minced garlic
2 tablespoons fresh chopped parsley
2 tablespoons capers, drained and rinsed

Pat the carrots dry. In a skillet over medium heat sauté the carrots in the butter and olive oil. Add 2 tablespoons of water and cook for 5 minutes. Add 2 more tablespoons of water and the garlic.

As the water evaporates, continue adding 2 tablespoons of water at a time until the carrots are just tender, leaving no water in the pan - about 10 to 15 minutes.

Allow the carrots to brown slightly, without scorching.

Add the parsley and capers, and toss. Cook for 1 additional minute and serve immediately.

Yield: 2 to 4 servings

Baked Mushrooms and Garlic

1 head garlic
1½ pounds white mushrooms, cleaned, and halved
(quartered, if large)
⅓ cup extra-virgin olive oil
2 to 3 sprigs fresh thyme, or a pinch of dried
Salt and freshly ground black pepper

Preheat oven to 400°.

Break up the garlic into individual cloves, peeling off the skin and trimming the stem ends.

In a roasting pan, just large enough to contain the ingredients in a single layer, combine the garlic, mushrooms, oil, thyme and salt and pepper to taste.

Bake for 35 to 40 minutes, stirring every 10 minutes or so, until the mushrooms and garlic are browned and tender. Remove from the oven and allow the vegetables to cool slightly before serving.

Yield: 4 servings

Baked Cucumbers

12 cucumbers, each about 8-inches long
4 tablespoons wine vinegar
5 teaspoons salt
¼ teaspoon freshly ground black pepper
1 tablespoon sugar
6 tablespoons butter, melted
1 teaspoon basil (or dill)
¼ cup minced onion
Fresh parsley, dill, or basil, for garnish

Peel the cucumbers and cut them in half lengthwise, scooping out the seeds with a spoon. Cut them into lengthwise strips about ⅜-inch wide. Then cut these strips into 4-inch pieces. In a stainless steel bowl, toss the cucumbers with the vinegar, salt, pepper, and sugar. Cover and let stand overnight.

Preheat oven to 375°.

Drain and pat dry the cucumbers, and toss them in a baking dish with the butter, basil, onion and pepper. Set them uncovered in the middle of the preheated oven for about 1 hour, tossing 2 or 3 times, until the cucumbers are tender, but still have a suggestion of crispness and texture. (They will barely color during the baking.)

Garnish with the fresh parsley, dill or basil.

Yield: 10 servings

This is decidedly different and definitely delicious!

BOSTON
SYMPHONY
ORCHESTRA
SEIJI OZAWA
Music
Director

V

Allegro con brio	2/4 ♩ = 108
Andante con moto	3/8 ♪ = 92
Allegro	3/4 ♩ = 96
Allegro	C ♩ = 84

VI

Allegro ma non troppo	2/4 ♩ = 66
Andante molto moto	12/8 ♩ = 50
Allegro	3/4 ♩ = 108
Allegro	2/4 ♩ = 132
Allegro	C ♩ = 80
Allegretto	6/8 ♩ = 60

VII

Poco sostenuto	C ♩ = 69
Vivace	6/8 ♩ = 104
Allegretto	2/4 ♩ = 76
Presto	3/4 ♩ = 132
Assai meno presto	3/4 ♩ = 84
Allegro con brio	2/4 ♩ = 72

VIII

Allegro vivace e con brio	3/4 ♩ = 69
Allegretto scherzando	2/4 ♪ = 88
Tempo di menuetto	3/4 ♩ = 126
Allegro vivace	¢ o = 84

Fennel with Parmesan Cheese

2 small fennel bulbs (about 1 pound)
1 teaspoon salt, plus additional for seasoning
3 tablespoons extra-virgin olive oil
Freshly ground black pepper
¼ cup freshly grated Parmesan cheese

Preheat oven to 450°. Oil a 13 by 9 by 2-inch baking dish.

Trim off the green tops of the fennel down to the bulb. If the outer layer is bruised, remove and discard that portion. Slice off a thin layer from the root end and discard it. Cut the bulbs lengthwise through the core into ¼-inch-thick slices.

In a large pot, bring 3 to 4 quarts of water to a boil. Add the fennel and 1 teaspoon of salt. Reduce the heat and simmer, uncovered, for 8 to 10 minutes, or until the fennel is crisp-tender. Drain the fennel well and pat dry.

Arrange the fennel slices in a single layer in the prepared dish. Sprinkle with the oil and salt and pepper to taste. Top with the cheese. Bake for 10 minutes, or until the cheese is lightly browned. Serve warm or at room temperature.

Yield: 4 servings

Louette's Leeks

5 to 6 leeks
1 tablespoon olive oil
Salt and pepper
Juice from 1 lemon

Wash the leeks thoroughly and dry them. Cut the leeks about 6 inches from the bottom. (Tops may be reserved for making soup at a later date, if desired.) Cut the white parts in half lengthwise, without separating the parts completely.

In a heavy pot heat the oil and add the leeks along with the salt and pepper to taste. Cook covered over low heat. After 15 minutes add the lemon juice and continue cooking for 35 to 40 minutes. (Caution: Check for liquid loss during this period; add up to ¼ cup of water, if necessary.)

Yield: 4 servings

This dish is very simple to make, and remarkably wonderful!

BOSTON
SYMPHONY
ORCHESTRA
SEIJI OZAWA
Music Director

Ikuko Mizuno
Violin

Louette's Leeks came to us from BSO violinist Ikuko Mizuno. She is a former Tanglewood Fellow and was the first woman to become a member of the BSO violin section in 1979.

This family recipe was given to Ikuko by her mother-in-law, who had been sent to Paris in the 1930s to learn to cook tasty and nutritional foods.

Mushroom Pie

8 ounces shiitake mushrooms
8 ounces portobello mushrooms
8 ounces button mushrooms
2 tablespoons oil, divided
1 small onion, chopped
1 clove garlic, minced
½ cup grated carrot
1 teaspoon dried thyme
Salt and pepper
1 tablespoon flour
1 (16-ounce) package frozen puff pastry, thawed
1 egg, beaten with 1 tablespoon milk

Wash and thoroughly pat dry the mushrooms, and cut into thick slices. Heat 1 tablespoon of the oil in a shallow pan and sauté the onion and garlic in it for 3 to 4 minutes. Add the carrot and thyme and cook for 2 more minutes. Remove the onion mixture from the pan and reserve. Add the remaining tablespoon of oil to the pan and sauté all the mushrooms for 2 minutes. Add the reserved onion mixture and salt and pepper to taste, and simmer for 8 to 10 minutes.

Mix the flour with 2 tablespoons of water, adding a little liquid from the mushrooms. Mix the flour in with the mushrooms. Cook for about 3 minutes; allow to cool. (This filling may be made ahead.)

Preheat the oven to 450°. Grease an 11 by 8-inch cookie sheet.

On a floured board roll out 2 puff pastry sheets to fit. Place one sheet on the cookie sheet, and mound the filling, leaving a 1 ½-inch border all around. Place the second sheet on top, cutting several vents in it. Seal the edges together using the egg as a "glue". Brush the top with more egg wash.

Bake for 10 minutes; lower the heat to 350°, and bake for 10 minutes more, or until golden brown.

Yield: 5 to 6 servings as a first course; 4 servings as a main dish

Note: If you prefer not to serve this delicious pie on a cookie sheet, you should make 2 smaller pies, because the dish is difficult to transfer from the cookie sheet to a serving tray in the single pie version.

Snow Peas and Cashews

¾ pound snow peas
1 (10-ounce) package frozen baby peas
4 tablespoons (½ stick) unsalted butter
1 teaspoon minced garlic
1 tablespoon chopped onion
1 cup unsalted cashews
½ teaspoon salt
¼ teaspoon black pepper
¼ cup chopped fresh parsley

Trim the ends of the snow peas, and remove the strings. Blanch the snow peas in boiling water until just tender - about 1 minute. Drain.

Separately, blanch the baby peas for one minute. Drain.

In a skillet melt the butter. Add the garlic, onion and cashews, and sauté for 1 minute. Add the salt, pepper and parsley. Combine the onion mixture with the peas and toss gently.

Yield: 6 servings

Note: If salted cashews are used, omit the ½ teaspoon salt from the recipe.

This is an unusual combination of ingredients
that works well - with a nice crunch!

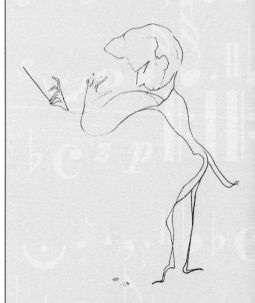

Guido Cantelli
by Olga Koussevitzky

Peperoni in Aceto Balsamico
(Sautéed Peppers in Balsamic Vinegar)

¼ cup extra-virgin olive oil
3 large red bell peppers, cored, seeded and thinly sliced
3 large yellow bell peppers, cored, seeded and thinly sliced
1 teaspoon sugar
½ teaspoon salt
3 tablespoons balsamic vinegar

In a large heavy skillet, heat the oil over medium-low heat. Add the peppers and cook, stirring occasionally, until tender and spotted with brown, about 25 minutes. (Do not raise the heat to speed up the cooking, or the peppers will burn.)

Add the sugar, salt and balsamic vinegar and stir well. Simmer until most of the liquid has evaporated - about 5 minutes more. Serve warm.

Yield: 6 to 8 servings

Note: The sweet-tart flavor of balsamic vinegar adds a subtle richness to bright red and yellow peppers. The peppers need long, slow cooking to tenderize them and bring out all their flavor.

"These two months have been beyond my fondest dreams."

~ Comment made by a TMC Fellow at the end of a Tanglewood Music Center season

Panzerotti
(Italian Potato Croquettes)

2 pounds boiling potatoes (about 5 large), peeled
Salt
3 large eggs, separated
½ cup freshly grated Parmesan cheese
Freshly ground black pepper
2 ounces mozzarella cheese, cut into ¼-inch cubes
1½ cups fine dry bread crumbs
Vegetable oil, for frying

Place the potatoes in a medium saucepan with cold water to cover. Add salt to taste, cover, and bring to a boil. Cook over medium heat until the potatoes are tender when pierced with a fork. Drain and mash the potatoes. (A masher, food mill, or ricer may be used.) Let them cool slightly.

Stir in the egg yolks and Parmesan cheese. Add salt and pepper to taste.

Take 3 tablespoons of the potato mixture and shape it into a 2½ by 1-inch log. Repeat with the remaining potato mixture. Push a few pieces of the mozzarella cubes into each log, then smooth the potato over them to completely enclose the cheese.

In a shallow dish, beat the egg whites until frothy. Spread the bread crumbs on a sheet of waxed paper. Dip the potato logs into the egg whites and then roll them in the bread crumbs. Pat them gently so that the crumbs adhere to the logs. Place them on a wire rack and allow to dry for 15 to 20 minutes.

Heat about ½ inch of oil in a deep heavy frying pan over medium heat. Fry the potato croquettes only a few at a time until golden brown, turning them once. (Note: The temperature of the cooking oil will become too low to properly brown the potato croquettes if too many are placed in the pan at one time.) Drain the croquettes on paper towels. Serve immediately, or set aside at room temperature until serving time. Then reheat them in a 350° oven for 10 minutes.

Yield: 18 to 20 croquettes

Variation: About 2 ounces of salami, cut into small cubes, may also be inserted in the croquettes along with the mozzarella.

BOSTON
SYMPHONY
ORCHESTRA
SEIJI OZAWA
*Music
Director*

*"I've been musically stretched
to my limits—they gave me the
best and they expected the
best from me."*
~ *A TMC violinist*

Oven-Browned Potatoes
with Pancetta and Rosemary

*6 pounds new potatoes, peeled
4 ounces (1 stick) unsalted butter, at room temperature
6 ounces thinly sliced pancetta, coarsely chopped
½ cup extra-virgin olive oil
2 tablespoons crumbled dried rosemary
1 teaspoon salt
⅛ teaspoon freshly ground black pepper*

Place the potatoes in a large pot and cover with cold water. Bring to a boil over high heat and cook for 15 to 20 minutes, or until the potatoes are still slightly firm when pierced with a knife. (It is important not to overcook the potatoes.)

Drain the potatoes and let them cool for several minutes.

Preheat the oven to 450°. Coat the bottom and sides of a large shallow baking pan with all the butter.

Cut the potatoes into large chunks and add them to the pan. Sprinkle the potatoes with the pancetta, olive oil, rosemary, salt and pepper. Roast in the oven for 1 to 1 ¼ hours, turning often, until all the butter and oil are absorbed, and the potatoes are very crisp. Turn the potatoes into a serving bowl and serve hot.

Yield: 8 to 10 servings

Note: Prior to roasting, the seasoned potatoes may be refrigerated for use the next day. Bring them back to room temperature before roasting. The recipe may also be doubled easily.

Pancetta is available in most markets and in Italian food shops. Bacon may be substituted, but it will provide a slightly different taste to the dish.

This recipe is great for a large group.

Gran-dad's Pennsylvania Dutch Potato Filling

6 medium potatoes, peeled and boiled till done
2 to 3 tablespoons butter
½ to 1 teaspoon salt
⅓ cup hot cream or milk
¼ cup shortening or oil, to coat pan to ¼-inch-depth for frying
1 cup chopped celery (including leaves)
3 to 4 medium onions, chopped
1 small bunch parsley, chopped
4 slices dried bread, cubed
1 to 2 eggs

Mash the hot boiled potatoes along with the butter, salt, and cream using a potato masher or electric mixer.

Heat the oil in a heavy saucepan, and sauté the celery, onions and parsley. When the onions are translucent, add the bread cubes and sauté together with the vegetable mixture, stirring until the cubes are lightly browned.

In a small bowl, lightly beat the eggs with a fork. In a large bowl mix together the mashed potatoes, the sautéed mixture and the eggs.

(The Pennsylvania Dutch use the recipe to this point for stuffing poultry. To use as a side dish, proceed as follows:)

Preheat the oven to 350°. Grease a casserole dish.

Place the mixture in the casserole. Moisten the top of the mixture with poultry or meat drippings, gravy, a bit of cream, or dot it with butter. Bake in the oven until hot throughout. The top should be lightly browned. (Cover during latter part of heating, if necessary, to keep casserole from drying out.)

Yield: 8 servings (as side dish)

BOSTON
SYMPHONY
ORCHESTRA
SEIJI OZAWA
Music Director

Elizabeth Ostling
Assistant Principal Flute

An authentic Pennsylvania Dutch recipe was given to us by Elizabeth Ostling, who joined the orchestra in 1994 as assistant principal flute.

"This recipe comes from my grandfather, who is 85. I know it is going to mean the world to him to see his Potato Filling recipe in the BSO Cookbook."

"The conducting classes with Lenny Bernstein were an experience you never forget. He was all over you like a great cloak, or dancing around you saying "Yes, yes or no, yes." You felt his eyes on you every second. It was exhilarating, exhausting, and hilarious all at the same time."

~ *A former TMC Conducting Fellow reminiscing about Leonard Bernstein*

Summer Squash Casserole

2½ pounds summer squash
¼ cup butter or margarine
2 cups seasoned stuffing mix
1 cup sour cream
1 (13½-ounce) can cream of chicken soup
1 cup grated carrot
¼ cup chopped onions

Preheat the oven to 350°.

Cut the squash into bite-size pieces. Cook until tender and drain. Set aside.

Melt the butter; mix with the stuffing in a bowl. Separately combine the sour cream, soup, carrot, onion and squash.

Spread half of stuffing mixture in a 13 x 9-inch pan. Spread squash mixture on the stuffing and top with remaining half of stuffing mixture.

Bake for 25 minutes.

Yield: 6 to 8 servings

This is a wonderful recipe to prepare ahead of time. Simply bake it when it's time to serve!

Zucchini Tarte

4 cups very thinly sliced zucchini (about 1 ½ pounds)
½ cup finely chopped onions
½ cup grated mozzarella cheese
½ teaspoon salt
½ teaspoon oregano
1 clove garlic, chopped
⅔ cup biscuit mix
½ cup freshly grated Parmesan cheese
2 tablespoons chopped fresh parsley
½ teaspoon seasoned salt
Dash of cayenne
4 beaten eggs
1 teaspoon dry mustard
¼ pound thinly sliced mushrooms, for garnish

Preheat oven to 350°. Grease a 13 by 9 by 2-inch pan.

Mix together in a bowl the zucchini, onions, mozzarella cheese, salt, oregano, garlic, biscuit mix, Parmesan cheese, parsley, seasoned salt, cayenne, eggs, and mustard. Pour the mixture into the greased pan and bake for 25 minutes, or until golden on top.

Sprinkle fresh mushroom slices on top as garnish.

Yield: 4 to 6 servings

Aaron Copland
by Olga Koussevitzky

Herb-Roasted Vegetables

3 sweet potatoes (about 2 pounds), peeled
1 red bell pepper, cored and seeded, cut into 2 by 1-inch wedges
1 yellow bell pepper, cored and seeded,
cut into 2 by 1-inch wedges
1 red onion, cut into 2 by 1-inch wedges
½ pound fresh asparagus, tough ends trimmed,
cut into 1-inch pieces
8 cloves garlic, peeled
3 tablespoons fresh chopped rosemary (or 3 teaspoons dried)
2 tablespoons fresh thyme (or 2 teaspoons dried)
2 tablespoons olive oil
½ teaspoon salt

Preheat oven to 500°.

Cut the sweet potatoes in half lengthwise and then into ½-inch slices. Put the potatoes, peppers, onions, and asparagus in a large bowl. Add the garlic, rosemary, thyme and olive oil and stir to distribute the seasonings. (The vegetables may be allowed to marinate at this point, if desired.)

Spread the vegetables evenly on a cookie sheet lined with heavy-duty foil, and sprinkle with salt. Bake in the oven for 18 to 20 minutes.

Yield: 4 to 6 servings

Chicken Rice Salad

2½ cups cooked rice (about 1 cup uncooked)
3 cups cooked chicken (about 1½ large boneless breasts),
cut into bite-size pieces
1¾ cups chopped celery
1 cup cooked peas
½ cup chutney
½ teaspoon curry powder
¾ cup Italian salad dressing
½ cup slivered almonds

In a large bowl, mix together the rice, chicken, celery, peas, chutney, curry powder, salad dressing and almonds.

Serve on a bed of lettuce.

Yield: 6 servings

Talk about a quick salad to make!

BOSTON
SYMPHONY
ORCHESTRA
SEIJI OZAWA
*Music
Director*

Cold Rice Salad

*4 cups chicken stock
2 cups long grain white rice
3 (6-ounce) jars artichoke hearts,
marinated in oil, marinade reserved
5 green onions, chopped
1 (4-ounce) can pimento-stuffed olives, sliced
1 large red or green bell pepper, cored, seeded and diced
3 large celery stalks, diced
¼ cup chopped fresh parsley
1 teaspoon curry powder
1 ½ cups mayonnaise
¼ cup oil and vinegar dressing
Salt and pepper*

In a medium-size saucepan bring the stock to a boil; stir in the rice, and return to a boil. Lower the heat, cover the pan, and simmer for 20 minutes, or until the liquid is absorbed. Cool.

Drain the artichokes, reserving the marinade liquid, and chop them. Add the artichokes to the rice along with the onions, olives, bell pepper, celery and parsley.

In a small bowl, combine the reserved marinade with the curry, mayonnaise, oil and vinegar dressing, and salt and pepper to taste. Toss with the rice mixture and mix thoroughly. Refrigerate until ready to serve.

Yield: 12 to 16 servings

Note: The pepper may be blanched if desired.

Chicken Pasta Primavera Salad

Basil Sauce:
¼ cup minced basil leaves
1 clove garlic, minced
½ teaspoon dry mustard
2 tablespoons tarragon vinegar
1 teaspoon lemon juice
½ teaspoon salt
1½ cups mayonnaise
½ cup sour cream

1 tablespoon oil
12 ounces fettuccine pasta
1 bunch broccoli, cut into small pieces
2 medium zucchini, cut into small pieces
1 red bell pepper, cored, seeded and thinly sliced
4 scallions, thinly sliced
1 (6-ounce) can pitted black olives, drained and sliced
1 (2-ounce) jar pimento, drained and sliced
3 cups cubed, cooked chicken breasts
(about 1½ large boned breasts)
⅔ cup freshly grated Parmesan cheese, divided
Salt and pepper

Make the Basil Sauce: In a bowl mix together the basil, garlic, mustard, vinegar, lemon juice, salt, mayonnaise and sour cream. Combine well and set aside.

Add the oil to a large pot of salted boiling water and cook the pasta until is "al dente", or firm to the bite. Drain.

While the pasta is cooking, in the another pot place the broccoli, zucchini and red pepper in water and bring to a boil; cook for 1 minute. Drain and place in a large bowl. Combine these vegetables with the scallions, black olives, pimento, and chicken.

After draining the pasta, place it in the bowl with the vegetables. Fold in two thirds of the basil sauce and ⅓ cup of the Parmesan cheese. Season with salt and pepper to taste. Refrigerate for 24 hours.

When ready to serve, add the remaining sauce and cheese.

Yield: 8 to 10 servings

Note: The recipe may be doubled easily.

Charles Munch
by Olga Koussevitzky

BOSTON
SYMPHONY
ORCHESTRA
SEIJI OZAWA
Music Director

Jascha Heifitz
by Olga Koussevitzky

Orzo Pasta Salad with Cumin-Lime Dressing

Dressing:
¾ teaspoon ground cumin
1 teaspoon ground coriander
¼ cup lime juice
1 tablespoon cider vinegar
1 teaspoon salt
⅛ teaspoon freshly ground black pepper
3 tablespoons olive oil
1 teaspoon salt

2 cups cooked orzo (about 6 ounces uncooked)
¼ cup chopped red bell pepper
¼ cup chopped yellow bell pepper
¼ cup chopped green bell pepper
¼ cup chopped green scallions
4 ounces sun-dried tomatoes, in oil, slivered
⅓ cup sweet corn kernels
⅓ cup artichoke hearts, cut into small pieces
¼ cup chopped Italian flat-leaf parsley (optional)

Make the dressing: In a small skillet, toast the ground cumin and coriander over moderate heat, stirring until fragrant - about 1 to 2 minutes.

In a small bowl, whisk together the lime juice, vinegar, salt, pepper and oil with the cumin and coriander. Set aside.

Make the salad: Mix the cooked orzo, peppers and green scallions. Add the sun-dried tomatoes and their oil to the orzo mixture. Mix well. Add the corn, artichokes and parsley, and mix thoroughly.

Pour the dressing over the salad and toss. Let the salad stand for 15 to 30 minutes before serving at room temperature.

Yield: 4 main course servings, or 8 to 10 servings as a side dish

This salad tastes even better the next day!

Ramen Noodle Salad

1 head Chinese cabbage
1 bunch green onions, chopped
2 (3-ounce) packages Ramen noodles
4 tablespoons (½ stick) butter
1 (2½-ounce) bag sliced almonds
2 tablespoons sesame seeds
½ cup sugar
¾ cup oil
3 tablespoons soy sauce
¼ cup white vinegar

Slice the Chinese cabbage into thin shreds (as in making cole slaw). In a bowl, combine the cabbage with the chopped onions, mixing well. Coarsely crush the Ramen noodles. (Discard the seasoning packet in the packages, or save for another recipe later.)

Melt the butter in a large skillet. Combine the crushed noodles, almonds and sesame seeds, and brown in the butter, stirring constantly. Remove from the heat and cool completely.

Combine the sugar, oil, soy sauce and vinegar in a saucepan and boil for 1 minute. Just before serving, toss the noodles with the cabbage mixture and pour on the dressing to taste. Serve immediately.

Yield: 6 servings

This is a different and delicious salad!

Salmon Pasta Salad

Lemon Dressing:
½ to ¾ cup olive oil
4 tablespoons lemon juice
2 tablespoons reserved salmon juice
2 cloves garlic, minced
1 teaspoon salt
1 teaspoon pepper
1 teaspoon dill
1 teaspoon lemon zest
½ cup freshly grated Parmesan cheese

1 (15-ounce) can pink salmon, juice reserved
1 pound rotini pasta, cooked, drained and cooled
½ cup provolone cheese cubes, ½-inch in size
½ cup chopped fresh parsley
Crisp greens, for garnish
Tomato wedges, for garnish

Make the dressing: In a medium bowl, whisk together the olive oil, lemon juice, reserved salmon juice, garlic, salt, pepper, dill and lemon zest. Mix in the cheese and set the dressing aside.

Break the salmon into chunks. Combine the salmon with the pasta, provolone chunks and parsley. Add the dressing and combine well. Serve over greens and garnish with tomato wedges.

Yield: 6 to 8 servings

Variation: Fresh salmon can be used, adding wine instead of salmon juice to the dressing.

Melon and Prosciutto Salad with Grilled Scallops

1 cantaloupe melon, seeded
1 large avocado, stone removed
Juice of 1 lemon
3 ounces prosciutto, cut into thin strips
2 bunches of fresh arugula, torn into pieces

Dressing:
2 teaspoons green pesto sauce
1 tablespoon white wine vinegar
4 tablespoons olive oil
1 red chili pepper, seeded and chopped
Snipped fresh chives
2 teaspoons chopped parsley
Salt and pepper
Oil, for brushing the pan
1 pound bay scallops (or sea scallops, cut in half)

Spoon out the melon flesh in small pieces and place in a bowl. Spoon out the avocado flesh in the same way, placing it in a separate bowl. Sprinkle the avocado with lemon juice (see note). Mix the avocado in with the melon; add in the prosciutto and arugula. Mix to combine.

Make the dressing: Place the pesto in a mixing bowl and add the vinegar. Gradually beat in the olive oil; then add the chili pepper, chives and parsley. Season with salt and pepper to taste, and set aside.

Heat a griddle pan to the smoking point and brush the surface with the oil. Cook the scallops quickly on the griddle for 1 minute on each side. Remove the scallops and add them to the salad bowl. Pour the dressing on the salad mixture, toss lightly and serve immediately.

Yield: 2 to 4 lunch servings

Note: If the lemon juice is not available, leaving the avocado stone in with the flesh will prevent its discoloring.

It is advisable to use gloves when working with chili peppers.

A very imaginative recipe! It also makes
a wonderful light summer supper!

BOSTON SYMPHONY ORCHESTRA
SEIJI OZAWA
Music Director

John Williams at Tanglewood

John Williams is a musician who can wear many hats. The latest has been his role as a faculty member at the Tanglewood Music Center. In 1998 he led a film seminar, which drew a full house in Seiji Ozawa Hall, and the following year he led a series of master classes. As a composer, conductor, and teacher, John is one of the great communicators.

Michael Tilson Thomas
by Olga Koussevitzky

Salad of Seared Scallops with Wild Mushrooms and Lemon

Vinaigrette:
¾ cup extra-virgin olive oil, divided
Juice of 2 lemons
Zest of 1 lemon
2 tablespoons minced shallots
1 teaspoon sugar
1 teaspoon Thai fish sauce
Salt and pepper

2 pounds mixed wild mushrooms,
"seasonal", cut into bite-size pieces
½ cup chopped chervil leaves
3 tablespoons finely snipped chives
24 Diver sea scallops, or "best available", sliced in half
30 chervil sprigs, for garnish

Make the vinaigrette: In a bowl combine ½ cup of the olive oil with the lemon juice, zest, shallots, sugar, fish sauce, and salt and pepper to taste. Mix well; set aside.

Heat the remaining olive oil until very hot in a skillet, and sauté the mushrooms in it. Season with the salt and pepper to taste, and toss with the chervil and chives.

Sear the scallops in a hot heavy pan, being careful not to overcook them.

Spread the mushrooms out on a large serving plate and arrange the scallops over the top. Spoon the vinaigrette over the scallops and mushrooms. Garnish with sprigs of chervil.

Yield: 4 servings as a main course salad

Note: Thai fish sauce may be found in some markets and in Asian food shops.

Bean Sprout Salad

2 pounds bean sprouts
3 scallions, chopped
¾ cup soy sauce
¾ cup water
2 tablespoons chopped ginger
1 teaspoon sesame oil

Place the bean sprouts in pot of boiling water for 1 minute. Remove; rinse with cold water and drain. Place them in a serving bowl, and add the scallions.

Mix the soy sauce, water, ginger, and sesame oil in a small pot over low heat. (Do not boil.) Remove from heat and pour over the bean sprouts and scallions. Mix thoroughly. Cover and refrigerate for 2 or 3 hours before serving.

Yield: 4 servings

Serving Suggestion: This is an excellent salad to accompany a meat or chicken main course.

Broccoli Salad

1 large bunch broccoli, chopped into bite-sized pieces
1 small onion, chopped
½ pound bacon, fried crisp, broken into pieces
1 cup shredded cheddar cheese

Dressing:
½ cup mayonnaise
1 tablespoon red wine vinegar
1½ teaspoons Dijon mustard
⅓ cup sugar
Pinch of salt

Blanch the broccoli and cool. Mix in thoroughly the onion, bacon and cheddar cheese. Set aside.

Make the dressing: In a bowl combine the mayonnaise, vinegar, mustard, sugar and salt. Pour the dressing over the broccoli mixture. Mix well and chill for 1 hour.

Yield: 4 servings

Variation: Top the salad with fried onion rings.

Salads

BOSTON
SYMPHONY
ORCHESTRA
SEIJI OZAWA
Music Director

Itzhak Perlman
Violin

Itzhak Perlman is beloved for his irrepressible joy in making music and his gift for sharing that joy with audiences. His artistry and charismatic personality propelled him onto the international stage of "The Ed Sullivan Show" at age 13.

In addition to a large collection of awards that includes many Grammys and Emmys, and a career full of great performances, Itzhak counts among his proudest achievements his collaboration with John Williams for the score of the Academy Award-winning film "Schindler's List," for which he performed the violin solos.

He kindly provided us with his unique Bean Sprout Salad recipe.

BOSTON
SYMPHONY
ORCHESTRA
SEIJI OZAWA
Music Director

Layered Vegetable Salad

Dressing:
2 cups sour cream
1 cup mayonnaise
1 cup plain yogurt
1 teaspoon Worcestershire sauce
1 teaspoon lemon juice
Salt and pepper

1 (16-ounce) package spinach, stemmed, blanched, squeezed dry, and chopped
1 head red lettuce, torn into ½-bite size
2 hard-boiled eggs, chopped
6 strips cooked bacon
1 head romaine lettuce, torn into ½-bite size
1 green bell pepper, seeded and finely chopped, divided
1 red bell pepper, seeded and finely chopped, divided
1 yellow bell pepper, seeded and finely chopped, divided
2 small yellow summer squash, thinly sliced
4 carrots, finely chopped
2 small green zucchini, thinly sliced
6 Italian plum tomatoes, seeded and diced
½ (10-ounce) package frozen green peas, unthawed
1 small red onion, thinly sliced
½ pound broccoli florets, blanched
Black and green olives, for garnish
Chopped parsley, snipped chives and dill, for garnish

In a bowl, mix together the sour cream, mayonnaise, yogurt Worcestershire sauce, lemon juice, and salt and pepper to taste. Set aside.

Using a straight-sided trifle bowl, arrange the vegetables in layers by color - let your eyes be your guide, working from the bottom to the top. Cut any vegetables into ½-bite size, if they are not already so. "Weigh down" each layer with the dressing, ending with dressing on the top-most layer. Refrigerate overnight to marry the flavors.

Layered Vegetable Salad continued

Suggested layers: (from top to bottom)

Dressing - with parsley, other herbs (if desired)

Black and green olives
Broccoli
Red onion
Peas
Tomatoes
Peppers

Dressing

Zucchini squash
Carrots
Summer squash
Peppers
Romaine lettuce

Dressing

Peppers
Egg and bacon
Red lettuce
Spinach

Yield: 12 to 14 servings

Comment: This is a great "do-ahead" salad for a party!

BOSTON
SYMPHONY
ORCHESTRA
SEIJI OZAWA
Music Director

Serge Koussevizky
by Olga Koussevitzky

William Gibson
Trombone

William Gibson was Principal Trombone with the BSO from 1955 to 1977.

Along with his wife Frances' recipe for the Marinated Carrot Salad, he sent this true story.

Following the final Beethoven Ninth performance in Symphony Hall, my trombone was stolen from the locker room. Six years later it was returned to me at Tanglewood. It had been purchased from a music store in New York by a student that I had auditioned and accepted for Tanglewood. As we rehearsed chamber music, I recognized the instrument as my own and broke the news to the unhappy student. Since the instrument now belonged to the insurance company, the return became a bit complicated. The student was in the midst of important concerts and begged to use it to the final days. Witnessed by the insurer, and with his permission, we exchanged a new 'bone for the old. Thanks to Tanglewood, my sound came back to me. And thanks to Tanglewood, the student has now a thirty-year career in a very fine orchestra."

Marinated Carrot Salad

5 cups cutup (on bias) carrots; parboiled, drained
1 medium Spanish onion, chopped
1 medium green bell pepper, cored, seeded, and chopped
½ cup salad oil
¾ cup wine vinegar
1 teaspoon Worcestershire sauce
1 teaspoon salt
1 (10¾-ounce) can tomato soup
¾ cup sugar
1 teaspoon prepared mustard
1 teaspoon ground black pepper

In a bowl mix together the carrots, onion, and green pepper. Set aside.

In another bowl, mix together the oil, vinegar, Worcestershire sauce, salt, tomato soup, sugar, mustard, and black pepper. Pour the marinade over the vegetables, and mix well. Chill at least 8 hours or overnight. (Will keep at least one week.)

Yield: 10 servings

This salad is a hit even with teenagers!

Bulgur Fruit Salad

½ cup uncooked bulgur
2 tablespoons or more golden raisins
¼ teaspoon cinnamon
1 cup apple juice
¼ cup chopped red apple
1 tablespoon chopped pecans

In a medium saucepan, combine the bulgur, raisins, cinnamon, and apple juice. Bring to a boil over medium-high heat. Reduce the heat to medium-low; cover, and simmer 12 to 15 minutes, or until the bulgur is tender and the liquid is absorbed.

Spoon the salad into a serving bowl. Cover and refrigerate at least 30 minutes to cool. Just before serving, stir in the apples and pecans.

Yield: 2 (1 cup) servings

Note. The amounts of raisins, chopped apple, and pecans may be adjusted for personal tastes.

Spinach Salad

Dressing:
½ cup cider vinegar
¾ cup sugar
1 teaspoon salt
⅓ cup ketchup
1 cup vegetable oil

1 (8-ounce) can water chestnuts, drained and thinly sliced
1 (8-ounce) can sliced bamboo shoots, drained
1 (16-ounce) can bean sprouts, drained
1 pound fresh spinach, stemmed, washed and torn
½ Bermuda onion, sliced into rings
½ pound fresh mushrooms, sliced
¾ pound bacon, cooked and crumbled

Make the dressing: Heat the vinegar in a saucepan; add the sugar and salt, and stir to dissolve. Remove from the heat, whisk in the ketchup and oil. Cover and refrigerate several hours, or overnight.

Similarly, chill the water chestnuts, bamboo shoots, and bean sprouts for several hours, or overnight.

To serve, combine in a serving bowl the spinach, onion, mushrooms, bacon, and the chilled vegetables. Pour the dressing over the salad and toss.

Yield: 6 servings

Variation: Serve the salad in pita pockets.

Surprisingly easy to make - and so delicious!

Pear and Endive Salad

Dressing:
2 tablespoons red wine vinegar
2 tablespoons Dijon mustard
4 tablespoons vegetable oil
Salt and pepper

½ cup toasted walnuts pieces
4 ounces prosciutto or Black Forest ham, cut julienne
10 ounces spinach leaves, stems removed,
torn into bite-size pieces
2 Belgian endive, thinly sliced
2 to 3 pears, peeled, cored and cut into bite-size pieces
2 ounces crumbled Gorgonzola cheese

Make the dressing: In a bowl, whisk together the vinegar, mustard, and oil. Add salt and pepper to taste. Set aside.

Make the salad: Mix the toasted walnuts, ham, spinach, endive, pears and cheese in a salad bowl. Add the dressing and mix well.

Yield: 6 servings

Note: To toast the walnuts: Preheat the oven to 350°. Place the nuts on a cookie sheet and bake for 8 to 10 minutes, taking care not to burn them. Allow to cool.

This is a great combination of flavors!

THE BOSTON POPS

*The Fourth of July on the Esplanade with
the Boston Pops Esplanade Orchestra*

Keith Lockhart succeeds John Williams as Pops Conductor

THE BOSTON POPS

In July 1885 BSO founder Henry Lee Higginson fulfilled another of his dreams. Charmed by the garden concerts he had attended as a music student in Vienna, he wondered whether the informal concerts would also appeal to Boston symphony-goers. By filling the hall with tables and chairs and arranging for refreshments to be served, Higginson transformed the staid hall into a cabaret for an evening. He asked Adolf Neuendorff to conduct a sprightly musical program that led off with a march, followed with a waltz and an overture, and concluded with a galop. The Music Hall audience loved it, and the Boston Pops Orchestra was born.

Dubbed "pops concerts" by the press and public, the concert series was initially called the "Boston Symphony Promenade Concerts." After moving into the new Symphony Hall, they became "The Symphony Hall Pops." Later they became the more familiar "Boston Pops," performing in Symphony Hall during May and June. Today the 92 members of the Boston Pops Orchestra are the same musicians who perform with the BSO, minus twelve of the orchestra's principals, who perform during this time as the Boston Symphony Chamber Players. During the period when the regular Pops members are on vacation or playing with the symphony, the Boston Pops Esplanade Orchestra, made up of local free-lance musicians, steps in to perform locally and on tour.

The inimitable Pops style comprises light classical repertory and American popular music. Every year, thousands of patrons revel in the Pops' one hundred or so performances in Symphony Hall and on tour. Capping each Pops season are free open-air performances on the Esplanade, highlighted by the nationally televised Fourth of July concert and fireworks display. There is also an annual series of Holiday Pops concerts in December.

Much of the Pops magic has emanated from its charismatic music directors. Early Pops conductors were of European background, but many came from within the ranks of the BSO, including Timothée Adamowski, Max Zach, and Gustav Strube. In 1930, the orchestra again turned to one of its own, a 35-year-old American-born violist named Arthur Fiedler. During Fiedler's legendary 49-year tenure, the Boston Pops emerged as a national institution, a musical ambassador abroad, and the most-recorded orchestra in the world. The PBS television program *Evening at Pops,* launched in 1969, kept both conductor and orchestra before a global audience.

It was Fiedler who first organized and conducted the free summer concerts at the Hatch Memorial Shell on the Esplanade. The six outdoor concerts are among the Pops most popular outings. The annual Fourth of July concert has evolved into the quintessential Independence Day celebration. Several hundred thousand music lovers enjoy the concert from their blankets on the Esplanade, and millions more tune in to the televised event.

Photo by: © Sylvia Gilman

Arthur Fiedler

225

Academy Award-winning composer John Williams succeeded Fiedler in 1980. Well known for his popular scores for over 80 films, he continued the legacy of traditional favorites, numerous recordings, and television tapings. He also added a new dimension to the pops experience with concerts that tapped the star power and magic of Hollywood and introduced works from contemporary composers.

Williams worked as a jazz pianist prior to his career as a composer. His works include several concert pieces, including two symphonies and numerous concertos. Following his retirement in 1993, Williams became Boston Pops Laureate Conductor. He is also Artist-in-Residence at Tanglewood.

In 1995 Keith Lockhart was named conductor of the Pops and he will lead the orchestra into the new millennium. Lockhart was 35, the same age as Fiedler when he began his tenure with the orchestra. In four seasons, Lockhart has conducted more than 200 concerts, taped 27 television shows, including 15 new programs for *Evening at Pops,* and led eight national tours. In 1996 the Boston Pops Orchestra signed a six-album recording contract with RCA Victor, the orchestra's original recording label, for which Fiedler made many hit recordings. In 1999, the Pops received its first-ever Grammy nomination for *The Celtic Album.*

Lockhart began his musical studies with piano lessons at the age of seven and holds degrees from Furman University and Carnegie-Mellon University. He has served as conductor for the Pittsburgh Civic Orchestra, and as assistant conductor of the Akron and Cincinnati Symphony Orchestras. Lockhart also served as associate conductor of the Cincinnati Symphony and Pops orchestras, and music director of the Cincinnati Chamber Orchestra. He is also music director of the Utah Symphony.

Today's Pops orchestra continues to celebrate a century of popular American music, from the classic Broadway musical compositions of Rodgers and Hammerstein to the film scores from *Star Wars* and *E.T.* The Boston Pops format has served as a model for such programming, which has become a part of most American orchestras' seasons. Higginson's vision in 1885 is now a celebrated aspect of our musical culture.

CAKES ~ COOKIES ~ PIES ~ DESSERTS

227

German Apple Cake

3 eggs
1 cup oil
2 cups sugar
1 teaspoon vanilla extract
2 cups sifted flour
2 teaspoons cinnamon
Dash of nutmeg
Dash of ground cloves
4 cups thinly sliced apples
1 cup chopped walnuts (optional)

Frosting:
4 ounces (1 stick) butter or margarine, at room temperature
8 ounces cream cheese, at room temperature
3 cups confectioners' sugar
1 teaspoon vanilla extract

Preheat the oven to 350°. Grease and flour a 13 by 9-inch pan.

In a mixing bowl beat the eggs and oil until foamy. Add the sugar, vanilla, flour, cinnamon, nutmeg, and cloves. Fold in the apples. (Mix in the walnuts, if desired.)

Pour the batter into the prepared pan and bake for 1 hour. (Check after 55 minutes for doneness.) Remove the cake from the oven and allow it to cool in the pan.

Make the frosting: In a bowl mix the butter, cream cheese, confectioners' sugar, and vanilla extract. Frost the cake with the mixture.

Yield: approximately 12 servings

Note: The cake will keep for at least one week.

Androscoggin Apple Cake

1 cup vegetable oil
1 cup sugar
3 eggs
1 cup whole wheat flour
1 cup all-purpose flour
1 tablespoon baking soda
1 tablespoon vanilla extract
1 teaspoon cinnamon
4 heaping cups peeled, cored and diced apples
1 cup walnuts
1 cup raisins

Preheat the oven to 350°. Grease a 13 by 9 by 2-inch baking pan.

Beat the oil, sugar and eggs in a bowl. Then beat in both flours, the baking soda, vanilla and cinnamon. While beating, fold in the apples, nuts and raisins, adding as much apple as can be coated with the batter.

Spread the mixture in the prepared pan. Bake for approximately 1 hour. Test with a toothpick for doneness. No icing is necessary.

Yield: 12 to 14 servings

BOSTON
SYMPHONY
ORCHESTRA
SEIJI OZAWA
*Music
Director*

A few years after Henry Lee Higginson established the Boston Symphony Orchestra, he realized that in order to keep his European musicians from deserting the orchestra, he would have to provide them with a longer season. Thus he initiated a series of nightly light-music concerts, modeled somewhat after the London Prom concerts. Since 1885 these popular concerts, now called the Pops concerts, have become an annual springtime tradition of the city of Boston.

The Pops has not always enjoyed its present popularity. There have been ups and downs. But when Arthur Fiedler took over in 1930 from Alfredo Casella and began to cater to public and current taste, the Pops assumed a popularity and success greater than ever before.

Pops conductor Keith Lockhart has not forgotten his roots.

At his first Opening Night at Pops in May 1995, his proud mother and father watched their son begin his Boston career.

A short time later, Keith returned to Furman University, his alma mater, to conduct a workshop. He has since repeated the "college reunion" trip, this time with the Boston Pops Esplanade Orchestra, to the delight of his university and the people of South Carolina.

Apricot Rum Cake

4 eggs
¾ cup oil
¾ cup apricot nectar
1 (18½-ounce) box yellow cake mix
¾ cup granulated sugar
5 ounces (1¼ sticks) butter
½ cup rum

Preheat the oven to 350°. Grease a Bundt pan.

In a bowl, mix the eggs, oil and apricot nectar. Add the cake mix and beat together for 4 to 5 minutes at medium speed. Pour the batter into the greased Bundt pan and bake for 50 minutes.

While the cake is baking, melt the sugar, butter and rum in a saucepan. As soon as cake is done, punch fork holes in top of the cake and pour the rum mixture on top of the cake, ensuring equal distribution around the cake's surface.

Allow the cake to cool for 1 hour before removing from the pan.

Yield: 12 servings

Note: For an increased apricot taste, add 1 to 2 teaspoons apricot liqueur in place of an equal amount of the rum.

Carrot Cake

2 cups sugar
1 cup shortening
4 eggs
1 teaspoon baking powder
2 cups flour
1 teaspoon baking soda
2 teaspoons cinnamon
½ teaspoon salt
3 cups grated carrot
1 cup walnuts, chopped

Frosting:
10 ounces confectioners' sugar
1 teaspoon vanilla extract
8 ounces cream cheese
6 tablespoons (¾ stick) unsalted butter

Preheat the oven to 350°. Grease and flour a Bundt pan.

In a mixing bowl, cream the sugar and shortening. Then add the eggs and mix well.

Into a bowl sift the baking powder, flour, baking soda, cinnamon and salt. Add the sifted dry ingredients to the egg mixture. Beat until smooth. Add the carrots and then the nuts. Mix together. Pour the batter into the prepared Bundt pan, and bake for 30 to 35 minutes.

Make the cream cheese topping: In a bowl blend together the confectioners' sugar, vanilla, cream cheese and unsalted butter, until they are creamy. (You may add more of any of the frosting ingredients if you wish.)

Allow the cake to cool at least 20 minutes before frosting it.

Yield: 8 to 10 servings

If you do not have a Bundt pan, this carrot cake
is so good that it warrants purchasing one!

BOSTON
SYMPHONY
ORCHESTRA
SEIJI OZAWA
*Music
Director*

Several years ago the Boston Pops played a hilarious arrangement of Lincke's "The Glowworm," entitled "The Glowworm Turns." It required a siren, and one night the battery for the siren was dead. The stage manager informed Harry Ellis Dickson, the conductor that night, that he'd fix it somehow. At the appropriate time the siren worked perfectly.

It wasn't long afterward that Harry found out that the power source for the siren was the battery from his own car, parked near the stage door!

Jessye Norman
Soprano

We welcome Miss Norman's repeat performance in the BSO cookbook.

Her beautiful voice and legendary career are well known worldwide. But did you know the National Museum of Natural History in Paris named an orchid for her? Or that she is the youngest recipient of the Kennedy Center Honor award? Or that she is a lifetime member of the Girl Scouts of America - and an avid cookie seller?

Miss Norman's lengthy list of philanthropic endeavors include board appointments of the New York City City-Meals-on-Wheels, the Elton John AIDS Foundation, and national spokesperson for both the Lupus Foundation and the Partnership for the Homeless.

Quick Dessert Cake

2 cups flour
3 teaspoons baking powder
¾ teaspoon salt
¾ cup milk
3 eggs, well beaten
6 ounces (1 ½ sticks) unsalted butter
¾ cup brown sugar
½ cup raisins
1 ½ teaspoons lemon extract
½ cup Grand Marnier liqueur (see note)
Confectioners' sugar (optional)

Sift together the flour, baking powder and salt into a large mixing bowl. Add the milk, eggs, butter, brown sugar, raisins, lemon extract and liqueur. Beat at medium speed for 4 minutes. Set aside to rest for 10 minutes.

Preheat the oven to 350°. Butter and lightly flour a 10-inch Bundt pan.

Beat the batter at high speed for 2 to 3 minutes, and pour the mixture into the Bundt pan. Bake for 45 to 55 minutes, or until the top is firm to the touch, and the edges have pulled away from the sides of the pan. (Be careful not to overbake the cake.)

Sift confectioners' sugar (if used) on top.

Yield: 8 to 10 servings

Note: The more inexpensive Triple Sec may be substituted for the Grand Marnier.

Chocolate Chip Cake

2 cups flour
3 teaspoons baking powder
1 teaspoon salt
1 ¼ cups sugar
½ cup shortening
¾ cup milk
2 eggs
1 teaspoon vanilla extract
¾ cup chopped nuts
1 (6-ounce) package chocolate bits, divided

Preheat the oven to 350°. Grease and flour 2 round 8-inch layer pans.

Sift together the flour, baking powder, salt and sugar into a bowl. Add the shortening and milk. Beat well (2 minutes with an electric beater). Add the eggs (unbeaten) and the vanilla. Beat well again. Stir in the nuts.

Pour the batter into the 2 layer pans. Add one half of the chocolate bits on each layer. Bake for 35 to 40 minutes. Cool.

Use a plain white frosting of your choice between the layers in assembly of the cake, and again on the top of the layered cake.

Yield: 6 servings

Variation: Reserve 2 tablespoons of the chocolate bits in Step 2. Top the frosted cake with the bits before serving.

Try this cake with a light coating of buttercream frosting.
It will become a family favorite!

BOSTON
SYMPHONY
ORCHESTRA
SEIJI OZAWA
*Music
Director*

Surprise Encores at Pops

Camaraderie and fun run through Pops performances, not only in the audience, but also on the podium.

In June 1999, at the annual Presidents at Pops concert, Keith Lockhart invited John Williams to be conductor for the evening. At the end of the concert, Keith suddenly appeared on the podium, and both conductors enthusiastically proceeded to conduct the "Stars and Strips Forever." The two maestros referred to the experience as "tag team conducting."

The following month, hundreds of thousands of concert-goers at the Fourth of July Esplanade concert witnessed a similar scene when Seiji Ozawa, sporting his Boston Red Sox cap, marched on stage and encouraged audience participation, while Keith Lockhart conducted the orchestra in the standard Souza score.

BOSTON
SYMPHONY
ORCHESTRA
SEIJI OZAWA
*Music
Director*

Pear Skillet Cake with Caramel Rum Sauce

1 cup firmly packed golden brown sugar
6 tablespoons (¾ stick) unsalted butter, cut into 4 pieces
1⅓ cups all-purpose flour
1⅓ cups granulated sugar
2 teaspoons cinnamon
1¼ teaspoons baking soda
½ teaspoon salt
2 large eggs
½ cup corn or vegetable oil
1 small pear, unpeeled, coarsely grated
1 tablespoon fresh ginger, peeled and grated
(or 1½ teaspoons powdered)
4 medium pears (preferably Bosc), about 1½ pounds,
peeled and cored, each cut into 6 wedges

Caramel Rum Sauce:
½ cup whipping cream
4 ounces (1 stick) unsalted butter
½ cup packed dark brown sugar
½ cup granulated sugar
3 tablespoons dark rum

Position the rack in the center of the oven and preheat the oven to 350°. Sprinkle golden brown sugar evenly over bottom of a large heavy ovenproof skillet (preferably cast iron), with 2½-inch sides. Add the butter and place the skillet in the oven until the butter melts - about 5 minutes.

Mix the flour, granulated sugar, cinnamon, baking soda and salt in a bowl. Using an electric mixer, beat in the eggs and oil; then mix in the grated pear and ginger. Set aside.

Remove the skillet from the oven, taking care to use pot holders or an oven mitt. Whisk together the butter and brown sugar in the skillet until thoroughly combined. Arrange the pear wedges in the skillet in a flower pattern, putting any extra pieces in the middle. Pour the batter over the pears, spreading evenly. (It will appear that you don't have enough batter, but just spread it evenly and it works out just fine!)

Bake until the cake is springy to the touch and a tester inserted in the middle comes out clean - about 1 hour.

Transfer the skillet to a rack, and let it set for 20 minutes. Loosen the edges with a knife. Place a large plate over the skillet and, using mitts, flip the skillet, turning the cake onto a platter.

Pear Skillet Cake with Caramel Rum Sauce continued

Make the sauce: Combine the whipping cream, unsalted butter, dark brown sugar, and the granulated sugar in a heavy medium saucepan over medium heat. Stir until the butter melts and the sugars dissolve. Increase the heat and boil it until it is slightly thickened, whisking occasionally - about 3 minutes. Mix in the rum. Cool slightly before serving.

Serve the skillet cake with the caramel rum sauce.

Yield: about 16 to 20 servings

Note: The sauce may be easily reheated in the microwave oven - about 30 to 60 seconds.

Serve this cake with ice cream or crème fraîche for a special treat. It is sinfully divine!

Scottish Short Bread

½ cup sugar
1 cup butter
2 cups flour
1 teaspoon salt

Preheat the oven to 350°.

Cream the sugar and butter in an electric mixer bowl; beat until light and fluffy. Add the flour and salt together, and mix well.

Divide the dough into 4 parts. Shape each part into a ball. On ungreased cookie sheets press or roll each ball into 6-inch rounds approximately ¼-inch-thick. With a knife, score each round into 8 wedges, leaving the wedges in place. Prick each wedge 3 times with a fork.

Bake for 18 to 25 minutes, or until the edges are light golden brown. Cool for 5 minutes. Prick each wedge again with a fork. Cut through and separate the wedges. Cool the short bread completely - about 15 minutes.

Yield: 32 pieces of shortbread

BOSTON
SYMPHONY
ORCHESTRA
SEIJI OZAWA
Music Director

Rolf Smedvig
Trumpet

This Icelandic terta (torte) was sent to us by retired orchestra member Rolf Smedvig.

It is a family recipe handed down from his mother, a true Icelander who traces her ancestry back to the 9th century.

Rolf retired from the orchestra in 1981 to tour the world with the Empire Brass.

Icelandic Vinarterta

Filling:
2 pounds prunes, pitted and cooked
½ cup prune juice
1 cup sugar
½ teaspoon cardamom seeds, split and ground
1 teaspoon vanilla extract

8 ounces (2 sticks) butter
1 cup sugar
2 eggs, slightly beaten
1 teaspoon vanilla extract
4 cups all-purpose flour
2 teaspoons baking powder
¼ cup milk

Make the filling: Place the cooked prunes, prune juice, sugar, cardamom and vanilla into a food processor and purée until smooth. Place the mixture into a pan and cook over low heat, stirring occasionally, until it is as thick as jam. Set aside and cool.

In a mixing bowl, cream the butter and sugar. Add the eggs and vanilla, and mix well. Sift together the flour and baking powder, then add the dry mixture alternately with the milk to the sugar mixture, beating well after each addition. The dough should be firm, but not stiff. Divide the dough into 10 equal portions and chill for at least 8 hours, preferably overnight.

Preheat the oven to 350°.

On a lightly floured board, roll each portion to about ¼-inch thickness, and trimmed so as to fit onto the back of an 8 or 9-inch square pan. (Save the trimmings for more layers, if needed.) Transport the dough on a rolling pin to the back side of the square pan. Bake each layer individually for 5 to 10 minutes, or until the edges start to brown. Remove the layer from the sheet with a spatula, and cool it on a rack. (Note: Allow the pan to cool before adding the next layer to be baked.) Repeat until all layers are baked.

Spread the filling on each layer, until you have a stack of 6, with the top layer not covered with the filling. If you have enough layers and filling left, make another stack of at least 4 layers. Wrap each stack tightly with a dry towel, plastic wrap or foil. Place a pan with some heavy object in it (for added weight) on top of the stack, and leave it so for a day or two.

Icelandic Vinarterta continued

When ready to serve, cut the crusty sides off the vinarterta. For easier handling, divide the cake into three blocks and cut ⅜-inch slices for serving.

Yield: about 20 to 24 servings per cake

Note: The individual blocks freeze well and will slice easily.

English Tea Cakes

1¾ cups flour
1½ teaspoons baking powder
¼ teaspoon salt
½ cup butter, or ¼ cup butter and ¼ cup shortening, softened
¾ cup fine sugar, plus additional for coating
1 egg
3 tablespoons milk
½ teaspoon vanilla extract
½ cup small raisins, or soft currants
1 egg white, beaten

Sift the flour, baking powder and salt into a bowl, and set aside.

With a mixer, cream the softened butter, sugar and egg until creamy. Add the milk and the flour mixture while the mixer is on low speed. Add the vanilla and raisins. Remove the mixture from the bowl and place onto some plastic wrap. Wrap it around the mixture and place it in the refrigerator for 1 hour or more.

Preheat the oven to 350°.

Place the beaten egg white in a small bowl and sprinkle some fine sugar onto waxed paper on a working surface. Roll teaspoons of chilled dough into walnut-size balls, and dip the tops first into beaten egg white and then into fine sugar. Place them on an ungreased cookie sheet and bake for 12 to 15 minutes, or until the edges begin to brown. Cool on a rack.

Yield: about 36 cookies

Note: The cookies can be stored in an airtight container for up to 2 weeks.

These delicate cookies have a lovely, crunchy sugar-egg glaze.

In May of 1938, Arthur Fiedler and the Pops presented for the first and only time, an entire ballet, with dancers, costumes, and simple scenery. It was the premiere performance of Walter Piston's "The Incredible Flutist."

Until the early seventies, when Fiedler began to conduct the Boston Ballet's annual Christmas performances of "The Nutcracker," this was the only experience he had conducting ballet! He would conduct about fifteen consecutive performances each December, one of which was always on his birthday, December 17.

On that night, after his bow, a huge birthday cake would always be rolled out onto the stage, and the audience would sing "Happy Birthday."

One evening, the Boston Red Sox team attended a Pops concert. During intermission, Arthur Fiedler and Harry Ellis Dickson introduced their first bass, Georges Moleux (a Frenchman who knew nothing about American baseball) to Walt Dropo, the Red Sox first baseman.

"Georges, meet Walt Dropo. He plays first base."

"What orchestra?" Moleux inquired.

"The Red Sox," Dropo replied.

"How many basses do you have?" Georges asked.

"Three," Walt stated.

"Must be a small orchestra," Moleux remarked, and left to go on stage.

Fantastic Fruit Cake

4 tablespoons (½ stick) butter or margarine
1 cup sugar
2 eggs
2 cups flour
2 teaspoons baking soda
½ teaspoon nutmeg
½ teaspoon cloves
½ teaspoon allspice
¼ cup bourbon
¾ cup applesauce
¾ cup cran-raspberry sauce
8 ounces dark raisins
8 ounces golden raisins
1 cup candied pineapple, diced
1 cup candied fruits, diced
1 cup dates, chopped
1 cup walnuts, chopped

Preheat oven to 325°. Generously coat a 10-inch Bundt pan with a nonstick spray.

In a large mixer bowl, cream the butter and sugar together until light. Beat in the eggs, one at a time. Sift together the flour, baking soda, nutmeg, cloves, and allspice. Add all but 3 tablespoons of the dry mixture to the creamed mixture, alternating it with the bourbon. Stir in the applesauce and cran-raspberry sauce.

In a bowl, toss the raisins, candied pineapple and fruits, dates and nuts with the remaining 3 tablespoons of the flour mixture. Add the mixture to the cake batter; stir until blended. Spoon the batter into Bundt pan.

Bake for 2 hours, or until a cake tester comes out clean. Cool the cake on a rack for 20 minutes. Invert the cake onto a cake tray prior to serving.

Yield: 16 to 20 servings

Use 2 regular or 5 mini-loaf pans in place of the Bundt pan to make hostess gifts!

Almond Poppy Seed Cake

4 ounces (1 stick) butter, at room temperature
2¼ cups sugar
½ cup oil
3 eggs
1½ teaspoons vanilla extract
1½ teaspoons almond extract
1½ teaspoons butter flavoring mix
1½ tablespoons poppy seeds
3 cups all-purpose flour
1½ teaspoons salt
1½ teaspoons baking powder
1½ cups milk

Glaze:
1¼ cups confectioners' sugar
½ teaspoon almond extract
½ teaspoon vanilla extract
Up to ¼ cup orange juice, divided

Preheat oven to 350°. Grease 2 large or 5 small loaf pans.

Cream the butter and sugar in a mixing bowl. Add the oil. Add the eggs 1 at a time, mixing after each addition. Add the vanilla extract, almond extract, butter flavoring and poppy seeds. Mix well.

In a bowl, combine the flour, salt and baking powder. Add the flour mixture and milk alternately to the cake mixture, while beating for 2 minutes.

Pour the mixture into the loaf pans and bake the larger pans for 1 hour, or the smaller pans for 25 minutes, or until brown. Cool the cake for 10 minutes before removing it from the pans.

Make the glaze: In a bowl, mix together the sugar, the almond and vanilla extracts, and 2 tablespoons of the orange juice. Add additional orange juice gradually, as necessary, until the glaze attains a drizzling consistency. Drizzle the glaze over the loaves. Cool completely. Wrap in foil to store or freeze.

Yield: 2 large loaves or 5 small loaves

Note: This cake can be made richer, if desired, by adding 1½ teaspoons butter flavoring to the batter and ½ teaspoon butter to the glaze.

Richard Ranti
Associate Principal Bassoon

At the age of nineteen, Richard Ranti, a native of Montreal, embarked upon his professional career as second bassoonist, and later as acting associate principal with the Philadelphia Orchestra.

He studied at the Curtis Institute and was a Fellow at the Tanglewood Music Center before joining the orchestra in 1989 as associate principal bassoon.

Richard promises this is a foolproof recipe.

Foolproof Lemon Loaf

½ cup oil
½ cup sugar
2 eggs
½ cup milk
1 teaspoon lemon zest
1½ cups flour
1 teaspoon baking powder
¼ teaspoon salt

Topping:
⅓ cup sugar
Juice of 1 lemon

Preheat oven to 325°. Grease a medium-size bread pan.

Mix together the oil and the ½ cup sugar. Set aside. Mix together the eggs, milk, and lemon zest. Combine with the sugar mixture.

Sift together the flour, baking powder and salt. Then blend the sifted ingredients into the milk mixture. Pour the mixture into the bread pan and bake for 1 to 1¼ hours. Remove and cool for 10 minutes.

Make the topping: Combine the sugar with the lemon juice. Pour the topping over the loaf. Allow it to cool completely, then wrap it in foil and refrigerate overnight.

Yield: One 1-pound loaf (about 8 servings)

Serving Suggestion: The lemon loaf goes well with sorbet.

Sweet Meringues

2 egg whites
1 teaspoon vanilla extract
½ teaspoon almond extract
Pinch of salt
¼ teaspoon cream of tartar
⅔ cup superfine sugar
3 ounces chopped pecans
6 ounces semisweet chocolate bits

Preheat the oven to 400°.

In a bowl, beat the egg whites, vanilla and almond extracts, and the salt into a froth. Add the cream of tartar; beat until stiff. Slowly add the sugar, a little at a time, until all is blended. Gently fold in the pecans and chocolate bits.

On cookie sheets, lined with foil, use a teaspoon of the mixture to make each meringue. (A larger size spoon may be used, if desired, to make larger meringues.)

Place the cookie sheets in the oven. Turn off the heat immediately and leave the meringues in the oven for 8 hours (or overnight). Do not open oven door at any time during this period!

Yield: about 60 meringues

BOSTON
SYMPHONY
ORCHESTRA
SEIJI OZAWA
Music Director

Roger Voisin
Principal Trumpet

Paris-born Roger Voisin's father, René, was one of the brilliant French trumpeters in the Boston Symphony Orchestra. At seventeen, Roger became the youngest member ever to join the Pops, and soon joined his father in the BSO's trumpet section. He followed Georges Mager as principal trumpet and served until his retirement in 1973.

In his active retirement, Roger was Chairman of the trumpet department of the New England Conservatory and has been a beloved faculty member at the Tanglewood Music Center. In 1999, at age 80, Roger retired from teaching. He is the organizer and director of the Boston Symphony Brass Ensemble, and has been recorded by Columbia Masterworks and Kapp Records.

Roger's charming wife, Martha, gave us this recipe for the perfect meringues. She enjoys cooking, and commented that this recipe is wonderful because "you can put them on a cookie sheet in the oven at night, and go to bed and forget about them until morning!"

Joseph Hearne
Bass

Jan Brett
Author and Illustrator

Double bass player Joe Hearne spends his extra time helping his wife, "New York Times" best-selling author Jan Brett, with her books. Joe helps with the air-brushed backgrounds for Jan's books and Jan brings her enthusiasm and talent to many BSO projects.

The Hedgehog Cookie recipe was inspired by their pet, a real hedgehog, named "Buffy," who lives in Jan's studio.

Hedgehogs Plain and Fancy

8 ounces (2 sticks) unsalted butter
⅔ cup sugar
1 egg
2⅓ cups all-purpose flour
¼ teaspoon baking powder
¼ teaspoon salt
1½ teaspoons vanilla extract
Sliced almonds
Mini-chocolate chips
Confectioners' sugar icing
Chopped nuts (walnuts, pecans, or almonds) for decoration

Using an electric beater, blend the unsalted butter and sugar. Add the egg and blend.

In a separate bowl, blend the flour, baking powder, salt and vanilla. Combine the butter mixture with the flour mixture until a dough is formed. In batches, roll the dough between 2 sheets of waxed paper. Refrigerate for 20 minutes to make handling easier.

Peel off top sheet. Cut ovals of dough with cookie cutter. (Use a round biscuit cutter that you have flattened into an oval as a cutter.) Chill the ovals in the refrigerator for 10 minutes.

Preheat the oven to 350°.

Place a cooled oval on a working surface and cut out a hedgehog's face with a small cutter. (The top of a honey jar makes a large hedgehog; and the top of a spice jar makes a smaller one!) Bake for 8 minutes.

While the cookies are still soft from the oven, press a sliced almond into the cookie for the ear, and make an eye with a toothpick. When almost cool, add a mini-chocolate chip for the snout.

To make a fancy hedgehog (it's crunchy!), frost with your favorite icing and press chopped pecans into the icing before it hardens.

Yield: 30 hedgehog cookies

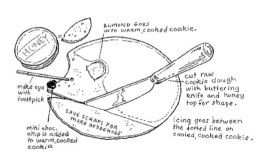

ALMOND GOES INTO WARM, cooked cookie.

HONEY

make eye with toothpick

SAVE SCRAPS FOR MORE HEDGEHOGS

mini choc. chip is added to warm, cooked cookie.

cut raw cookie dough with buttering knife and honey top for shape.

icing goes between the dotted line on cooled, cooked cookie.

242

Mandelbrot

3 eggs
½ cup oil
1 scant cup sugar
1 teaspoon vanilla extract
¾ teaspoon salt
3 cups sifted flour
2 teaspoons baking powder
1 cup ground nuts, or raisins
Dash of cinnamon (optional)

Preheat the oven to 350°.

In a bowl beat the eggs well one at a time. Add the oil and again beat well. Add the sugar and continue beating the mixture. Add the vanilla and mix well.

Separately, combine the salt, flour and baking powder. Add the flour mixture one spoon at a time to the sugar mixture. Mix well, then add the nuts and the cinnamon (if used).

Grease a 13-inch by 9-inch pan or cookie sheet. If possible, use a layer of parchment paper or baking paper on the pan. Moisten your hands, then shape the mixture into 2 narrow loaves, patting them with your hands to even them out. Bake for 30 minutes, or until brown.

Remove from pan carefully with a spatula, and slice the loaves while they are still warm into 1-inch strips with a serrated knife, cutting on the diagonal. Return the mandelbrot to the oven for an additional 10 minutes.

Yield: 2 dozen mandelbrot

Note: Cookies last indefinitely and may be frozen.

Variation: Ginger or orange peel may be added to the mixture.

BOSTON
SYMPHONY
ORCHESTRA
SEIJI OZAWA
Music Director

The Search for Keith Lockhart

In February 1995 a successor to John Williams had finally been found after a two year search. Rumors as to who would be the next Pops conductor had flown around Boston for months, but there had been silence from the orchestra. It was to be the then relatively unknown Keith Lockhart.

The day prior to the landmark press conference Keith was flown into Boston under an assumed name and driven immediately to a hotel outside the city. The following morning he was picked up by a volunteer instead of the official driver, driven to Symphony Hall, and escorted through the kitchen to make his surprise entry before the hordes of waiting reporters and the glaring cameras.

Today the personable Pops conductor would be easily recognized as a result of Pops telecasts, recordings, and tour appearances.

The choice of recording materials was usually up to Arthur Fiedler and the recording company.

Fiedler once ran across a piece called "Jalousie," a tango by an unknown Danish composer, Jacob Gade, in a second-hand music store. He bought the sheet music for fifteen cents. It became a hit at the Pops concerts, and Fiedler subsequently suggested it for a Pops recording to fill in the last five minutes available for the recording session.

After much argument, Fiedler won out, and the three minute and forty-five second recording was made. It was the first concert record to sell over a million copies!

This was in 1935; about twenty years later a man came to Symphony Hall and introduced himself to Arthur. "My name is Jacob Gade," he said. "I have just arrived from Denmark, and I want to thank you for making me rich."

Biscotti with Brandy and White Chocolate

8 tablespoons (1 stick) unsalted butter, at room temperature
¾ cup sugar
2 eggs, at room temperature
1 teaspoon vanilla extract
2 tablespoons brandy
2 cups plus 2 tablespoons flour, divided
1½ teaspoons baking powder
¼ teaspoon salt
1½ cups white chocolate chunks
1 cup walnuts (optional)

Preheat the oven to 325°. Line a baking sheet with parchment paper.

In the bowl of an electric mixer, cream the butter and sugar. Add the eggs one at a time, mixing thoroughly. Add the vanilla and brandy. With the mixer on a low setting, add the flour, baking powder, and salt. With your hands, mix in the chocolate.

Turn mixture out onto the counter, and using a little extra flour for your hands, shape the dough into 3 logs, each approximately 8 by 3 by ½-inches. Carefully transfer the dough logs onto a baking sheet, leaving 3 inches between each log.

Bake for 25 minutes, or until light brown. Leaving the oven on, remove the baking sheet from the oven, and allow it to cool for 10 minutes.

Using a sharp knife, cut the logs into ½ to 1-inch slices. Return the slices to the baking sheet, with the cut side up and bake for 10 minutes. Flip the slices to the other side, and bake for an additional 10 minutes. Remove the cookies from the oven and cool on a rack. Store in a covered airtight container.

Yield: approximately 3 dozen biscotti

Serving Suggestion: These biscotti go well with various coffees and teas.

Chocolate Sugar Cookies

3 squares unsweetened chocolate
8 ounces (2 sticks) butter or margarine
1 cup sugar
1 egg
1 teaspoon vanilla extract
2 cups all-purpose flour
1 teaspoon baking soda
¼ teaspoon salt
Additional sugar for coating

Microwave or heat the chocolate and butter until the butter is completely melted. Stir until the chocolate completely melts. Stir in the sugar, then the egg and vanilla. Mix thoroughly. Mix in the flour, baking soda, and salt. Chill for about 30 minutes, or until the dough is easy to handle.

While the mixture is cooling, preheat the oven to 375°.

Shape the cooled mixture into balls about 1-inch in size; then roll them in sugar. (If crispier cookies are desired, flatten them slightly with the bottom of a glass.) Place the balls on ungreased cookie sheets. Bake for 8 minutes, or until set. Remove; cool on a rack.

Yield: about 42 cookies

The first "Evening at Pops" program was aired in July 1969, five months before Arthur Fiedler's seventy-fifth birthday.

Because the programs eventually achieved not only nationwide but also worldwide audience acceptance, Arthur Fiedler and the Pops attained universal popularity. So much so that, a few years after "Evening at Pops" was first televised, when Seiji Ozawa became music director of the BSO, a musician was in a taxi on his way to a rehearsal at Symphony Hall.

The talkative taxi driver asked, "How's Arthur? And how's that Japanese assistant of his?"

Beacon Hill Cookies

½ teaspoon salt
2 egg whites
½ cup sugar
½ teaspoon vinegar
½ teaspoon vanilla extract
½ cup flaked coconut
¼ cup chopped walnuts
1 (12-ounce) package chocolate chips, melted

Preheat the oven to 350°. Grease a cookie sheet.

In a bowl add the salt to the egg whites, and beat until foamy. Add the sugar gradually, beating after each addition. Continue beating until stiff peaks form. Add the vinegar and vanilla, and beat well. Fold in the coconut, chopped nuts and melted chocolate chips.

Drop teaspoons of the batter onto the greased cookie sheet. Bake for 10 minutes.

Yield: 2 to 2 ½ dozen cookies

These cookies are lovely with ice cream or sorbet.

Walnut Butter Cookies

4 ounces (1 stick) butter, softened
½ cup brown sugar
2 eggs, separated
1 teaspoon vanilla extract
2 cups sifted flour
Ground nuts for coating
Choice of jam (strawberry, raspberry or apricot) for filling

Preheat the oven to 350°. Grease a cookie sheet.

Cream the butter and sugar in a bowl. Mix in well the egg yolks, vanilla and flour.

Place the egg whites in a small bowl. Place the nuts in another bowl, or on waxed paper on a work surface. Make walnut-size balls of dough. Dip each ball into first the egg whites and then the nuts. Make a dent in each ball, placing in each depression some jam of your choice.

Put the balls onto the greased cookie sheet and bake for 20 minutes. Cool.

Yield: 1 ½ to 2 dozen cookies, depending on the size of the balls

Arthur Fiedler, John Williams, and Keith Lockhart have all made Christmas holiday recordings that are still popular with the public.

In December 1998 Keith Lockhart and the Boston Pops released "Holiday at Pops." Keith broke the record for one-day sales of a single CD at a local music store when he appeared for an autographing session.

True to his word, Keith signed over 600 CDs for those attending one evening.

Currier & Chives

Currier & Chives' Head Chef Matt Daignieult shares his recipe for these great cookies.

Although Boston area-based, the caterer drives to Tanglewood to provide special dinner and picnics on the grounds each summer.

Lemon Puckers

8 ounces (2 sticks) butter, softened
3 ounces cream cheese
1 cup sugar
1 egg yolk
½ teaspoon lemon zest
2½ cups flour
½ teaspoon salt
1 cup finely chopped walnuts
3 tablespoons lemon juice
¾ cup sifted powdered sugar

Cream the butter and cream cheese in a mixing bowl. Mix in the sugar and then the egg yolk. Add the lemon zest and mix well.

Separately, mix the salt with the flour; then add small amounts at a time to the butter mixture. Blend well after each addition. Mix in the walnuts and refrigerate the dough for 2 hours.

When the dough is ready to bake, preheat the oven to 325° and lightly grease a cookie sheet.

Form the dough into 3 logs, each approximately 6 inches long. Flatten the logs slightly. Cut twelve 3 by 1-inch ovals from each log.

Bake the cookies on the greased cookie sheet for 18 to 20 minutes or until they are golden brown. Cool the cookies on a rack and glaze them with a mixture of the lemon juice and powdered sugar.

Yield: about 36 cookies

Note: For a more rounded and flatter cookie, reduce the amount of walnuts to ¾ cup.

Anise Cookies

1 cup sugar
4 ounces (1 stick) margarine, melted
4 eggs
1 teaspoon oil of anise
1 tablespoon baking powder
3 cups flour

Frosting:
1 heaping cup confectioners' sugar
½ teaspoon vanilla extract
Milk, for the glaze
Sprinkles (optional)

Preheat the oven to 350°. Spray a cookie sheet.

Mix the sugar, melted margarine, eggs and anise oil in a mixer at low speed. Stir in the baking powder and flour by hand; then mix and knead it in the mixing bowl.

Drop tablespoon-size dough balls onto the sprayed cookie sheet. Bake for 12 to 15 minutes. (Between batches keep the remaining dough refrigerated to make it easier to work with.)

Make the frosting: In a bowl, mix together the confectioners' sugar, vanilla extract, and milk, using just enough milk to make a glaze consistency. Let the cookies cool at least 1 hour before frosting them. You can add sprinkles to the glaze by dipping the cookie into the glaze and then into the sprinkles.

Yield: 24 to 30 cookies

BOSTON
SYMPHONY
ORCHESTRA
SEIJI OZAWA
*Music
Director*

One evening Frank Sinatra came to a concert. During intermission, he came backstage and was greeted by a number of musicians - one of them was Jean LeFranc, former first viola player with the BSO. LeFranc, a quiet, unassuming Frenchman who, although he had lived in the United States for a number of years, knew virtually nothing about this country or the people who inhabited it, and his English was unintelligible. What occurred beyond Symphony Hall did not concern him.

After the performance, LeFranc came to Harry Ellis Dickson and asked, "Who is this man?"

"Haven't you heard of Frank Sinatra?"

"Mais oui, I know the Franck Sonata. Played it many times, but who is this man?"

BOSTON SYMPHONY ORCHESTRA
SEIJI OZAWA
Music Director

Victor Romanul
Violin

Victor Romanul joined the violin section of the orchestra in 1992.

He learned to cook by watching his grandmother, the immortal soprano Stella Roman(ul). Her enormous talent led Richard Strauss to cast her in a starring role in the premiere of his opera "Die Frau ohne schatten" at La Scala. But Victor remembers a grandmother more than a great performer. "She used to visit when I was little and make the Romanian recipes she had grown up with," he says. "It was she who inspired me with the mystery of becoming a musician, and it is she whom I copy in my passionate approach to music."

His contribution to the BSO cookbook is a natural loop. "Bringing a recipe to this cookbook combines my first exposure to great music in both the symphonic and familial senses."

Holiday Cookies

8 ounces (2 sticks) butter, softened
1 cup brown sugar
½ cup sugar
2 eggs
1 teaspoon vanilla extract
½ teaspoon ground cloves
¼ teaspoon ground ginger
½ teaspoon orange zest
2½ cups flour
1 teaspoon baking soda
1 (12-ounce) package chocolate chips
1 cup chopped nuts

Preheat the oven to 325°.

Mix the butter and both sugars in a bowl. Add the eggs and vanilla, mixing well. Mix in the cloves, ginger and orange zest. Add the flour and baking soda, mixing well. Add the chocolate chips and nuts, again mixing thoroughly.

Drop small walnut-size balls of dough onto an ungreased cookie sheet. Bake for 10 to 15 minutes.

Yield: about 3 dozen cookies

Note: To make a more rounded, flatter cookie reduce the nuts to ¾ cup and the chocolate chips to 8 ounces. Use a wet glass bottom to press down on the cookies.

Variation: Rolled oats may be substituted for one half of the flour.

The Best Pie Crust Ever!

2½ cups flour
1 teaspoon salt
1 cup shortening, cold, cut into pieces
1 tablespoon vinegar
½ cup milk

Method #1:
Combine the flour and salt in a mixing bowl. Add the shortening and, working quickly, use a pastry blender, two knives, or your fingertips to cut in the shortening until the mixture resembles coarse crumbs.

Combine the vinegar and milk, and sprinkle over the mixture 1 or 2 tablespoons at a time. Toss after each addition. When you can gather the dough into a ball, divide the dough into halves. Flatten each half slightly, wrap in waxed paper and refrigerate for 30 minutes to 1 hour. (Dough can be frozen at this point, if desired, by first wrapping well in plastic wrap.)

Method #2:
Stir together the flour and salt into a food processor bowl. Arrange shortening pieces around the bowl and imbedded in the flour mixture. Combine the vinegar and milk, and sprinkle evenly over the surface of the flour mixture. Process by turning blades on and off quickly about 8 times. Proceed as above in forming a ball and dividing it into halves.

Yield: 2 large or 3 small pie crusts

You will never buy a pie crust again
after you have made this recipe!

Well-known guest conductors were never invited to guest conduct during Arthur Fiedler's first twenty-five years at the Pops.

There was, however, a young conductor, a Harvard graduate, who, after having won first prize in a musical quiz sponsored by the "Boston Post," was invited to conduct Wagner's "Die Meistersinger" Prelude at an Esplanade Concert. He immediately impressed the orchestra, and later became rather famous in his own right.

His name was Leonard Bernstein.

Aunt Gertrude's Swedish Apple Pie

*4 to 6 Granny Smith apples, peeled, cored and sliced
(enough to fill pie pan ⅔ full)
1 tablespoon sugar
1 teaspoon cinnamon,
or ½ teaspoon each of cinnamon and nutmeg*

For the Topping:
*5⅓ ounces (about 1¼ sticks) margarine, melted
1 cup sugar
1 cup flour
1 egg
¼ cup chopped nuts
⅛ teaspoon salt*

Preheat oven to 350°.

Fill a 9-inch pie pan two-thirds full with the apples. Sprinkle with the sugar and cinnamon.

In a small bowl, combine the margarine, sugar, flour, egg, nuts, and salt. Pour the topping over the apples. Pat down lightly and evenly.

Bake for 45 minutes, or until golden.

Yield: 8 servings

This is a great recipe for anyone opposed to pie crusts!

Southern Pecan Pie

1 cup brown sugar
2 tablespoons butter
3 eggs, beaten
1 cup or more whole pecans
½ cup each light and dark corn syrup, combined
½ teaspoon salt
1 teaspoon vanilla extract
1 prepared uncooked pie crust

Preheat the oven to 350°.

Cream the brown sugar and butter in a bowl. Mix in the eggs, the combined syrups and salt. Stir in the vanilla and pecans. (Alternatively, the pecans may be withheld here, and spread on the pie crust first. The mixture is then poured over them in the next step.)

Pour the mixture into the pie crust. Bake for about 50 minutes.

Yield: 8 servings

Variation: You may add ½ teaspoon ginger and 1 teaspoon lemon juice to the recipe.

BOSTON SYMPHONY ORCHESTRA
SEIJI OZAWA
Music Director

James Cooke
Violin

"This recipe comes from my grandmother and for as long as I can remember, it was always part of our Thanksgiving dinner. It now brings back a flood of loving memories," says James Cooke, who has been a BSO violinist since 1987.

"My recollections of joining the BSO are a little different," he says. Asked to audition at Tanglewood, James was invited to spend the night at Seranak, the former summer home of Serge Koussevitzky. "I spent a sleepless night surrounded by portraits of Serge Koussevitzky, then went back to the Shed where the orchestra was rehearsing the Mahler First," he remembers. "I was completely overwhelmed that I might be joining an orchestra with such sound and rich tradition."

Blueberry-Strawberry Pie

2 unbaked pie crusts ("Best Pie Crust Ever" recipe, p. 251)
1 tablespoon butter
4 tablespoons flour
¾ cup white sugar
½ cup brown sugar
½ teaspoon salt
3 heaping cups blueberries, picked over and stems removed
1 heaping cup hulled and quartered strawberries
1 tablespoon tapioca

Preheat oven to 400°.

You may alternatively prepare a different pie crust recipe. Ensure that it makes 2 crusts for a 9 or 10-inch pie pan. Line the pan with 1 crust and set aside.

Cut the butter into the flour, both sugars and the salt. Toss the berries in these crumbs.

Sprinkle the tapioca on the bottom pie crust. Pour the berries and crumb mixture into the shell. Cover with the top crust. Make several vents in the top crust. Brush it lightly with water; and sprinkle with sugar.

Bake until golden brown - about 40 minutes or more, depending on your oven. Allow the pie to cool until warm before serving, to allow the liquids to congeal.

Yield: 8 servings

A perfect blending of two favorite fruits!
The blueberries and strawberries make a perfect blend
in a pie that smells great and tastes wonderful!

Crustless Cheese Pie

Filling:
16 ounces cream cheese
3 eggs
¾ cup sugar
1 teaspoon almond extract
¼ teaspoon salt

Topping:
1 cup sour cream
1 teaspoon vanilla extract
3 tablespoons sugar

Preheat the oven to 350°. Butter a 9-inch pie dish.

Make the filling: In a bowl, mix together the cream cheese, eggs, sugar, almond extract and salt. Mix well until the ingredients have a smooth consistency. Pour the mixture into the buttered pie dish, and bake for 25 minutes, or until a golden crust forms. Set aside to cool.

Make the topping: In a bowl mix together the sour cream, vanilla, and sugar. Mix well until the ingredients have a smooth consistency. Once the pie has cooled for at least 10 minutes, pour the topping onto the pie leaving formed crust showing. Chill overnight.

Yield: 6 to 8 servings

Serving Suggestion: Pie may be served as is, or fresh strawberries or blueberries may be placed on top in a decorative pattern.

BOSTON SYMPHONY ORCHESTRA
SEIJI OZAWA
Music Director

Geralyn Coticone
Piccolo

Geralyn Coticone plays the piccolo in the woodwind section of the orchestra.

Along with her recipe, Geralyn provided the following comments:

"The summer before I joined the BSO, a colleague in the National Symphony Orchestra gave me a copy of the first BSO cookbook as a going-away present. I thoroughly enjoyed reading all the recipes (and trying a few from the wonderful musicians that I respected so much). Little did I know that I would be contributing a recipe to the latest new cookbook."

"I hope you enjoy this easy recipe as much a I do."

Wayne Rapier
Oboe

Retired BSO oboe Wayne Rapier is the founder of Boston Records, a nonprofit corporation that relies on financial contributions to produce unique CD recordings of live recitals. Most recordings have featured BSO orchestra members, including Harold Wright, Ann Hobson Pilot, and Wayne himself. He is also a commercial pilot.

This New England pie was given to us by Wayne and his wife Toni.

Cranberry Surprise Pie

6 to 7 ounces chopped cranberries
½ cup chopped nuts
½ cup frozen blueberries
⅓ cup shredded coconut
1 ½ cups sugar, divided
1 egg
½ cup flour
6 tablespoons (¾ stick) melted butter

Preheat the oven to 325°.

Spread the cranberries to cover the bottom of an 8-inch pie pan. (Chop more cranberries, if necessary, to fully cover the bottom.) Cover the cranberries with the nuts, blueberries and coconut. Sprinkle 1 cup of the sugar over them.

In a bowl beat the egg well; add the remaining ½ cup of sugar and mix thoroughly. Add the flour and butter; mix well. Spread evenly over the cranberry mixture.

Bake for 45 minutes.

Yield: 8 servings

Serving suggestion: Serve the pie warm with vanilla ice cream.

Cran-Apple Crisp

5 cups sliced tart apples (about 6 medium-sized)
1 ½ cups fresh or frozen cranberries
⅓ cup granulated sugar

Topping:
½ cup all-purpose flour
½ cup brown sugar
1 teaspoon cinnamon
¼ cup butter or margarine

Preheat the oven to 375°. Grease a 9-inch square pan.

Layer the apples and cranberries in the pan, sprinkling them with granulated sugar as you layer.

Make the topping: In a bowl, mix together the flour, brown sugar, and cinnamon. Cut in the butter until light and crumbly. Sprinkle this topping evenly over the apple-cranberry mix.

Bake in the oven for 45 minutes. Serve while still warm.

Yield: 6 to 8 servings

Serving Suggestion: Serve the crisp with a scoop of ice cream or hard sauce.

July 4, 1979 was the first Independence Day Esplanade Concert in fifty years not to be conducted by Arthur Fiedler, due to his illness. It was at Harry Ellis Dickson's suggestion that Arthur's wife Ellen would narrate Aaron Copland's "Lincoln Portrait," which she had done previously with the Maestro. Before she appeared on the stage that night, with Dickson conducting, the audience was told, "For fifty years there has been a Fiedler on this stage, and tonight is no exception."

Lemon Ice Torte
with Strawberry-Raspberry Sauce

Crust:
3 cups blanched slivered almonds, toasted
½ cup sugar
5 tablespoons butter
¼ teaspoon ground cinnamon

Filling:
⅓ cup strawberry preserves
3 pints lemon sorbet or sherbet

Sauce:
1 cup sugar, divided
½ cup water
1 vanilla bean, split lengthwise (or ½ teaspoon vanilla extract)
1 (20-ounce) package frozen unsweetened raspberries
1 (20-ounce) package frozen unsweetened strawberries
1 pint fresh strawberries
Fresh mint sprigs, for garnish

Make the crust: Combine the almonds and sugar in a processor and chop finely. Transfer the mixture to a medium-sized bowl. Separately, combine the butter and cinnamon. Mix into the almonds. Transfer the combined mixture to a 9-inch springform pan. Using plastic wrap as an aid, press the almond mixture firmly 2 inches up the sides and then over the bottom of the pan. Freeze for 15 minutes.

Preheat the oven to 350°.

Place the pan with the crust on a cookie sheet and bake for 20 minutes. If the crust sides slip, press them back with the back of a fork. Transfer the pan to a rack and cool the crust completely.

Make the filling: Melt the strawberry preserves in a small heavy saucepan. Pour the preserves into the cooled crust and spread to cover the bottom. Cool.

Soften the sorbet or sherbet slightly and spread into the pan. Cover and freeze until firm. (Can be prepared 1 day ahead.)

Make the sauce: Combine ½ cup of the sugar and ½ cup water in a medium heavy saucepan. Scrape in the seeds from the vanilla bean; add the pod. If using vanilla extract, do not add it here, but rather after the frozen fruit is added (see below). Simmer for 5 minutes. Add the remaining ½ cup sugar and stir to dissolve.

Lemon Ice Torte with Strawberry-Raspberry Sauce *continued*

Add the frozen raspberries and frozen strawberries. Cover and bring to a simmer. Cool. Cover and refrigerate until well chilled. (If vanilla extract was used, it should be added after the sauce cools slightly.) (Recipe can be prepared to this point 1 day ahead.)

If the vanilla pod was used, remove it from the sauce. Cut between the crust and pan sides with a small sharp knife. Remove the pan sides. Spoon ½ cup of the sauce over the center of the torte. Mound fresh strawberries in the center. Garnish with fresh mint sprigs. Cut the torte into slices and serve with remaining sauce.

Yield: 10 to 12 servings

Variation: If available, one 20-ounce package frozen unsweetened rhubarb may be substituted for the raspberries. Add the rhubarb to the recipe before the frozen strawberries, bringing the mixture to a boil. Reduce the heat, cover and simmer until the rhubarb is tender, about 5 to 8 minutes. Then add the frozen strawberries and proceed as above.

After Arthur Fiedler's death in 1979, Harry Ellis Dickson was one of several conductors being considered to succeed the maestro of the Pops. When John Williams was selected, Harry made the following comments:

"I think that getting John Williams was a stroke of genius. Not only a fine musician, he is warm and sensitive, a person of great decency, and very modest; I don't know if I have ever met a more humble conductor. He is a dear man, and I feel very good about working with him."

BOSTON SYMPHONY ORCHESTRA
SEIJI OZAWA
Music Director

When John Williams began his illustrious career as Pops conductor, he was well aware that the Pops concert format was an informal one, with people eating and drinking during the performance.

The din caused by the glass-ware and utensils prompted on inquiry from him, however.

John wondered if they could serve "quieter food."

Mocha Brownie Torte

1 (21½-ounce) package fudge brownie mix
¼ cup water
2 eggs
½ cup finely chopped nuts
1½ cups whipping cream, chilled
⅓ cup brown sugar
1 tablespoon instant coffee
Shaved chocolate, for sprinkling

Preheat the oven to 350°. Grease and flour two 9 by 1½-inch round layer pans.

Blend the dry brownie mix, water and eggs. Stir in the nuts; distribute the mixture equally in the two pans. Bake for 20 minutes; remove the pans from the oven and cool the cakes for 5 minutes in the pans. Then remove the cakes from the pans and place them on wire racks to cool completely.

In a chilled bowl, beat the cream until it begins to thicken. Gradually add the sugar and instant coffee. Continue beating until stiff.

Spread one half of the cream mixture on the top of one cake. Place the unfrosted cake on top, and frost it with the remaining cream mixture. Sprinkle on the chocolate shavings. Chill at least 1 hour.

Yield: 10 to 12 servings

Note: Torte may be made one day in advance and refrigerated overnight.

This is a delicious "do ahead" dessert.

Sweet Noodle Pudding

12 ounces wide noodles, cooked and drained
⅓ cup sugar
16 ounces fat-free cottage cheese
8 ounces plain yogurt (or sour cream)
1 teaspoon cinnamon
4 ounces (1 stick) margarine, melted
1 cup golden raisins (optional)
1 teaspoon vanilla extract
1 (15-ounce) can crushed pineapple, drained, juice reserved
4 eggs
Milk (quantity needed that, when added
to reserved pineapple juice, equals 2 cups total liquid)
Crushed corn flakes, for topping
Additional cinnamon and sugar, for topping

Preheat oven to 350°. Grease a casserole.

Put the cooked noodles, sugar, cottage cheese, yogurt, cinnamon, margarine, raisins, vanilla and pineapple into the greased casserole. In a bowl, beat the eggs; mix in the 2 cups pineapple liquid mixture. Pour over the noodle mixture. (The recipe may be refrigerated at this point overnight.)

Top with the crushed corn flakes, and sprinkle with additional cinnamon and sugar. Bake for 1 hour or until brown.

Yield: 12 servings

Note: The recipe can be made in smaller casseroles, if desired.

BOSTON
SYMPHONY
ORCHESTRA
SEIJI OZAWA
Music Director

Alfred Schneider
Violin

Soloist, chamber player, and orchestra member all describe Alfred Schneider's versatile career. A graduate of the Eastman School of Music and a student of the Tanglewood Music Center, he has performed with the Rochester Civic Orchestra, the Rochester Philharmonic, and the St. Louis Symphony. An aficionado of chamber music, Alfred and three BSO colleagues founded the Gabrielli String Quartet and have performed throughout New England.

This sweet noodle pudding is a favorite recipe of the Schneider family.

BOSTON
SYMPHONY
ORCHESTRA
SEIJI OZAWA
*Music
Director*

John Williams' association with the Boston Pops was marked by many major accomplishments.

Under Arthur Fiedler the Pops was well-attended and financially successful. But it was always a second cousin to the Boston Symphony until Williams' arrival. He was the perfect choice to succeed Fiedler. He is a man with a serious classical background and training (he is a graduate of the Juilliard School in New York), and has a knowledge and feeling for American popular music.

During his tenure he raised the Pops to a new level of popularity both here and around the world.

Apple Indian Pudding

2 medium apples, peeled, cored and sliced
⅓ cup corn meal
½ cup molasses
½ cup sugar
1 teaspoon salt
1 scant teaspoon ginger
1 quart milk
1 tablespoon butter
1 teaspoon cinnamon

Preheat oven to 325°. Grease a casserole dish.

Mix well in a bowl the apples, corn meal, molasses, sugar, salt, ginger, milk, butter, and cinnamon. Then place the mixture in the prepared casserole dish. Bake for 1 ¼ to 2 hours. (Check for doneness after 1 ¼ hours, and adjust final cooking time accordingly.) Stir 3 or 4 times during the first hour.

Yield: 4 to 6 servings

Bread Pudding with Caramelized Pears

2 eggs
3½ cups milk
1⅔ cups sugar, divided
1 tablespoon vanilla extract
1½ teaspoons cinnamon
¾ teaspoon grated nutmeg
⅛ cup raisins (optional)
8 ounces dried bread, crusts removed
1 cup water
1½ to 2 pounds (about 5 to 6 medium)
Anjou or Bosc pears, peeled, cored and halved
Heavy cream (optional)

In a bowl beat the eggs. Add the milk, ⅔ cup of the sugar, vanilla, cinnamon, nutmeg, and the raisins, if desired. Mix; add the bread and soak at least 20 minutes. Break up the bread thoroughly, removing any tough or hard bits.

In a large heavy pan bring 1 cup of water to a boil with the remaining 1 cup of sugar. Add pear halves and simmer gently until tender. Remove the pears from the syrup with a slotted spoon, and set aside. Bring the syrup to a boil, and continue boiling until the syrup is caramelized. Place a scant teaspoon of the syrup in the bottom of each of 12 custard cups, and then top with a slice of the reserved pears.

Preheat the oven to 350°.

Fill the cups with the bread pudding mixture. Place the cups in a pan on a towel, and add boiling water until the water level is 1 inch up the sides of the cups. Bake for 30 to 35 minutes, or until a knife inserted in the middle of the cup comes out clean. Cool the puddings in the pan.

To serve, run a knife around the edge of the custard cups and invert the puddings onto a dessert plate. Serve warm, cool or at room temperature with heavy cream as an accompaniment, if desired.

Yield: 12 to 14 servings

Strawberries Romanoff

*2 quarts ripe strawberries, cleaned,
hulled, and cut into quarters, or sliced
½ cup rum
Rind of 1 grapefruit, cut into very thin slivers,
with no white membranes
Rind of 1 orange, cut into very thin slivers,
with no white membranes*

*Custard:
3 eggs, beaten slightly
3 tablespoons sugar
½ pint light cream
½ pint heavy cream
Sugar
Vanilla extract
½ cup crumbled macaroons*

Place the strawberries in a bowl. Pour the rum over them. Boil the rinds until tender, drain and add to the strawberries. Let the mixture stand for 3 hours.

Fill a large bowl with ice cubes (to be used to cool the custard).

Make the custard: In the top of a double boiler cook the eggs, sugar and light cream over medium heat, stirring constantly. Remove the pan from the stove immediately when the liquid coats the spoon that you are stirring it with. Take care not to overcook the custard. (Overcooking will cause the custard to resemble scrambled eggs, although it will not affect the taste.) Place the pan in the bowl of ice cubes. The custard needs to be cooled completely.

Whip the cream and add the sugar and vanilla to taste.

To serve, chill a large crystal bowl. Into it pour the mixture of strawberries, fruit rinds, custard and whipped cream. Top with the crumbled macaroons. (Chill well after adding the strawberries.)

Yield: 6 to 8 servings

Variation: In place of the whipped cream, use 1 pint of vanilla ice cream.

*This wonderful dessert dish is just as
tasty without the whipped cream or macaroons!*

Marblehead Berries

1 pint strawberries
1 tablespoon kirsch
½-inch piece vanilla bean (or 1 teaspoon vanilla extract)
¼ cup powdered sugar
⅔ cup sour cream
1 tablespoon light cream

Gently wash, hull, and cut the strawberries in half lengthwise. Place the strawberries in a glass serving bowl and sprinkle with the kirsch. Place in the refrigerator for 2 hours or more.

Meanwhile, in a bowl, place the vanilla bean in the powdered sugar. Cover and let stand for 2 hours or more. Remove the vanilla bean and mix in the sugar with the sour cream. Mix in the light cream. Gently fold the cream mixture over the strawberries, and let stand for 1 hour or more. Serve chilled.

Yield: 4 servings

Photo: Courtesy of Ginny Martens

BOSTON
SYMPHONY
ORCHESTRA
SEIJI OZAWA
Music Director

New Year's Eve with the Boston Pops

The members of the Symphony Hall house crew are our unsung heroes. Early in the morning of December 31, the crew, along with eight strong high school students, prepares to transform the hall into a ballroom for the annual New Year's Eve Party.

A number of Pops tables and chairs are cleared away, the floor opens, and extra tables and chairs are lowered into the basement. Boxes and boxes of festive decorations and party favors are unpacked. The stage is dismantled and redecorated for the evening and the hall is polished. All of the details are in place for a Pops-style New Year's Eve celebration.

At the end of the evening, when the last guests have left, the house crew begins the immediate clean-up. After a one-day break, they are back at work, storing the tables and chairs, removing the stage decorations, and reinstalling the banks of seats for the return of the symphony.

Fruit Pizza

1¾ cups sifted cake flour
¾ cup corn starch
3 teaspoons baking powder
1 teaspoon salt
1 cup sugar, divided
⅓ cup salad oil
1 cup milk, divided
1½ teaspoons vanilla
2 eggs, separated

Topping:
1 (8-ounce) package whipped cream cheese
¼ cup 10x powdered sugar
Variety of fruit selections from:
canned/drained Mandarin orange slices,
halved red seedless grapes, halved pineapple chunks,
red cherries, strawberries, or ground nuts

Preheat the oven to 350°.

Sift the flour, corn starch, salt and ½ cup of the sugar into a mixing bowl. Make a well and add the salad oil along with ½ cup of the milk and the vanilla. Blend. Beat for 1 minute at medium speed. Add the remaining ½ cup of milk and the 2 egg yolks. Beat for 1 minute.

In a glass bowl, beat the 2 egg whites until soft peaks form. Gradually add the remaining ½ cup of sugar. Beat until very stiff. Fold into the batter.

Put the batter into 2 layer cake pans. (This will make 2 separate bases for 2 fruit pizzas.) Bake for 12 to 15 minutes. If you need only one pizza base now, the other may be frozen before the cheese and fruit are added.) Cool.

When the cake is cool, spread the whipped cream cheese on top of a cake layer. Sprinkle lightly with powdered sugar. Use fruit and nuts as desired.

Suggested use of fruit and nuts: (Drain all fruit on a paper towel before assembling.) Place canned and drained Mandarin orange slices on the outer edge, with the halved grapes arranged in a second row. Follow with a row of pineapple chunks, and place cherries or strawberries in the center. Sprinkle finely ground pecans between rows of fruit and around the cherries.

With a biscuit cutter, cut an outline around the center. The orange slices indicate each serving.

Yield: 8 to 16 servings

Serving Suggestion: This fruit pizza makes a great luncheon dish for a vegetarian meal!

Englemot

½ cup cream
½ cup milk
½ cup sugar
4 ounces (1 stick) butter, or margarine
½ teaspoon salt
1 egg, beaten
6 cardamom pods
1 envelope (1 tablespoon) dry yeast
3½ to 4 cups flour
1 pint whipped cream, sweetened
10 ounces lingonberry liqueur

Bring the cream and milk to a boil in a pan; add in the sugar and butter. When the sugar is dissolved and the butter is melted, add the salt and egg. Remove the pan from the heat and let the milk mixture cool down at least to room temperature.

Mash the seeds from the cardamom pods and add them to the mixture. Dissolve the yeast in the milk mixture. Add enough flour until the mixture is no longer sticky. Allow it to rise to double its size. When it has risen, punch it down and allow it to rise until doubled once again. Make it into one large braid and allow it to rise still again.

Preheat oven to 350°.

Bake the bread until it is lightly browned; then remove it from the oven and allow it to cool. When cooled, break the braid into small pieces and layer the bread pieces in a bowl. Place a layer of sweetened whipped cream on the bread layer. Then place a "layer" of lingonberry liqueur on top. Repeat the procedure with another layer of bread pieces. Continue until the bowl is full. Allow it to sit throughout the day in the refrigerator to "season".

Yield: 12 servings

Note: This Swedish bread may be made 1 day ahead.

Note: Use caution in adding the liqueur, since it is quite strong.

Variation: This is a delicious bread by itself.

BOSTON
SYMPHONY
ORCHESTRA
SEIJI OZAWA
*Music
Director*

The planners of Symphony Hall preserved the original formula for the paint used in the hall's interior. Each spring the lower maroon walls of the hall used to be painted green for the Pops season, then repainted in the fall for the winter concerts, a practice discontinued some years ago. Since 1900 the walls have carried over 130 coats of paint! It is no wonder that some of the older subscribers voiced the opinion that the hall seems to be getting narrower!

BOSTON
SYMPHONY
ORCHESTRA
SEIJI OZAWA
*Music
Director*

Symphony Clusters

*1 cup canned chow mein noodles
1 cup lightly salted or unsalted peanuts
4½ (7-ounce) plain chocolate candy bars
12 ounces baking raisins*

Crush the chow mein noodles to break up the larger pieces. Ensure that most of the nuts are similarly broken into halves. Break up the chocolate bars, and melt the pieces in the top of a double boiler, being careful not to get the water vapor into the mix, inasmuch as it will make it grainy.

When the chocolate is melted, add the nuts, noodles and raisins, and mix thoroughly, making sure that all the added components are thoroughly coated with the melted chocolate. Using a teaspoon, drop bite-size chunks of the molten mix onto cookie sheets lined with waxed paper. (This procedure is easier if an extra spoon is used to assist in moving chunks onto the paper.) Put the sheets of chocolate in a cool place and allow the candy to harden thoroughly before removing it from the waxed paper. It is best to keep the chocolate clusters in a cool place or in the refrigerator until use.

Yield: 60 to 180 clusters, depending on size

Note: If, at any time, the mix is so thick that it is hard to work with, optionally melt some of the remaining chocolate. But if the chocolate is kept quite thick, the clusters will have good height and appearance, and will not flatten out. Additionally, making smaller clusters equals more work!

TANGLEWOOD

An evening Concert at Tanglewood

Sentinel Pines at the Tanglewood entrance

TANGLEWOOD

Photo by: © Stu Rosner

Since the 1930s the BSO's summer home at Tanglewood, amidst the beauty of the Berkshire hills, has occupied a special place in the hearts of music lovers. In the small town of Lenox, Massachusetts, the BSO's summer program of orchestral and chamber music and brilliant guest artists found a natural home. The 526 acres of grounds, including the Bernstein Campus and the Tappan and Highwood estates, are manicured expanses of woods and grass. A cluster of buildings, including the Koussevitzky Music Shed and Seiji Ozawa Hall, were designed for music and, together with picnicking on the lawn, provide the ideal landscape for music.

Tanglewood received its start in August 1934, through the diligence of Berkshire-area arts patron Gertrude Robinson Smith. Smith's persistence and love of music paid off in a series of concerts performed by members of the New York Philharmonic. The venture's success inspired the promoters to repeat the program the following summer. Then, in 1936, at the invitation of the festival committee, Serge Koussevitzky and the BSO gave their first performance in the Berkshires.

Later that same year, Mrs. Gorham Brooks and Miss Mary Aspinwall Tappan donated the 210-acre Tappan family estate, called Tanglewood, to Koussevitzky and the BSO. In 1937, a large audience crowded into a tent for the first concert. The weather quickly pointed out the downside of open-air concerts: Torrential rain and a thunderstorm drowned out the music and leaked onto the musicians. The next day, Smith went to work to raise funds for a permanent structure.

Photo by: © Stu Rosner

Built at a cost of $100,000, the Music Shed was inaugurated in 1938 and is still used today. It has a seating capacity of almost 6,000. In 1959, the installation of the Talbot Orchestra Canopy, along with other improvements, produced the Music Shed's world-famous acoustics. On the shed's 50th anniversary in 1988, it was named in honor of Koussevitzky.

Attracting more than 375,000 visitors each summer, Tanglewood offers music lovers a vast quantity of music in a wide range of musical forms and styles. In addition to BSO concerts every weekend, the season includes more than forty Tanglewood Music Center concerts of orchestra, opera, and chamber music during July and August. Each year in late July, the Festival of Contemporary Music mixes previously introduced 20th century works with fresh new pieces. The Boston Pops performs its signature blend of light classics, symphonic jazz, and classical music at Tanglewood. Recently, a weekend of jazz has been added to close the summer season.

Picnics on Tanglewood's green lawn before the evening concerts have become a tradition for many music lovers. Tanglewood, through a sponsored program, provides free admission to the lawn for children under 12. For many youngsters picnicking on the lawn with their families, this becomes their first concert experience. The picnics are especially popular before the Pops concerts and Tanglewood on Parade, one of the summer's highlights. Tanglewood on Parade features both the BSO and the TMC Orchestra, and serves as a showcase for TMC students. Along with the music, hot-air balloons and the

bagpipe-playing Berkshire Highlanders add to the festive spirit. Whether they unpack cartons of fried chicken or set out elaborate table settings complete with candelabra, thousands of concert-goers picnic in a party atmosphere. The thunder of live cannons at the conclusion of the eagerly awaited *1812 Overture* and the post-concert fireworks display always make this evening a memorable one.

The Tappan Manor House now serves as a Visitors Center. There are gift shops, music stores, and cafeterias. Motivated by a desire to offer visitors insight into the history of Tanglewood, the late Carrie Peace instituted the Tour Guide program. This component has been an integral part of Tanglewood for many years.

Tanglewood boasts hundreds of volunteers working in a variety of roles to keep the summer festival running. They help plan the Opening Night Gala, assist customers in the gift shops, serve refreshments in the Tent Club, and arrange flowers on the tables at the Highwood Sunday brunch and Supper Club. As always, the volunteers continue to work as program guides and ushers in the Music Shed and Ozawa Hall.

Each summer Tanglewood provides the perfect setting where, to paraphrase that popular Broadway musical, the hills truly are alive with the sound of music.

PICNICS AT TANGLEWOOD

Tanglewood

A Family Picnic

Menu

English Cucumber Soup
Mediterranean Pasta Salad
Chocolate Mint Brownies

Wines

Ca'vit Pinot Grigio 1997
Domaine du Colombier Crozes-Hermitage 1996
Côtes du Rhône (White), Coudoulet de Beaucastel 1996

English Cucumber Soup

3 medium English cucumbers, unpeeled
3 cups (fat-free) chicken broth
3 cups nonfat yogurt
3 tablespoons white wine vinegar
1 to 3 cloves garlic
1 teaspoon salt
½ teaspoon pepper
1 to 2 packets of sugar substitute (optional)

Cut the cucumber into chunks to facilitate processing.

Combine the cucumbers with the chicken broth, yogurt, vinegar, garlic, salt, pepper, and sugar substitute (if used). Put the mixture into a processor, and purée. Refrigerate at least 1 to 2 hours.

Yield: about 12 servings

Dave Sturma, Director of Tanglewood Facilities and BSO Liaison to the Berkshires, ensures that the beauty of the Tanglewood grounds is renewed each season. He has an interesting comment about selecting your picnic site at Tanglewood:

"People sitting on the lawn for evening concerts are more likely to be 'mosquito bait' the closer they sit to the wooded areas at the edges of the lawn."

Yehudi Menuhin
by Martha Burnham Humphrey

Mediterranean Pasta Salad

Dressing:
⅔ cup olive oil
3 tablespoons red wine vinegar
4 tablespoons (¼ cup) finely chopped fresh basil, divided
2 tablespoons chopped green onion
2 tablespoons freshly grated Parmesan cheese
1¼ teaspoons salt
¼ teaspoon pepper

12 ounces rotini pasta, cooked and drained (about 6 cups)
1 small red bell pepper, cored, seeded, cut into thin strips
1 small green bell pepper, cored, seeded, cut into thin strips
1 small yellow bell pepper, cored, seeded, cut into thin strips
10 or 12 cherry tomatoes, halved
½ cup ripe black olives, pitted and halved
¼ cup pine nuts, toasted
8 ounces feta cheese, cubed
½ teaspoon oregano

In a blender, process the oil and vinegar with 2 tablespoons of the basil, the green onion, Parmesan cheese, salt and pepper. Set the dressing aside.

In a large bowl combine the cooked pasta with the peppers, cherry tomatoes, olives and nuts. Pour the dressing over pasta mixture and toss well.

Roll the cheese cubes in the remaining 2 tablespoons of basil to coat, then add them to the salad. Sprinkle on the oregano and toss again.

Yield: 12 servings

Chocolate Mint Brownies

2 (1-ounce) squares unsweetened chocolate
4 ounces (1 stick) margarine
2 eggs
1 cup sugar
½ teaspoon peppermint extract
½ cup flour
¼ teaspoon salt
½ cup walnuts, chopped (optional)

Frosting:
2 tablespoons margarine
1 cup confectioners' sugar
1 tablespoon milk
½ teaspoon peppermint extract

Glaze: (optional)
1 (1-ounce) square unsweetened chocolate
1 tablespoon margarine

Preheat oven to 350°. Grease an 8 or 9-inch square baking pan.

Melt the chocolate squares and margarine in a double boiler over low heat. Beat the eggs until frothy and stir in the sugar, chocolate mixture and peppermint. Add the flour, salt and nuts; mix well.

Spread the batter in the greased baking pan. Bake 20 to 25 minutes. Cool.

Make the frosting: Work the margarine into the confectioners' sugar. Add the milk and peppermint, and mix well. Spread over the cooled brownies.

Make the glaze (if used): Melt the chocolate square and the margarine together. Mix well. Drizzle over the frosted brownies.

After adding the frosting (and the optional glaze), refrigerate the brownies. When ready to serve, cut the brownies into 2-inch squares.

Yield: 16 brownies

Leonard Bernstein

Composer and conductor Leonard Bernstein was a beloved figure at Tanglewood for fifty years. Although he traveled around the globe performing music, Tanglewood had a special effect on him. "All he had to do was breathe that air," family members remarked.

After all that Tanglewood had given to him, he felt it was his responsibility to give back. Thus, the maestro devoted the summers of his final years to sharing his musical genius with students at the Tanglewood Music Center.

Picnic on the Lawn

Menu

Vegetarian Pâté
Sweet and Sour Chicken
Broccoli Salad
Herbed Onion Bread
Sour Cream Marble Coffee Cake

Wines

Roses (really - try them!):
George Duboeuf Syrah, Vin de Pays d'Oc Rosé 1996
Vin Gris de Agar (California) 1996
Domaine Ott 1996 - save the lovely bottle!

Vegetarian Pâté

½ cup walnuts
1 (10-ounce) can baby green peas, drained
4 hard boiled eggs
2 large onions, chopped
2 tablespoons oil

Chop the walnuts in a food processor (but not too fine). Remove the nuts from the processor and place them in a large bowl.

Process the green peas until almost smooth, and place them in the bowl with the nuts. Repeat with the hard boiled eggs.

In a skillet, sauté the onions in 2 tablespoons of oil until translucent, but not brown. Add the onions to the other ingredients in the bowl. Mix well and refrigerate covered at least 1 to 2 hours.

Serve with crackers.

Yield: 8 servings

Variation: For a low-cholesterol version, use only the egg whites.

Sweet and Sour Chicken

½ cup brown sugar
¼ cup pineapple juice
¼ cup water
¼ cup salad oil
¼ cup soy sauce
2 garlic cloves, minced
2 teaspoons sesame seeds
1 teaspoon ground ginger
2 frying chickens, cut in eighths

In a bowl, make a marinade by mixing together the brown sugar, pineapple juice, water, salad oil, soy sauce, garlic, sesame seeds, and ginger. Put the chicken in a plastic bag and pour in the marinade mixture. Seal the bag tightly and let it marinate in refrigerator overnight.

Preheat oven to 350°.

Place the chicken and marinade in a baking pan at least 13 by 9-inches in size, which has been coated with a nonstick spray. Bake covered for 20 minutes. Uncover and bake an additional 30 minutes more.

Raise the oven temperature to 400°, and bake the chicken an additional 10 to 15 minutes, or until chicken juices are clear.

Yield: 8 servings

The Three Birthdays

Three birthdays were celebrated on one glorious summer Sunday afternoon, on July 23, 1995, at Tanglewood.

Seiji Ozawa was turning 60, violinist Itzhak Perlman was turning 50, and cellist Yo-Yo Ma was turning 40.

Seiji Ozawa conducted the first half of the afternoon concert, after which the musical party of special birthday offerings began. John Williams had composed a special "Happy Birthday" piece, which he and the orchestra had secretly rehearsed. This was a complete surprise to all three honorees, but especially for Seiji, who had rehearsed the orchestra that morning, after which he was quickly hustled off the grounds so Maestro Williams and the orchestra could prepare the piece for the afternoon concert.

This grand birthday party was enjoyed by over 5,000 people in the Shed and another 10,000 picnicking on the lawn.

**Dimitri Mitropoulos
by Olga Koussevitzky**

Broccoli Salad

4 cups broccoli florets
½ cup raisins
1 medium onion, chopped
4 slices crispy fried bacon, crumbled
¼ cup sunflower seeds

Dressing:
1 cup mayonnaise
2 tablespoons vinegar
2 tablespoons sugar

Combine the broccoli, raisins, red onion, bacon and sunflower seeds in a bowl.

Make the dressing: Combine the mayonnaise, vinegar, and sugar in a small bowl. Pour over the salad and serve immediately.

Yield: 4 servings

Note: The vegetables will stay crisp if the dressing is not added until just before serving the salad.

Herbed Onion Bread

8 tablespoons (1 stick) butter or margarine, divided
3 cups finely chopped onions
6 cups buttermilk baking mix
2 eggs
2 teaspoons minced fresh basil
3 teaspoons finely snipped fresh dill

Preheat oven to 375°. Grease a round 9 by 2-inch baking pan.

Melt one half of the butter in a skillet and sauté the onions in it until tender.

Combine in a large bowl the baking mix, eggs, milk, basil and dill, mixing just until blended.

Spoon the mixture into the greased pan. Bake for 60 to 70 minutes.

Melt the remaining half of the butter and brush it on the top of the bread.

Yield: 1 loaf (about 6 to 8 servings)

Sour Cream Marble Coffee Cake

1 cup sugar
8 tablespoons (1 stick) butter
2 eggs
1 teaspoon baking soda
8 ounces (½ pint) sour cream
2 cups flour
1 teaspoon baking powder
Pinch salt
1 ½ teaspoons pure vanilla extract

Filling:
½ cup chopped walnuts
2 tablespoons flour
1 tablespoon cinnamon
¼ cup cocoa or chocolate chips
½ cup brown sugar

Preheat the oven to 350°.

Cream together the sugar and butter in a bowl. Continue mixing, adding one egg at a time.

In another bowl, mix the baking soda in the sour cream and then add it to the egg mixture. Sift together the flour, baking powder, and salt; then gradually blend it into the egg mixture. Mix in the vanilla and set aside.

Make the filling: Combine the walnuts, flour, cinnamon, cocoa and brown sugar in a bowl.

Place one half of the batter into a greased tube or springform pan. Sprinkle on one half of the filling; then cut it through with a knife. Add the remaining batter, and top with the rest of the filling.

Bake for 45 minutes.

Yield: 12 to 14 servings

Bernstein's Final Concert

"Bernstein weather" was a euphemism well known to concert-goers at Tanglewood. No matter how dreary the weather, the skies somehow would clear on most days when Leonard Bernstein was conducting at Tanglewood.

However, August 19, 1990, did not follow the pattern. "It was a cold, rainy and gray day," remembered one concert-goer. "It seemed more like a dark November day." The dark clouds were like a prelude to a concert that no one who attended will ever forget. Leonard Bernstein conducted Beethoven's Symphony No. 7 to a rousing ovation.

Soon after the concert the seventy-two-year-old maestro noted that he had conducted his first major concert at Tanglewood, and that he had just conducted his last concert in the same venue exactly fifty years later. His prophetic words rang true; the music world mourned his loss two months later.

Tanglewood

Seafood Picnic

Menu

Tomato and Orange Soup
Tapenade
Paella Salad
Chocolate Delight Bars

Wines

Crisp White Wines from Australia:
Giesen Sauvignon Blanc Marlborough 1997
Tyrrells Semillon-Sauvignon Blanc 1997
A special treat:
Cloudy Bay Sauvignon Blanc Marlborough 1997

Tomato and Orange Soup

2 cups tomato juice
2 cups orange juice
3 tablespoons lemon juice
Celery salt
Chopped parsley, for garnish
Snipped chives, for garnish

In a bowl, mix together the tomato and orange juices. Add the lemon juice, and celery salt to taste.

Garnish with the parsley and chives

Yield: 4 servings

Note: This soup may be served chilled for a picnic, or hot for a home meal.

Tapenade
(Olive Pâté)

7 ounces pitted black olives
1 (2-ounce) can anchovies
2 cloves garlic, minced
1 tablespoon lemon juice
1 tablespoon brandy
½ cup extra-virgin olive oil
Salt and black pepper

Drain the olives and anchovies; then place them in a food processor. Chop, but do not purée. Place the olive mixture in a bowl along with the garlic, lemon juice and brandy. Stir in the oil, and salt and black pepper to taste. Mix well and refrigerate for 24 hours, or at least overnight.

Serve with crackers.

Yield: about 8 servings (1 ½ cups)

Note: The tapenade should be made at least 24 hours in advance.

Tanglewood

Audiences at Tanglewood have changed over the years, and so has the tolerance of the management. In the early years people dressed formally; men were discouraged from attending without a tie. Women who showed up in shorts were given wrap-around skirts to cover their legs. Today it is different - casual clothes are the rule, and on a warm afternoon or evening the grass customers sometimes appear in bathing suits!

Many patrons bring blankets and food and combine their picnics on the grass with a live Boston Symphony concert.

Tanglewood

Paella Salad

3 tablespoons red wine vinegar
1 tablespoon lemon juice
1 clove garlic, finely chopped
2 tablespoons chopped fresh parsley
2 scallions, finely chopped
1 large tomato, peeled, seeded and diced
½ cup olive oil
Salt and freshly ground black pepper
1 red bell pepper, cored, seeded and cut into strips
1½ cups chopped cooked chicken
(about 1 medium boneless breast)
½ pound cooked shrimp (about 12 to 15 medium-size)
½ pound chorizo, cooked and cut into cubes
2 cups chicken stock
1 cup white rice
¼ teaspoon saffron
1 cup frozen peas, thawed

In a large bowl, stir together the vinegar, lemon juice, garlic, parsley, scallions, tomato, oil, and salt and pepper to taste. Add the red pepper, chicken, shrimp and sausage. Mix well and set the mixture aside.

Bring the stock to a boil in a large saucepan. Add the rice and saffron; stir, and lower the heat. Cover, and cook for 15 to 20 minutes, or until the rice is tender and the stock has been absorbed. Remove the rice from the heat, and let it stand for 5 minutes.

Add the rice to the large bowl containing the chicken, shrimp and sausage mixture. Toss gently, but thoroughly, and taste for seasoning. Add more salt and pepper, if necessary. Add the peas, mix well, and cover tightly. Let it sit at room temperature until lukewarm. Refrigerate for several hours. Prior to serving, take the salad out of the refrigerator to allow it to warm slightly.

Yield: 6 to 8 servings

Note: Chorizo can be found in most large supermarkets.

Chocolate Delight Bars

8 tablespoons (1 stick) unsalted butter, at room temperature
1 egg yolk
2 tablespoon water
1 ¼ cups flour
1 teaspoon sugar
1 teaspoon baking powder
6 ounces butterscotch morsels
6 ounces semi-sweet chocolate morsels

Frosting:
2 large eggs
¾ cup sugar
6 tablespoons (¾ stick) unsalted butter, melted
2 teaspoons vanilla extract
2 cups nuts, very finely chopped

Preheat oven to 350°.

Beat the butter, egg yolk and water until blended. Stir in the flour, sugar and baking powder. Press into a 13 by 9 by 2-inch pan.

Bake 10 minutes. Remove from the oven, and immediately sprinkle with butterscotch and chocolate morsels. Return the pan to the oven for an additional 1 or 2 minutes.

Remove the pan from the oven and smooth the morsels.

In a small bowl, beat the 2 eggs with sugar until lemon-like in color. Stir in the melted butter and the vanilla. Spread the mixture over the chocolate-butterscotch layer and sprinkle with nuts.

Return pan to oven and bake for additional 40 minutes. Allow to cool completely before cutting into small squares.

Yield: 24 squares

The Tanglewood "Swallows" Chorus

Tanglewood is one of the most remarkable of summer music festivals, and its location makes it one of the most beautiful as well. It is set in over 500 acres of sweeping lawns, tall pines, and wide walking paths. The many buildings seem to nestle into the landscape, and even the Koussevitzky Shed, which seats almost 6,000 people, does not overwhelm its surroundings.

The open-sided Shed will some-times entice a full-throated bird to sing along with the orchestra. One year a band of swallows nested in the eaves. They proved somewhat disruptive when they would swoop over the heads of the audience, making their own bird calls.

Something had to be done about the swallows. The solution came from a staff member who heard that swallows avoid owls. Fake owls were placed around the eaves, and it worked like a charm. The swallows took up other quarters away from the Shed.

Tanglewood

I

Adagio molto	C ♪ =	88
Allegro con brio	₵ ♩ =	112
Andante cantabile con moto	3/8 ♪ =	120
Allegro molto e vivace	3/4 ♩ =	108
Adagio	2/4 ♪ =	63
Allegro molto e vivace	2/4 ♩ =	88

II

Adagio molto	3/4 ♪ =	84
Allegro con brio	C ♩ =	100
Larghetto	3/8 ♪ =	92
Allegro	3/4 ♩ =	100
Allegro molto	₵ ♩ =	152

III

Allegro con brio	3/4 ♩ =	60
Adagio assai	2/4 ♪ =	80
Allegro vivace	3/4 ♩ =	116
Allegro molto	2/4 ♩ =	76
Poco andante	2/4 ♪ =	108
Presto	2/4 ♪ =	116

IV

Adagio	₵ ♩ =	66
Allegro vivace	₵ o =	80
Adagio	3/4 ♪ =	84
Allegro vivace	3/4 ♩ =	100
Allegro ma non troppo	2/4 ♩ =	80

Fish Lover's Delight

Menu

Curried Zucchini Soup
Orange and Raisin Slaw
Picnic Salmon
Kiss Cookies

Wines

Dry White Wines from Alsace:
Schlumberger Gewürztraminer 1992
Domaine Schoffit Pinot Blanc 1996
To splurge a little:
Zind-Humbrect Pinot d'Alsace 1996
For Red Wine Lovers:
Laurel Ridge Willamette Valley (Oregon) Pinot Noir 1996

Curried Zucchini Soup

8 young green zucchini (about 2 pounds), unpeeled
4 tablespoons butter
4 tablespoons finely chopped onions
2 teaspoons curry powder
1 teaspoon salt
1 cup milk
3½ cups chicken broth

Scrub the zucchini; then thinly slice them. Melt the butter in a pan with a cover, and add the zucchini and onions. Cover tightly and simmer 10 minutes, shaking the pan occasionally. Do not let the vegetables brown.

Add the curry, salt, milk and broth. Bring to a boil, lower the heat, and simmer until the zucchini is tender - about 15 minutes. Place the pan's contents into a processor, and purée at high speed for 1 minute, or until smooth.

Serve cold or hot.

Yield: 4 to 6 servings

Orange and Raisin Slaw

4 cups (about 1 pound) cabbage, sliced thinly
1 (11-ounce) can mandarin oranges, drained
⅓ cup raisins
2 tablespoons minced onion
⅓ cup mayonnaise
⅓ cup sour cream

Combine the cabbage with the drained oranges and raisins.

Separately combine the onion, salad dressing and sour cream. Add it to the cabbage mixture.

Chill for at least 1 hour.

Yield: 6 to 8 servings

Picnic Salmon

1 tablespoon honey
1 tablespoon grain mustard
1 tablespoon vinegar (balsamic, cider, etc)
1 pound salmon fillets, skin removed
Lemon or lime slices (for garnish)

Preheat oven to 500°.

Mix together the honey, mustard and vinegar for a glaze and brush it on top of the salmon fillets. Bake for approximately 10 minutes and check for doneness. (Put the tip of a knife in thickest part; the flesh should be opaque. Use caution not to overcook.)

Serve chilled. Garnish with lemon or lime slices.

Yield: 4 servings

Note: Measurements are for 1 pound of salmon. If increasing the portions by using a side of salmon, the tail piece (which is thinner) will cook faster. Cover tail with aluminum foil for last few minutes of cooking. If fillets are being cooked as well as a side, remove the fillets first.

Variation: Salmon may be served hot or at room temperature.

	V			
Allegro con brio	2/4	♩	=	108
Andante con moto	3/8	♪	=	92
Allegro	3/4	♩	=	96
Allegro	C	♩	=	84
	VI			
Allegro ma non troppo	2/4	♩	=	66
Andante molto moto	12/8	♩	=	50
Allegro	3/4	♩	=	108
Allegro	2/4	♩	=	132
Allegro	C	♩	=	80
Allegretto	6/8	♩	=	60
	VII			
Poco sostenuto	C	♩	=	69
Vivace	6/8	♩	=	104
Allegretto	2/4	♩	=	76
Presto	3/4	♩	=	132
Assai meno presto	3/4	♩	=	84
Allegro con brio	2/4	♩	=	72
	VIII			
Allegro vivace e con brio	3/4	♩	=	69
Allegretto scherzando	2/4	♪	=	88
Tempo di menuetto	3/4	♩	=	126
Allegro vivace	¢	𝅝	=	84

Tanglewood

Kiss Cookies

½ pound (2 sticks) butter, room temperature
¾ cup granulated sugar
2 cup flour
2 cups chopped walnuts
8 ounces chocolate "kisses"

Cream together the butter and sugar in a bowl. Combine the flour and walnuts; then add them to the creamed mixture. Chill the mixture for at least 30 minutes.

Wrap a small amount (about 1 tablespoon) of dough around each chocolate and place them 1 inch apart on an ungreased cookie sheet. Chill again before baking.

Preheat oven to 375°.

Bake for about 15 to 20 minutes. Watch the cookies carefully. Their edges should be just lightly browned. Remove the cookies from the oven; cool; then remove them with a spatula.

Yield: about 44 cookies

Not only are these cookies tasty, but
fun for kids to make as well!

Sandwich Picnic

Menu

Ratatouille Niçoise
Round Bread Sandwich
Dream Bars

Wines

Light, delightful Beaujolais wines would be perfect!
Mommessin Brouilly 1997
George Duboeuf Julienas 1997
Château de Pizay Régnie 1996

Ratatouille Niçoise

4 eggplants, peeled
4 zucchini, peeled
1 pound tomatoes, peeled and seeded
2 green bell peppers, cored and seeded
3 large onions
1 cup olive oil
4 garlic cloves, minced
1 teaspoon dried parsley
1 teaspoon thyme
Salt and pepper

Cut the eggplants, zucchini, tomatoes, green peppers and onions into ½-inch dice. In a large saucepan, heat the olive oil, and cook the onions and garlic for one minute. Then add the eggplant, zucchini, tomatoes, peppers, parsley and thyme. Simmer covered for 1 ½ hours, stirring occasionally. Season with salt and pepper to taste.

May be served hot or cold.

Yield: 16 to 20 servings

Keith Lockhart is a very busy man. Not only is he in Boston for the Holiday Pops season in December and the regular Pops season from early May to mid-July, but he also tours extensively with the Boston Pops Esplanade Orchestra. Additionally, he is music director of the Utah Symphony and guest conducts with other national orchestras.

Keith and the orchestra have cemented the Pops' reputation as "America's Orchestra," crisscrossing the country in the years since Keith became conductor. From New England through the Atlantic states, down to Florida, out to Arizona, up the Pacific seaboard, and even to Vancouver, British Columbia, the Pops have made its musical presence felt. In December 1998, Chicago and Cleveland, both cities rich with a musical heritage, fell under the spell of the "Holiday at Pops" concerts.

For violinists, the most common mishap during performances is a string breaking. When this happens during a violin concerto, the soloist grabs the concertmaster's violin and plays on.

When the young violinist Midori was playing Bernstein's Serenade at Tanglewood, her E string snapped. Although a very young talent (only 14 years old!), she had the presence of mind to accept the concertmaster's violin and continue, only to have the E string break again. This time she took the assistant concertmaster's violin and finished the piece.

Round Bread Sandwich

1 large round loaf peasant-style bread
Olive oil
Chopped parsley
Assorted sliced meats
Assorted sliced cheeses
2 red or green peppers, roasted, peeled, seeded and sliced
½ cup fresh chopped basil
1 red onion, thinly sliced
1 large or 2 medium tomatoes, thinly sliced

Slice the bread in half. Remove the soft center, reserving it for another use. Sprinkle the inside of the crusts with olive oil and chopped parsley.

Assemble the sandwich by layering the meats, cheeses, peppers, and onion on one half of the loaf. Sprinkle the basil over all. Cover with the remaining half and wrap the entire loaf tightly in plastic wrap. Keep it tightly wrapped at least 2 to 3 hours. Then slice it in 8 to 16 slices, depending upon the size of the bread, and the amount of filling.

Yield: 8 to 10 servings

Note: Exact amounts of meats and cheeses is not given. Desired thickness of sandwich will dictate exact amounts.

Peppers may be roasted (whole) by placing on a pan under the broiler for 5 to 10 minutes. Carefully watch them. As the skins char, rotate them until all sides have been blackened. Remove the peppers and place them in a paper bag, sealing the top tightly. Allow the peppers to steam for 10 minutes. Remove them from the bag and rub the blackened skin off. Proceed coring and seeding the peppers as normal. (Ensure that the bag is sitting on a plate or board, or is in the sink while the peppers are steaming. The oil from the peppers will eventually leak through the bag!)

Dream Bars

4 ounces (1 stick) butter
½ cup brown sugar
1 cup flour

Filling:
2 eggs
1 cup brown sugar
½ teaspoon salt
1 teaspoon pure vanilla extract
2 tablespoons flour
1 cup chopped walnuts or pecans
Confectioners' sugar (optional)

Preheat the oven to 375°. Coat a 9-inch square pan with nonstick spray.

Make the crust: In a bowl, mix well the butter, brown sugar and flour and spread the mixture into the prepared pan. Bake for 10 minutes. Remove the crust and cool. Leave the oven on.

Make the filling: In a mixing bowl beat the eggs with the brown sugar, salt, and vanilla. Add the flour and walnuts. Mix well. Pour the mixture into the cooled baked crust. Bake for 20 minutes; then remove from the oven and cool. Remove from the pan, and dust with confectioners' sugar, if desired. Cut into small squares.

Yield: 12 to 16 small bars

Tanglewood

Bernard Haitink
Principal Guest Conductor

Long a favorite both with the orchestra and audiences in Boston and Tanglewood, Bernard Haitink has served as Principal Guest Conductor of the BSO since 1995, and recently agreed to extend his tenure in this position.

When he was first engaged to be the principal guest conductor, the maestro stated that he was not only looking forward to continuing his work with the BSO in Boston, but also experiencing the musical scene at Tanglewood for the first time.

A Romantic Picnic

Menu

Cold Strawberry Soup
Marinated Chicken
Roasted Potato Salad
A Chocolate Cake for Lovers

Wines

What is more romantic than a bottle of bubbly?
Brut Saumur Saphir 1996
Domaine Chandon Blanc de Noirs
For a special date:
Bollinger Special Cuvée

Cold Strawberry Soup

4 cups strawberries, hulled
1 ½ cups sugar
¾ cup sour cream
1 cup light cream
1 ½ cups dry white wine

Place the strawberries and sugar in a processor or blender. Pulse a few times. Add the sour cream and pulse again to combine. Then add the light cream and wine. Pulse to desired consistency. Chill well.

Yield: 4 to 6 servings

Marinated Chicken

2½ cups orange marmalade
½ cup soy sauce
½ cup orange juice
¼ teaspoon ginger
¼ teaspoon garlic powder
2 (4 to 5 pound) chickens, cut into pieces
1 (11-ounce) can mandarin oranges
1 cup slivered almonds

Combine in a bowl the orange marmalade, soy sauce, orange juice, ginger and garlic powder. Place the chicken pieces in a foil-lined pan and pour the marinade over the chicken. Place in the refrigerator overnight.

Preheat the oven to 350°.

Place the chicken in the oven and bake for 1 hour. About 10 minutes before the chicken is done, add the mandarin oranges.

Prior to serving, sprinkle the chicken with the slivered almonds.

Yield: 6 to 8 servings

Note: If the chicken is roasted whole, cooking time will be increased at least 30 minutes longer.

Gregor Piatigorsky
by Martha Burnham Humphrey

Danny Kaye
by Olga Koussevitzky

Roasted Potato Salad

2½ pounds small red bliss or Yukon gold potatoes
1 clove garlic, chopped
5 tablespoons olive oil, divided
Salt and pepper
1½ teaspoons red wine vinegar
1 tablespoon grainy mustard
3 teaspoons snipped chives
2 teaspoons fresh rosemary

Preheat oven to 425°.

Scrub the potatoes, cut into bite-size pieces and place them in a baking dish. Scatter the garlic and 3 tablespoons of the olive oil over the potatoes. Add salt and freshly ground pepper, to taste, and toss the potatoes to coat them evenly. Roast for 30 to 40 minutes, tossing the potatoes approximately every 10 minutes, to allow for even cooking.

Beat the vinegar and mustard in a large bowl. Whisk in the remaining 2 tablespoons of olive oil until smooth. Add the potatoes and mix gently. Cool to room temperature and add the chives and rosemary.

Yield: 6 servings

A Chocolate Cake for Lovers

1 (18½-ounce) box Swiss or Devil's Food Chocolate Cake mix
1 (12-ounce) can sweetened condensed milk
1 (12-ounce) can butterscotch caramel fudge
Nondairy whipped cream, for topping
3 crushed chocolate-caramel candy bars

Bake the cake according to the package instructions. Cool.

In a sauce pan over low heat, mix the condensed milk with the caramel fudge.

Poke holes in the cooled cake and drizzle the sauce mixture over the surface until all is absorbed.

Top the cake with the nondairy whipped cream and the crushed candy bars.

Yield: 12 to 16 servings

*Ina Wilhelm parted with this
favorite recipe. She and her
husband, orchestra member
Ron Barron, host a bed and
breakfast in the town of Rich-
mond during the Tanglewood
season. This Brie is waiting on
the coffee table when their
guests return from an evening
Shed performance.*

Picnic for a Summer's Eve

Menu

**Brie with Basil and Sun-Dried Tomatoes
Stuffed Scampi
Spinach Salad with Prosciutto Dressing
Mango Cake**

Wines

*Rich White Burgundy (or California Chardonnay) -
but a French wine is more romantic!
Mirassou Monterey County 1996
Le Manoir Murisaltien Mâcon-Fuisse 1996
To splurge on someone special:
Louis Jadot Meursault Les Charmes 1996*

Brie with Basil and Sun-Dried Tomatoes

*1 pound Brie cheese, softened
3 tablespoons minced Italian flat-leaf parsley
3 tablespoons fresh basil strips
2 tablespoons chopped pine nuts (pignoli)
2 cloves garlic, minced
8 sun-dried tomatoes, minced
3 tablespoons freshly grated Parmesan cheese*

Remove the rind from the Brie and place the cheese on a serving
plate. Allow the Brie and other ingredients to come to room
temperature before proceeding.

Combine the parsley, basil, pine nuts, garlic, sun-dried tomatoes and
Parmesan cheese. Spread the mixture on the top and sides of the
Brie. Refrigerate for 2 to 3 hours; then bring to room temperature
before serving.

Serve with crackers.

Yield: about 10 to 12 servings

Tanglewood

Stuffed Scampi

*1 clove garlic, chopped
¼ cup fresh bread crumbs
¼ cup grated Parmesan cheese
¼ cup olive oil
1 ½ pounds (24 to 30) large shrimp,
peeled and deveined (tail intact)
Lemon juice
Black pepper*

Preheat the broiler.

Mix together garlic, crumbs, cheese and oil in a bowl. Stuff each shrimp with the mixture and lay them on a cookie sheet. Place the sheet on the highest oven rack and broil the shrimp about 2 minutes per side.

The stuffed shrimp can be served hot, at room temperature, or chilled, with freshly squeezed lemon juice and ground pepper to taste.

Yield: 4 servings

Note: The recipe serves 6 to 8 as an appetizer.

Spinach Salad with Prosciutto Dressing

Dressing:
*6 tablespoons olive oil
½ cup chopped prosciutto
2 tablespoons minced garlic
6 tablespoons white wine
6 tablespoons lemon juice
2 tablespoons sugar
Salt and pepper*

*1 (10-ounce) bag stemmed spinach, or baby spinach leaves
2½ cups sliced fresh mushrooms
½ cup toasted walnuts
½ cup freshly grated Parmesan cheese*

Make the dressing: Heat the oil in a pan over medium heat and add the prosciutto and garlic. Sauté for 3 minutes. Add the wine, lemon juice and sugar. Simmer for 5 minutes. Cool. Add the salt and pepper to taste. The dressing may be made a couple days in advance.

Place the spinach, mushrooms and walnuts in a salad bowl. Add the dressing; then sprinkle on the cheese.

Yield: 8 servings

Mango Cake

*2 cups mango flesh (about 2 or more mangos)
2 cups ground almonds
½ cup sugar
1 teaspoon baking powder
5 eggs
Powdered sugar, for dusting*

Preheat the oven to 375°. Grease and line a 10-inch round cake pan.

In a processor, purée the mango flesh until smooth and measures 2 cups. Set aside.

Place the almonds, sugar and baking powder in the processor and combine well - about 30 seconds. Pour in the mango purée and combine them well. Add the eggs 1 at a time, pulsing the processor after each addition.

Pour the batter into the cake pan. Bake in the oven for 1 hour. Cool the cake in the pan for 10 minutes before removing. Dust the cake with the powdered sugar. Serve at room temperature.

Yield: 8 to 10 servings

**Serge Koussevitzky at Tanglewood
by Martha Burnham Humphrey**

A Berkshire Picnic

Menu

Bagnetto Parsley Sauce
Greek Pasta Salad
Sliced London Broil
Bosc Pears in Burgundy Wine

Wines

Start with a fruity white wine:
Pinot Grigio, from Morasutti or Fontana Candida
Then follow with a good Pinot Noir:
Navarro Mendocino 1995
David Bruce Sonoma County 1995
To splurge:
Saintsburg Carneros

Bagnetto Parsley Sauce

1½ (2-ounce) cans anchovies
3 cups parsley
1 small onion
1 small plum tomato
½ green pepper
½ red pepper
2 cloves garlic
¼ cup olive oil
¼ cup wine vinegar
Salt and pepper

In a processor, purée the anchovies, parsley, onion, tomato, both peppers, and the garlic, until the mixture has a thick sauce consistency. Put the sauce into a bowl with the olive oil and wine vinegar. Season with salt and pepper to taste. Mix well to combine, and refrigerate. When ready to serve, bring the sauce back to room temperature.

Serve with fresh sliced French bread to dip.

Yield: 4 to 8 servings

Variation: The recipe may also be used as a sauce by increasing the olive oil to ½ cup.

Greek Pasta Salad

1 pound fusilli pasta

Dressing:
½ cup olive oil
1 teaspoon red wine vinegar
1 teaspoon dried oregano
½ cup chopped parsley
1 teaspoon salt

1 cup sliced red onion
1 cup diced cucumber
1 cup diced red or green bell peppers
1 (6-ounce) jar marinated artichoke hearts, rinsed and drained
¾ cup black Greek olives
1½ cups cubed feta cheese

Boil the fusilli in salted water for 9 to 10 minutes, or until "al dente". Drain and rinse well in cold water (to stop further cooking), and place the pasta in a large serving bowl.

Make the dressing: Combine the olive oil, vinegar, oregano, parsley, and salt in a bowl. Add the onion, cucumber, bell pepper, artichoke hearts, olives and cheese, along with dressing, to the pasta. Mix well to combine all the ingredients.

Serve at room temperature.

Yield: 12 servings

Tanglewood

"I was volunteering at the Glass House one day and completing a sale for a lovely couple. When the purchases were totaled, the gentleman said he would pay with his credit card. It was our procedure to check the name and expiration date on the card. When I noted the gentleman's name, Yo-Yo Ma, I cried out, 'You're Yo-Yo Ma? May I have your autograph?' He very graciously gave it to me and it now is displayed in a prominent place in our home."

~ A Tanglewood Volunteer

Tanglewood

Sliced London Broil

2 tablespoons Dijon mustard
2 tablespoons soy sauce
2 tablespoons olive oil
2 tablespoons brown sugar
1 tablespoon chopped garlic (optional)
1 ¼ pounds flank steak (London broil)

In a bowl, combine the mustard, soy sauce, olive oil, brown sugar, and the garlic (if used). Place the marinade in a plastic zip-lock bag. Add the steak to the bag, seal and marinate overnight in the refrigerator.

Prepare the grill or preheat the broiler. Grill or broil the steak for about 5 minutes per side to desired doneness. Let the meat rest for a few minutes before carving.

Slice the meat thinly on a bias.

Yields 4 to 6 servings

Variation: The steak may be cut smaller and used as an appetizer, yielding 8 to 10 servings

Bosc Pears in Burgundy Wine

2 cups Burgundy wine
1 cup sugar
4 to 6 whole cloves
1 cinnamon stick
6 Bosc pears, peeled, cored and halved

In a pan, combine thoroughly the wine with the sugar. Add the cloves and cinnamon stick. Bring to the mixture to a simmer and add the pears. Simmer until tender, about 10 to 15 minutes. Remove the pears from the liquid.

Continue to cook the liquid for 15 minutes, allowing it to thicken. Pour the liquid over the pears. Cool before serving.

The pears will keep for 1 to 2 weeks.

Yield: 6 to 12 servings (using one-half and one whole pear servings, respectively)

Meat Lover's Picnic

Menu

Creamed Zucchini Soup
Teriyaki Tenderloin
Orzo in Tabbouleh Seasoning
Favorite Fudge Cake

Wines

Start with a dry Alsatian white wine:
Pierre Sparr Gewirztraminer 1996
Hugel Alsace Gentil 1996
Then a classic California Cabernet Sauvignon:
Hawk Crest 1996
Napa Ridge 1996
To splurge:
Stag's Leap Wine Cellars Napa Valley 1996

Dimitri Mitropoulos
by Olga Koussevitzky

Creamed Zucchini Soup

5 to 6 small to medium zucchini, cut into 1-inch cubes
1 large onion, thinly sliced
1½ teaspoons curry powder
3 cups chicken broth
1 cup heavy cream
½ cup milk
Salt and freshly ground pepper
Snipped chives, for garnish

Place the cut zucchini in a saucepan, then add the onion slices. Sprinkle with curry powder and stir to coat the pieces. Add the chicken broth and bring the mixture to a boil. Cover and simmer for 45 minutes.

Spoon the mixture into a blender or food processor. Blend to a fine purée. There should be 4 cups of soup.

Pour the soup into a bowl that is large enough to accommodate the addition of the remaining ingredients. Add the cream, milk, and salt and pepper to taste. Chill the soup thoroughly.

Serve sprinkled with snipped chives.

Yield: 6 to 8 servings

Tanglewood

Teriyaki Tenderloin

Marinade:
½ cup soy sauce
½ cup oil (vegetable, soy, olive or combination)
½ cup sherry, or dry white wine
1 (4 to 5-pound) beef tenderloin, trimmed

Mix together in a bowl the soy sauce, oil and wine to make a marinade. Place the tenderloin in a bowl or container and pour the marinade over it. Cover. Marinate the tenderloin fillet at least 4 hours (overnight, if possible) in the refrigerator, turning the meat at least once.

Preheat the oven to 475°.

Roast the tenderloin for approximately 30 to 40 minutes or until a meat thermometer registers the desired doneness. Allow the meat to rest at least 10 minutes before carving. It is best sliced and served at room temperature.

Yield: 8 to 10 servings

Note: The recipe can be done ahead and transported to the picnic.

Orzo in Tabbouleh Seasoning

4 ripe tomatoes, chopped
2 cucumbers, peeled, seeded, finely chopped
½ large onion, minced
¼ cup fresh mint, minced
¼ cup parsley, minced
Juice of 2 lemons
¼ cup olive oil
Salt
1 ½ cups orzo pasta, cooked, drained and cooled

In a bowl mix together the tomatoes, cucumbers, onion, mint, parsley, lemon juice, and olive oil, until well blended. Add salt to taste.

Place the orzo pasta in a medium to large bowl and add the vegetable mixture to it. Mix well to combine the ingredients.

Refrigerate for at least 4 hours. Serve the salad cold, or at room temperature.

Yield: 6 to 8 servings

Favorite Fudge Cake

½ pound semi-sweet chocolate chips
¾ cup sugar
¼ cup boiling water
4 large eggs
11 tablespoons (1⅓ stick) butter
1 tablespoon vanilla extract
¼ cup all-purpose flour
1 cup chopped walnuts (optional)

Preheat the oven to 350°, with the rack in the center. Grease a 9 or 10-inch cake pan.

Chop the chocolate and sugar in a processor. With the machine running, add the boiling water to blend, and continue, adding 1 egg at a time, the butter, vanilla and flour. (It may be necessary to stop and scrape down sides of bowl from time to time.)

When all is blended, mix in the walnuts. Pour the batter into the greased cake pan and bake for about 30 minutes. Check the center with a toothpick for doneness. Allow the cake to cool before removing it from the pan.

Yield: 10 to 12 servings

Note: This cake freezes very well. Several can be made at one time in disposal cake pans, frozen, and then used when it's time to picnic!

Tanglewood

Gregor Piatigorsky
by Olga Koussevitzky

Picnic for a Crowd

Menu

Tortellini and Artichoke Salad
Spicy Gazpacho with Shrimp
Jailbird Soufflé

Wine

Three different white wines, all matching the spicy and mild food mix:
Sancere, Sauvion et Fils, 1996
Robert Mondavi, Fumé Blanc 1996, 1997
Hugel Pinot Blanc 1997

Tortellini and Artichoke Salad

2 (7-ounce) boxes cheese tortellini, cooked and drained well
2 tomatoes, chopped
2 (6-ounce) jars marinated artichokes, chopped,
drained and liquid reserved
1 (6-ounce) can sliced or chopped black olives
½ pound feta cheese, crumbled
3 scallions chopped
¾ cup olive oil, or marinade from
artichokes plus enough oil to make ¾ cup
⅓ cup vinegar
2 cloves garlic, crushed
Salt and pepper
Snipped dill and/or chopped basil
Pecans or walnuts (optional)

In a large bowl, mix together the tortellini with the tomatoes, artichokes, olives, feta cheese, and scallions.

In a small bowl, whisk the olive oil, vinegar, garlic, and salt and pepper to taste. Add the dill and/or basil, as desired. Pour the oil mixture on tortellini mixture. Toss well. If using nuts, sprinkle on top as a garnish, or stir into the salad itself

Yield: 6 to 8 servings

Serving Suggestion: The salad may be served warm, but is best cold at a picnic!

Spicy Gazpacho with Shrimp

2 garlic cloves, peeled
1 teaspoon salt
1½ cups small bread pieces, crusts removed
¼ cup red wine vinegar
⅓ cup olive oil
1 teaspoon ground cumin
2½ cups tomato juice or vegetable juice, divided
2 pounds tomatoes, peeled, seeded and minced (about 3 cups)
1 green bell pepper, cored, seeded, and finely chopped
1 red bell pepper, cored, seeded and finely chopped
⅓ cup minced scallion
⅓ cup peeled, seeded and minced cucumber
⅓ cup minced red onion
1 cup ice water
¼ cup minced fresh parsley
Hot pepper sauce
Salt and pepper
½ pound medium shrimp (about 15) peeled,
deveined and cooked

On a work surface mince and mash the garlic together with the salt, until a paste is formed.

In a blender combine the garlic paste with the bread, vinegar, oil, cumin and 1 cup of the tomato juice, and blend the mixture until smooth.

In a large bowl, combine thoroughly the bread mixture with the tomatoes, bell peppers, scallions, cucumber and onion. Stir in the remaining 1½ cups tomato or vegetable juice and chill the soup, covered, for 3 hours, or until it is very cold.

When ready to serve, thin the soup with one cup ice water, or enough water to obtain the desired consistency; add the parsley, hot pepper sauce, and salt and pepper to taste.

Serve the soup with the shrimp on the side.

Yield: 6 to 8 servings

Tanglewood

**Igor Stravinsky
by Olga Koussevitzky**

Jailbird Soufflé

*¼ cup cold water
1 (¼-ounce) envelope unflavored gelatin
½ cup fresh lemon juice
1½ cups sugar, divided
3 eggs, separated
1 teaspoon vanilla extract
1 cup heavy cream*

In the bowl of food processor, add the cold water; sprinkle gelatin over it and allow it to soften for 10 minutes. Meanwhile, heat the lemon juice in a pan.

Pulse the processor once, then add the juice. Add 1 cup of the sugar, the egg yolks and vanilla to the processor; process for 5 minutes. Scrape the sides of the bowl and let the mixture cool.

Prepare a 1-quart soufflé dish with a foil collar around it, using masking tape to hold it in place.

In a separate bowl, whip the cream; then fold it into the mixture. Add the remaining ½ cup of sugar. Beat the egg whites until stiff, but not dry. Fold them into the mixture. Pile the mixture in the soufflé dish, smoothing the top.

Refrigerate overnight.

Yield: 4 servings

Serving Suggestion: When ready to serve, decorate with whipped cream rosettes, a lemon slice cut halfway through and twisted, and with a few mint leaves.

"Pick-a-Chick" Salad Picnic

Menu

Wild Rice and Chicken Salad
Curried Chicken Salad
Chicken Salad Mold
Steamed Corn
Never-Fail Day-Ahead Chocolate Cake

Wines

For something different, try a light German wine:
Kurt Darting Riesling Kabinett 1996
Joh. Jos. Prüm, Riesling 1996
Or, for a standard and lovely Chardonnay:
Fetzer Mendocino 1996
Gallo of Sonoma 1996

Wild Rice and Chicken Salad

1 ½ boneless chicken breasts, cooked and cut into 1-inch cubes
1 ½ cups cooked wild rice (about ½ cup uncooked)
1 large tart apple, unpeeled, cored and coarsely chopped
⅓ small red onion, chopped
½ large red bell pepper, diced
½ cup dried currants
2 tablespoons balsamic vinegar
2 tablespoons olive oil
¼ teaspoon black pepper

Combine in a bowl the chicken chunks with the wild rice, apple pieces, onion, red pepper, and currants. Add the vinegar and olive oil, and mix well. Add the ¼ teaspoon black pepper, or to taste. Refrigerate until ready to serve.

Yield: 4 servings

Variation: To make a wrap: Heat mountain bread or lavasch in a microwave oven until pliable, approximately 20 to 30 seconds. Place the rice and chicken salad along one end of the bread and roll, tucking in the sides. Wrap in foil. Foil can be peeled back as the bread is eaten.

Serving suggestion: This salad can be served with an accompanying green salad.

If you walked the grounds at Tanglewood on the morning following an afternoon or evening concert, you would never suspect that a crowd of thousands had walked and picnicked there on the previous day. Each path appears raked and the sweeping lawns look pristine and green.

When Director of Tanglewood Facilities Dave Sturma was asked how the grounds are kept so perfect in appearance, he answered that the lawns are mowed to a particular length, and an underground sprinkler system provides a heavy soaking at night.

**Artur Rubenstein
by Olga Koussevitzky**

Curried Chicken Salad

*4 cups cooked chicken, cut in chunks
(about 2 large boned breasts)
5 cups small apple chunks (about 5 or 6 medium apples)
5 stalks celery, chopped
¼ large onion, finely chopped
1 cup golden raisins
1 cup chopped walnuts
¼ cup brown sugar
1 tablespoon curry powder
2 cups sour cream
Juice of 3 lemons
Salt and ground white pepper*

In a large bowl combine the cooked chicken chunks with the apples, celery, onion, raisins, walnuts, brown sugar, and curry powder. Stir in the sour cream and lemon juice. Season with salt and white pepper, to taste. Mix well.

Chill the salad thoroughly before serving.

Yield: 10 to 12 servings

Variation: Nonfat sour cream may be substituted for dietary considerations.

Variation: Grapes and slivered almonds may be substituted for the raisins and walnuts.

Chicken Salad Mold

4 cups diced cooked chicken (about 2 large boned breasts)
4 tablespoons chopped stuffed olives
4 tablespoons chopped black olives
4 tablespoons chopped sweet pickles
1 ½ cups diced celery
1 cup toasted almonds, slivered
4 hard cooked eggs, chopped
2 tablespoons chopped onions
4 tablespoons pimento
3 tablespoons prepared mustard
¾ to 1 cup mayonnaise
1 (15-ounce) can pineapple chunks, well-drained

Grease a large ring mold.

In a bowl, mix well the chicken, both kinds of olives, pickles, celery, almonds, eggs, onions, pimento, mustard, and mayonnaise. Pack the mixture into the mold. Chill.

When ready to serve, unmold the salad on large platter lined with lettuce leaves, or other greens, and fill the center with the pineapple.

Yield: 6 to 8 servings

Steamed Corn

4 ears corn, husked and cleaned

Place the corn in a zip-lock plastic bag. Microwave for 4 minutes on high. Remove the corn from the microwave, wrap it in silver foil, and carry it to the picnic site in a separate bag. The corn will retain the heat and will be enjoyed hot for at least 1 to 2 hours after cooking.

Yield: 4 servings

**Sir Thomas Beecham
by Olga Koussevitzky**

Never Fail Day Ahead Chocolate Cake

*1 (18½-ounce) box Devil's food or dark chocolate cake mix
1 (4-ounce) box instant chocolate pudding
1 cup sour cream
4 eggs
1 cup rum
½ cup water
⅓ cup salad oil
6 ounces chocolate chips*

Preheat the oven per cake directions.

Grease well and flour a Bundt pan. Mix together in a bowl the cake mix, chocolate pudding, sour cream, eggs, rum, water, and salad oil. When combined, beat for 1 or 2 minutes on high speed of electric beater. Fold in the chocolate chips.

Pour the batter into a prepared cake pan. Bake in the preheated oven for 50 minutes. Cool on a rack before inverting onto serving plate.

Yield: 8 to 10 servings

Note: It is important to use salad, and not olive, oil in this recipe.

Variation: For an alcohol-free cake, an equal amount water may be substituted for the 1 cup of rum.

Picnic Brunch

Menu

Refreshing Yogurt Soup
Layered Party Salad
Raspberry Velvet Tart

Wines

Mimosas made with orange juice (⅓)
and a California sparkling wine (⅔):
Domaine Chardon Brut
or a Spanish sparkling wine:
Paul Cheneau Brut (Spain)

Refreshing Yogurt Soup

3 cups plain yogurt
½ cup milk
½ cup raisins
½ cup chopped walnuts
2 sprigs mint, chopped
2 sprigs basil, chopped (optional)
1 large cucumber, chopped
1 small green onion, chopped
2 sprigs savory, chopped (optional)
Salt

In a large bowl, mix together the yogurt, milk, raisins, walnuts, mint, basil (if used), cucumber, onion, and savory (if used). Add salt to taste.

Chill thoroughly before serving

Yield: 4 to 6 servings

This soup is at its refreshing
best when served on a hot summer day!

Layered Party Salad

½ (10-ounce) package fresh spinach, torn into pieces
Salt and pepper
6 hard-boiled eggs, chopped
½ pound boiled ham, cut into pieces
1 (10-ounce) package frozen peas, thawed and drained
1 red onion, thinly sliced
2 cups mayonnaise
1 cup sour cream
½ pound Swiss cheese, cut into small pieces
6 strips cooked bacon, crumbled
¼ cup toasted almond slices

Layer the spinach in the bottom of a large bowl and add some salt and pepper.

Then layer the egg and ham. Top with additional salt and pepper, as desired.

Next layer the peas and onion slices. Mix the mayonnaise and sour cream, and spread over the peas and onions.

Top the salad with the Swiss cheese pieces, the bacon bits and the toasted almonds.

Cover the bowl with plastic wrap and refrigerate.

Yield: 6 servings

Note: Almonds may be toasted by placing them on a cookie sheet and baking for 8 to 10 minutes in a 350° oven, taking care not to burn them.

Raspberry Velvet Tart

1 prepared, baked crust in an 8-inch tart loose-bottom or springform pan, cooled (or "Best Pie Crust Ever", p. 251)

Filling:
2 cups fresh red raspberries, or frozen, thawed and drained
½ cup heavy cream
4 tablespoons (½ stick) butter
12 ounces quality white chocolate, finely chopped

Line the baked pie crust with the berries.

Slowly heat the cream and butter in a pan over low heat, until the butter is melted and steam is coming from the liquid. Be careful not to boil. Immediately pour the liquid over the chocolate in a bowl, whisking it in until combined. Pour the mixture over the berries.

Refrigerate. (Recipe may be made ahead.)

Yield: 8 servings

Tanglewood

The Whispering Bench

Walk to the back of Tanglewood's formal garden and you will find the lovers' bench. It is known as the whispering bench and was originally owned by Nathaniel Hawthorne. The seats on each side include space in between that is suitable for a chaperone. The idea is that the lovers whispered to each other and the sound carried around the chaperone. It remains a favorite of Tanglewood visitors.

The Whispering Bench at Tanglewood

COMMITTEES & CONTRIBUTORS

Cooking with Music

Executive and Steering Committees

William Along   Gwenda Schanzle
Co-Chairmen

Mary Marland Rauscher
Vice-Chairman

For the BSAV:

Mary Blair   † Hannah Campbell   Linda Clarke

John Farrenkopf   Augusta Leibowitz   Maria Isabel Veliz

Margaret Williams-DeCelles

† *In Memoriam*

For the Boston Symphony Orchestra:

Roberta Kennedy, *Manager, Symphony Shop*

Patricia Krol, *Director of Volunteer Services*

Pauline McCance, *Cookbook Project Liaison*

Kim Noltemy, *Director of Marketing*

Cooking With Music

In the preface of *The Boston Symphony Cookbook*, published in 1983, Chairman Judy Gardiner of the Cookbook Committee stated that, "This is a book for music lovers who love to cook, and for good cooks who love music". That statement still holds true for this second volume, *Cooking With Music: Celebrating the Tastes and Traditions of the Boston Symphony Orchestra.*

From its earliest beginnings as a simple idea and concept, throughout its growth and development period of recipe solicitation, testing and selection, and finally, its culmination in design, layout and manuscript compilation, the book required thousands of volunteer hours for its successful completion. The following listing reflects the names of those volunteers who enthusiastically and selflessly gave of their time and energy, and who believed in a project that would truly produce once again "a book for music lovers who love to cook, and for good cooks who love music".

The Advisors, Office Volunteers, Recipe Testers, Editors and Writers

Robyn Aldo

William and Elinor Along

Marian Alper

Pat Amend

Elvira Balzano

Brian Bell

Mary Blair

Pat Bonita

Judy Borger

Peg Bradley

Barbara Bradstreet

Laura Brown

Melinda Brown

Gail Bucher

Felicia Burrey

Anita Busch

† Hannah Campbell

Catherine Catchpole

Cynthia Curme

Barbara Davidson

Nicole Desrosiers

Susan Donnelly

Mary Drummey

Karin Dumbaugh

Stella Easland

Goetz and Elizabeth Eaton

Marie Eaton

Jeanne Ebert

Ginger Elvin

Paula Emerick

John and Alice M. Farrenkopf

Pamela Foggo

Leslie Wu Foley

Pattie Geier

Maxine Goldblum

Robin Hamilton

Barbara Hammel

Helen Hammond

Margaret Hargrove

Bettina Harrison

Bess Hartley

Noriko Hata

Joyce Hatch

David and Mary Ellen Hautanen

Pam Hill

Bert Hirshberg

Cynthia Holmes

Nancy Horton

Patricia Jensen

Patricia Krol

Helene Leavitt

Augusta Leibowitz

Barbara B. Leith

Arlene Levine

Shari Loessberg

Mary Lopez

Phyllis Lozo

Diane Lupean

Patricia Manhard

Janice Marnell

Claire Timmerman Marotta

Sybil Masters

Pauline McCance

Jane McGregor

Linda McLear

Pat Meigs

Karen Methven

Rita Meyer

Kevin Montague

† *In Memoriam*

316

Patti Newton
Teddie Preston
Charlotte Rafferty
Mary Marland Rauscher
Dorothy Robbins
Chris Ruigomez
Zabelle Russian
Esther Engel Salzman
Idah R. Salzman
Hessie Sargent

Gwenda Schanzle
Terri Scheff
Linda Sperandio
Mara Sprogis
Sylvia Stein
Danette Stephens
Yvonne Stewart
Dave Sturma
Lillian Sturm-Katz
Betty Sweitzer

Olivia Thompson
Kristin Tyrrell
Maria Isabel Veliz
Meghan Robinson Wander
Margaret Weimer
Kate Weiss-Gordon
Margaret Williams-DeCelles
Robin Worcester
Amy Yentsch
Anne Zakrosky
Eva Zervos

Recipe Contributors:

Lorna Adler
Nancy Agnew
Robin Aldo
William and Elinor Along
Dorsay Alpert
Carol Amaya
Elizabeth Amis
Elaine C. Andersen
Meg Anderson
Patricia Anderson
Scott and Nina Andrews
Dorothy Arnold
Sally Aronson
Stefan Asbury
Ron Barron
Judith Barr
Kate Begier
Maisy Bennett
Clara Stagliano Benson
Bonnie Bewick
Blantyre (Chef Michael Roller)
Pat Bonita
Barbara Bonney

Judy Borger
Helen Bradley
Jane Breslau
Anita Busch
Lucille Butler
Leone Buyse
Laura Carlo
Joan Carlton
Catherine Catchpole
Sarah Chang
Judy Clark
Linda Clarke
Barbara Clemens
Marilyn Cohen
Bobbi Cohn
Kathryn Conant
James Cooke
Martha Corbett
Geralyn Coticone
Joan Curhan
Currier & Chives
   (Chef Matt Daignieult)
Kim Dalzell

Nader Darehshori
Nelson and Ruth Darling
Margaret J. Dee
Beatrice deLalla
Ron and Joyce Della Chiesa
James and Ginette DePreist
Nicole Desrosiers
Harry Ellis Dickson
Kit Dornbush
Diane Droste
Mrs. John Eaton
Deborah Elfers
Frances P. Elliott
Ginger Elvin
Joan Elwood
Mrs. Richard Emmet
Mary A. Epstein
Rachel Fagerberg
Hortense Feldblum
Beverly Fendrick
Una Fleischmann
Linda Flint
Pamela Frank

Marion Gardner-Saxe

Pattie Geier

William and Frances Gibson

Chad Gifford

Jana Gimenez

Nancy Glynn

Thelma Goldberg

Maxine Goldblum

Joyce Goldweitz

Ralph Gomberg

Ina Gordon

Brigitte Graneau

Gail Hamel

Robin Hamilton

Barbara Hammel

Margaret Hargrove

Bettina H. Harrison

Amy Harris

Joseph Hearne and Jan Brett

Pat Henneberry

Bert Hirshberg

Cynthia Holmes

Nancy Horton

Sandra Jenkins Howard

Phyllis Hubbard

Phyllis Huberman

Bo Youp Hwang

Joanna R. Inches

The Inn at Stockbridge
  (Len Schiller)

Sherry Jones

Edna Kalman

Elita Kang

Carol Kaplan

Daniel Katzen

Jean Kennedy

Donna Kim

Ada Klein

Carol Kosakoff

Elizabeth Lavigne

Helene Leavitt

Augusta Leibowitz

Barbara B. Leith

Laurence Lesser

Carol Levinson

Amnon Levy

Susan Litt

Keith Lockhart and Lucia Lin

Elaine London

Mary Lopez

Cynthia Lovell

Phyllis Lozo

Diane Lupean

Lisa Mafrici

Olivia Manice

John Marksbury

David Mazzotta

Diana McClinton

Jo Ann McGrath

Jonathan Menkis

Karen Methven

Elizabeth Meyer

Rita Meyer

Ruth Miller

Ikuko Mizuno

Kevin Montague

Amy Moore

Patty Morse

Judith Mosse

Ellen Moyer

Betsy Moyers

Abby Sue Nathan

Mary Newman

Ruth Nordiff

Chris Nordstrom

Jessye Norman

Megan O'Block

John Oliver

Anita Oren

Elizabeth Ostling

Fredy and Katherine Ostrovsky

Seiji and Vera Ozawa

Lois C. Parlow

Claire Pedranti

Itzhak Perlman

Ann Hobson Pilot

Anne L. Powis

Carol Procter

Wendy Putnam

Charlotte Rafferty

Richard Ranti

Wayne and Toni Rapier

Mary Marland Rauscher

Diane Read

Suzanne Read

Red Lion Inn
  (Chef Douglas Luf)

Norma Reiner

Joan Reopell

Jane Rice

Dorothy Robbins

Lilia Roberts

Gloria Rodhouse

Victor Romanul

Elaine Rosenfeld

Rosalind Rothman

Carolyn Rowland

Matthew Ruggiero

Janet Russell

Alma Sahagaian

Esther Engel Salzman

Idah R. Salzman

Phyllis Sandrew

Marion Santoro

Mary Sarin

Gwenda Schanzle

Alfred Schneider

Virginia Scott

Meredith Shapiro

Blanche Siegfried

Johanna Hill Simpson

Mrs. Edward Simpson

Manny and Natalie Slater

Roland and Kikue Small

Rolf Smedvig

Josephine Smith

Thurman Smith

Fainna Solasko

Lee T. Sprague

Susan V. Stanton

Sylvia Stein

Barbara Steiner

Julie Steinhilber

Isaac Stern

Ellie Stoddard

Linda Stoker

Anne B. Stone

Jean R. Stone

Jennifer Suesse

Kirk Sullivan

Richard Svoboda

Nancy Vale

Maria Isabel Veliz

Roger and Martha Voisin

Mark and Martha Volpe

Frederica von Stade

Norma Wachtell

Anna Walther

Phyllis Walt

Megan Robinson Wander

Therese Ward

Susan A. Waterman

Christine Watson

Patricia Watts

Robert S. Weill

Julie Weiss

Richard and Helen Westerfield

Rosemary Westra

Wheatleigh (Chef Peter Platt)

Mrs. Henry Wheeler

Ina Wilhelm

John and Samantha Williams

Margaret Williams-DeCelles

Nancy Winterbottom

Larry Wolfe

Robin Worcester

Ami Yentsch

Mari Young

Amy Zander

Eva Zervos

Marge Zupanec

Acknowledgments

The BSO Cookbook Committee wishes to thank the following individuals for their valuable contribution to the creation and production of *Cooking With Music*:

Dan Gustin, former Acting BSO Managing Director, for his initial approval of and continuing enthusiasm for the new BSAV project;

BSO Managing Director Mark Volpe and Director of Finance and Business Affairs Tom May for their final authorization of and financial commitment to the cookbook;

General Manager Robin Brown, Executive Chef Edward Gannon, and the staff at the Four Seasons Hotel, along with photographer Jim Scherer, for their artistic assistance in the production of the cover photo;

Sametz Blackstone Associates, Boston for the concept and design of the cover;

Caroline Smedvig, BSO Director of Public Relations and Marketing, for her assistance with the copy material for Seiji Ozawa and her support of the marketing plan;

BSO Orchestra Manager Ray Wellbaum, and BSO staff members Bernadette Horgan, Dennis Alves, Jana Gimenez, and Karen Leopardi for their assistance with the copy material on Seiji Ozawa, Keith Lockhart, John Williams, and the guest artists;

Susanna Bonta, Caleb Cochran, and Sean Kerrigan of the BSO Press Office, and BSO Archivist Bridget Carr, who assisted us immeasurably during the research phase of our book;

Richard Stebbins for his research and assistance in developing the copy material on Symphony Hall and its history;

Marc Mandel and Eleanor McGourty of BSO Publications and Deborah Asbrand, who utilized their editorial skills to polish most of the copy material in the book. Doris Chung and Sarah Manoog of the BSO Marketing Department for their advice and assistance on art development;

Harry Ellis Dickson, for the use of his wonderful anecdotes about the musicians and public figures who played such vital roles in the history of the Boston Symphony Orchestra;

Northeastern University Press, for permitting us to use anecdotal excerpts from *Beating Time* by Harry Ellis Dickson (Copyright 1995 by Harry Ellis Dickson. Reprinted with the permission of Northeastern University Press);

Houghton Mifflin Company, for permitting us to use anecdotal excerpts from *Arthur Fiedler and the Boston Pops* by Harry Ellis Dickson (Copyright 1981 by Harry Ellis Dickson. Reprinted with the permission of Houghton Mifflin Company);

Joseph Hearne and Jan Brett for the use of the artwork on pages 68 and 242, and their subsequent assistance in the artistic development of those pages.

Fareed Zakaria, Managing Editor of *Foreign Affairs* magazine, and wine columnist for the *webzine slate.com* who provided us with a lovely wine list to accompany the Tanglewood picnics;

The Olga Koussevitzky caricatures on pages 56, 167, 181, 195, 201, 207, 211, 212, 216, 219, 280, 294, 297, 301, 304, 306, 308 and 310 are reprinted with the kind permission of The Koussevitsky Music Foundation, Inc., copyright owner.

Patricia Humphrey Frederick, who graciously granted us permission to reprint the musical sketches of her mother, Martha Burnham Humphrey;

Photographers Mary Blair, Tom Gauger, Sylvia Gilman, Marc Glassman, Chris Lee, Michael Lutch, Ginny Martens, William Mercer, Stu Rosner, Lincoln Russell, Walter Scott, Steve J. Sherman, Christian Steiner, Julie Steinhibler, Miro Vintoniv, the family of Heinz H. Weissenstein, Margaret Williams-DeCelles, and Ira Wyman, who all so graciously permitted us to use their camera's eye to "see" some of the Boston Symphony's history.

GUEST CHEFS

Photo by: © Miro Vintinov

INDEX

A

G

GRAINS AND CEREALS (ALSO SEE RICE)

H

I

J

K

L

LAMB

S

Mail or fax to:
Symphony Shop
Symphony Hall
Boston, MA 02115
(617) 638-9380 fax
(617) 638-9383 phone

Please send me

COPIES @ $29.95 EACH	
+ $1.50 PER COPY MA SALES TAX (MA RESIDENTS ONLY)	
+ $3.95 SHIPPING AND HANDLING	$3.95
+ $2.00 SHIPPING AND HANDLING PER ADDITIONAL BOOK	
GRAND TOTAL ENCLOSED	

❑ Enclosed is my check made out to **Boston Symphony Orchestra, Inc.**
❑ Please charge the full amount to:

    ❑ American Express   ❑ Diners Club

    ❑ Visa   ❑ Discover Card

    ❑ MasterCard

NAME

ADDRESS

CITY

STATE   ZIP

CARD NUMBER   EXP. DATE

NAME (AS IT APPEARS ON CARD)

- -

Mail or fax to:
Symphony Shop
Symphony Hall
Boston, MA 02115
(617) 638-9380 fax
(617) 638-9383 phone

Please send me

COPIES @ $29.95 EACH	
+ $1.50 PER COPY MA SALES TAX (MA RESIDENTS ONLY)	
+ $3.95 SHIPPING AND HANDLING	$3.95
+ $2.00 SHIPPING AND HANDLING PER ADDITIONAL BOOK	
GRAND TOTAL ENCLOSED	

❑ Enclosed is my check made out to **Boston Symphony Orchestra, Inc.**
❑ Please charge the full amount to:

    ❑ American Express   ❑ Diners Club

    ❑ Visa   ❑ Discover Card

    ❑ MasterCard

NAME

ADDRESS

CITY

STATE   ZIP

CARD NUMBER   EXP. DATE

NAME (AS IT APPEARS ON CARD)

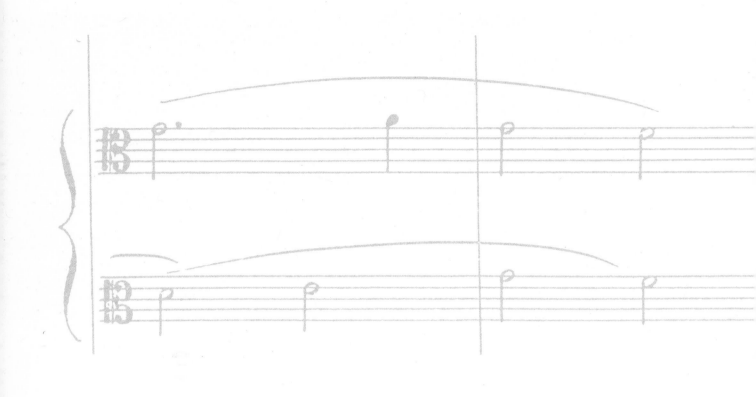